ADVENTURER AT HEART

To my mum
Janice Anne Fa'avae
who was also a mum to many others.
I'd love to see you again.

ADVENTURER AT HEART

NATHAN FA'AVAE

AN AUTOBIOGRAPHY

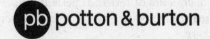 potton & burton

ABBREVIATIONS

AF	atrial fibrillation
AMS	acute mountain sickness
AR	adventure racing
CP	checkpoint/control point
FFS	for fuck's sake
ICU	intensive care unit
PC	passport control [another name for CP]
PFD	personal flotation device
RV	recreational vehicle
SPOT	GPS tracking device
TA	transition area
UCI	Union Cycliste Internationale

First published in 2015 by Potton & Burton
98 Vickerman Street, PO Box 5128, Nelson, New Zealand
pottonandburton.co.nz

© Nathan Fa'avae
www.nathanfaavae.nz

Edited by Mike Wagg
Front cover by Chris Chisnall Design

Printed in New Zealand by printing.com

ISBN 978 1 927213 62 9

CONTENTS

INTRODUCTION

On 14 November 2005 as the sun was setting over the South Island of New Zealand, I ran a half marathon along a desolate beach. To my left was the Tasman Sea, alive with frightening-size swells, crashing with almighty force after travelling hundreds of uninterrupted miles from Australia. To my right were the prized Southern Alps, a mountain range of global significance and heart-held treasure to many New Zealanders, with snowcapped peaks, glaciers, mighty rivers and a rich history. With me were three other people – my team. Weary and sore, we ran as best we could. The sand made the running energy-consuming, and the tidal river we had just crossed was deep and cold, leaving us shivering. As the kilometres passed underfoot and the goal drew closer, our excitement and spirits were peaking. Soon we'd be able to stop, truly stop.

The significance of the stop was not just completing a half marathon on a beach at night. The significance was that this was the final leg of the Adventure Racing World Championships that had begun 114 hours ago. We'd been racing non-stop and had already completed 147 km kayaking, 225 km mountain biking and 187 km mountain running. Added to that, we'd squeezed through caves, abseiled off cliffs and rafted through a gorge. We'd suffered exposure to a southerly storm, torrential rain and flooded rivers. We'd had mechanical gear failures, broke the stern off a double kayak in pounding surf, and travelled for hours through dense untracked rainforest navigating with just a map and compass. We'd fought the tortures of sleep deprivation and extreme fatigue, and suffered the pains of extended periods of physical exercise. Covering the final kilometres with swollen knees and blistered feet, our senses were in a heightened state – relief and achievement almost within grasp. Relief that we could finally rest, achievement that we had made it: survived the environment, the course, the challenges and the competition. We were returning.

This race had more than the usual race-ending emotions for me. It was the Adventure Racing World Champs on home soil and it also marked the end of my professional adventure-racing career. I had just spent four years competing full-time on the international circuit. While this was a relatively short period, adventure racing is a very tough and taxing sport. I didn't realise it at the time, but I had also spent 12 years training for those four years. Many people will say that adventure racing is the toughest sport in the world. I couldn't make that claim, as I haven't done every sport, but what I do know is that it certainly has tested me in every way imaginable. In 2005 I captained the New Zealand team to victory in the World Championships in what our main rivals and defending world champions titled the 'perfect race'. We won by the biggest-ever winning margin – 14 hours. This book is the story of how I got to that point in my life, the journey and the influences that shaped me into becoming a world champion athlete – attaining the highest level in my chosen sport – and then what I did after that.

As I get older I'm becoming less social, less frontman, more caveman. I rarely speak of my achievements, but when people do prise stories out of me about adventure in faraway places they invariably say, 'I look forward to reading your book', and I'm left wondering 'Why?' Fundamentally, I consider myself a humble person, so writing about myself doesn't sit easily with me. Although I've toyed with the idea for many years and reached a level of acceptance that I would write a book at some point (probably when I was so old and decrepit that it's the only thing remaining I could do), I was never in a hurry, mainly because I didn't perceive I had anything of interest to write about. However, after avidly reading a few biographies of Kiwi sportspeople, I came to a realisation that everyone's life is fascinating. The simple and trivial – like the fact they did a paper run as a kid, or had a family bach at the beach, a dog named Sue, or went skiing during school time – is what made their stories interesting. The normal, ordinary things that happen in life were the bits I enjoyed most, and which I also want to share.

So I have written a book and I can define my motivation to three core reasons. The first being the challenge of writing – I thrive on challenge. Second, I hope my pathway, learning, conclusions and somewhat staunch views about things will be thought-provoking and helpful to people. Third, I sensed this would be a valuable process for me to go through, essentially midlife, or perhaps post-midlife. At this 'crisis' point some people have an affair, buy a sports car, or enter the Coast to Coast multisport race – me, I decided to write a book. But the biggest believer and instigator for me finally putting pen to paper is my wife, Jodie, whose motivation is somewhat different. She's sees a book as something to sell – in our household I bring home the beans and she counts them!

Here it is then: the story of a half-caste Samoan who prior to becoming a world champion athlete struggled through school, was very average at sport, always slightly overweight, dabbled in crime, drugs and alcohol, found himself exploring, developed a passion for the outdoors and made a career out of it while battling with a heart condition, built a house, is raising a family and floundering at golf. That's about it.

CHAPTER ONE
NATHAN FA'AVAE

Hitchhiking from Motueka to Nelson with a mate when I was a teenager, an older couple picked us up, immediately quizzing us about what we were doing, where we were going, and where were we from. We informed the lady we were both local, from Nelson, and she promptly asked if we were born there. My mate told her he was born in Gisborne but had lived in Nelson since he was four. She gave him a hard stare and said, 'You're not really a local then, are you.' Thankfully my own local status was enough to get us a ride home as I was born in Nelson in 1972, the same year Nike was founded (who despite their involvement in globalisation, price-fixing and sweatshops, still make bloody good running shoes). My 5 April birth date makes me an Aries, the Ram, a stubborn, thick-skinned animal that can survive in harsh environments. My favoured Aries traits are, on the light side:

- adventurous and energetic
- pioneering and courageous
- enthusiastic and confident
- dynamic and quick-witted.

And on the dark side:

- selfish and quick-tempered
- impulsive and impatient
- foolhardy and daredevil.

Yep, that's me alright, I can't argue with that.

My mother Jan was born and raised on the West Coast by her mother Maureen and Scottish father Peter Taylor. They lived primarily around the mining towns of Millerton and Granity, north of Westport – a rugged place to live, especially back then, but also scenically majestic. Granddad Peter was injured in a mining accident resulting in him being paralysed on one side for the last 35 years of his life. Despite his disability, his determination and strong will remained. Taking up to five times longer to do most jobs than an able person, he kept an amazing flower garden, massive vegetable patch and cared for a number of fruit trees. He used to walk to the library, some days carrying a heavy bag of novels, which was a half-day trip for him even though it was only 500 metres down the road. He was a tough bugger and had a low tolerance for silly behaviour, or 'acting the goat', as he would call it. A keen sportsman and soccer player in his day, he really enjoyed following his grandchildren's sport. Maureen was a storybook nana to us kids. She spoiled us with ample presents, home baking and love, despite the fact we sometimes 'drove her up the wall'. Seeing us kids happy gave her great pleasure, and we loved to go to Nana and Granddad's, first stop the cookie jar. Peter passed away first (partly, I suspect, due to the cost of the care-home he was in, his Scottish blood never at a healthy pressure when it came to spending money), while Maureen fell victim to Alzheimer's disease and drifted in and out of reality in her final years.

One day I went around to their house to do the lawns and found Nana and Granddad locked in a raging argument. Eventually I managed to calm them down enough to find out what was going on. Granddad told me that Nana had made his lunch, called him in, they ate, cleaned up afterwards, and then she forgot all about it. She then set to and made a second lunch. Granddad was back in his chair for an afternoon snooze when Nana called him back. Nearly choking on his false teeth, he yelled, 'I've had me bleeding lunch already!' Nana wasn't having a bar of that nonsense and insisted he get to the table pronto. That's when I arrived. So I joined them, and through his swearing, Granddad reluctantly managed to eat another hearty meal. I loved spending time with them both and appreciated their generosity. Nana's baking was divine and on special occasions such as birthdays, Christmas and Easter, the gifting was excessive. I would get paid $20 to mow their small lawn – about ten times the amount my mates were getting from their grandparents for the equivalent job.

My father Filemoni is Samoan. He lived in Samoa for the first 20 years of his life and then studied quantity surveying at Victoria University in Wellington. Being the eldest son in his family and the son of a church minister, he enjoyed a few privileges uncommon to most young Samoans. Growing up in the Pacific Islands was a life of freedom and adventure, including a warm climate, swimming, beaches, riding horses and fishing. Rugby is a big part of island life and my dad was a keen rugby player and also partial to the late-night partying that often goes with that sport. In Wellington he played competitive rugby and despite the colder climate enjoyed his time in New Zealand. In the early 1970s he returned to Samoa and began to work utilising his degree.

On completing her school education on the West Coast, my mother moved to Christchurch to study early childhood education (kindy teaching) and did a stint on Norfolk Island through Volunteer Service Abroad after gaining her qualifications. She then travelled to Samoa to help establish the first pre-school centre and there she met my dad. Mum was a strong, independent young woman, especially for the late sixties. One night she went to a social and, as she walked in, Dad, who apparently was a bit of a smooth customer, said, 'We don't see many Palangis around here', which got Mum's attention, but probably not for the right reasons, although he assured her they'd be dancing together before the night was out.

The family were not entirely thrilled about Filemoni dating a Palangi, or 'white girl', perhaps because they knew that in time he'd move to New Zealand. A year later their relationship was cemented when my older brother Braden was born in Apia, the capital of Samoa. Having had some birth complications, Mum was told she probably wouldn't be able to carry any more children, but not long after she discovered she was pregnant again – the Ram was on his way.

CHAPTER TWO

NO FISH

I had a good childhood, growing up in what was a middle-class working family in probably the best town in New Zealand, and consider myself lucky in that sense. By the time I started school Dad had built us a brand-new family home on the hills above Tahunanui Beach with expansive views over Tasman Bay, the Waimea Plains and across to the distant mountain ranges later to become Kahurangi National Park. I didn't know it at the time but the jagged skyline that encompasses Tasman Bay would play a significant part in my life, as in years to come those hills would consume hundreds of my days and nights, providing sanctuary, exploration and untold lessons. My bedroom, however, looked the other way, beyond a datura tree onto a few acres of farmland that was home to some horses, and a forestry plantation that grew to the ridgeline. Essentially we lived in suburbia but we wore gumboots and spent hours out on the fields and in the trees. We kept free-range chickens and pet rabbits, some of which were wild ones that my brother and I had caught by simply running them down until they were exhausted.

Dad still played rugby and we'd go and watch some of his games. From what I can gather, he was a good player with a reputation as a man not to be messed with on the pitch. His nickname was 'Bom Bom' and he's still known by that name to some of his rugby friends even now. Story has it that in one of his first games for Nelson they played a visiting team notorious for rough and foul play, with fights almost guaranteed. There was one particularly feared man in that team who had a streak of evil in him, an angry fella who took out his life frustrations on the rugby field. During the game, this guy deliberately fouled my dad, who promptly popped him with a left jab followed by a long right that laid him out cold. News of the two-punch victory swept the local scene: 'File stood up from the maul and – "Bom Bom" – knocked him out!' A legend was born.

My brother and I spent quite a few Saturdays in the grandstands while Dad played rugby and pulled out his boxing skills now and then. I can remember a lady scowling at me during one game and saying, 'Your dad is a savage – he should be sent back to the Islands.' I hadn't a clue what she meant at the time, but evidently her husband was being stretchered off the field courtesy of Bom Bom. Beer and rugby go together, and Dad liked to celebrate the wins and lament the losses in the clubrooms after each game. Braden and I would be in the car and every so often Dad would bring us out more chips and drinks. I don't ever recall it being an issue – there were other kids in other cars – even though sometimes we could be there until quite late at night. It created tension with Mum, though, who sometimes came and got us, probably to save us from the drunken drive home with Dad who would be well over the legal limit. One game there was a stoppage and when they carried the player off it was Dad, who had broken his leg. It turned out that was the end of his rugby career, aged thirty. Once he mended, he started playing golf, and that's been his sport ever since.

My chosen sport through school years was soccer. It was a game I was good at, understood and enjoyed. I made rep teams from time to time and played a hugely successful season in goal when our regular keeper suffered an injury. I was so good that I was known that year as 'Safe Hands' – I hardly let a ball get by and our team won the league convincingly – but after that I wanted to be out on the field. I dabbled a bit with rugby but never completely comprehended the finer points of the game. I played a bit of cricket too but I was so hopeless that I never got into it properly. Braden, by comparison, was a natural sportsman. He was good at everything – soccer, rugby, cricket; he was in representative teams, usually selected for tournament teams, and qualified for a few national sides. He had the ability to reach the top in any sport he had chosen, I have no doubt about it. He possessed an abundance of talent and excelled at academics and music as well. He dated the headmaster's daughter and even went to golf school, which pleased Dad immensely. Truth be told, he was A grade and I was B grade. I could see that but I didn't care and Mum and Dad never suggested or implied any such thing. I wasn't jealous; I was inspired.

Braden and I spent most days after school playing sport. We would play soccer, rugby, cricket or kicks until it got dark. While the path wasn't direct, that was the start of me becoming a sportsman, with sport the mainstay in my life. I can still smell the grass of the winter afternoons and evenings at Greenmeadows playing fields where Braden and I played together hour after hour, day after day. We'd bike down there with a bag of balls each, rugby or soccer, and kick them around for hours, either through the uprights on the rugby field or taking turns at goalkeeper while the other peppered in the shots. We even knew how to turn the floodlights on if we wanted to play after dark – an 11- and 12-year-old with four fully lit-up fields all to themselves. Although I would normally lose games against him, the occasional win would go a long way.

My primary school years were happy ones and followed a familiar routine. Because Mum was a teacher she would be home for the school holidays and always did interesting things with us, including travelling around and making it to Auckland most years to visit Dad's family there. We went to all sorts of places around the country accompanying Braden to numerous sports tournaments too. As an educator herself, Mum made the decisions around our schooling, and she had some fairly radical views for her era. She was interested in alternative education principles, such as the teaching of A. S. Neill and the Summerhill School, founded on the philosophy that the school should fit the child, instead of the other way round. Looking back, she empowered us from a very young age to make our own decisions, to take responsibility and, most of all, gave us ample room to explore and make mistakes. Both Braden and I had complete freedom to choose what schools we went to. So when Braden finished primary school he insisted on going to Nelson College Preparatory School, because he believed the sporting opportunities there to be greater than at the intermediate schools at the time. At 10 years old, he already knew what he wanted. A year later, I followed, for no other reason than that's where Braden went.

Braden was naturally successful – in his teenage years he was the lead singer in a popular college rock band, heaps of people knew him and he often had his photo in the local newspaper – so I started to get known through association. 'Oh, you're Braden's brother, cool.' I couldn't have agreed more, it was cool. Even so, although we were close growing up and spent vast quantities of time together, we used to fight frequently too – often wrestling matches that would elevate to hitting and punching. Being the weaker one, I made up for what I lacked in strength with violence and aggression, sometimes wielding a weapon in pursuit. I've chased him with cricket bats, golf clubs, an axe, even Mum's car once. Dad brought us some boxing gloves each and they were great – we couldn't lace them up fast enough!

Although they were generally satisfactory, my primary school reports often said the same thing: 'Nathan has not reached his potential.' I was polite and well-mannered and had plenty of friends. I only got the strap once, for throwing mud at girls on the playground. Actually, I was targeting one particular girl, a girl I really liked. Instead of hitting me and yelling 'Naughty, naughty boy!', it's a pity the principal didn't just sit me down and say, 'You obviously really like this girl but you don't have the skills to communicate that to her, so why don't I help you to write her a card, and you can pick a flower from the office garden and give it to her after school.' But he hit me and then had to face the fury of my mother who was vehemently opposed to corporal punishment, and told him sternly that if he ever hit me again he'd better book himself a one-way ticket to Timbuktu. Overall, though, I was a studious kid, did what I was told, volunteered for road patrol, was in the chess club and soccer team, and had the lead role in a school production, *The Flying Doctor*. Braden had a leading role in a show too – he starred as Little Black Sambo and his teacher smeared him in cocoa paste to get him darker.

I grew up in a welcoming home. We regularly had guests and people staying, and it was common to have more than just our family at the dinner table. For a few years my younger cousin Marisa from Auckland lived with us when her family decided she would get a better education in Nelson. Marisa and I used to spend lots of time together but invariably it would end in tears, classic pecking order stuff – Braden would pick on me, I'd pick on Marisa. Mum and Dad regularly hosted Samoan college students, and spending weekends at our place, away from the boarding hostels, was a highlight of their stays. So when I turned 10 and pulled on my uniform and trotted off to Nelson College, I knew the Samoan senior students that weekended with us really well. Many of them were in the First XV rugby team. Knowing people in the right places has been the story of my life in some respects.

The Form 1 'preppies' were the lowest form of life in the system, the easiest prey for the bullies, especially the third-formers, who themselves had predators in the shape of fourth-formers, and so on. The teacher gave us all a nickname based on our initials. I was known as 'No Fish', which was pronounced 'nophish'. Luckily for me, Braden and his Form 2 mates were quite capable chaps and were not afraid of the third-formers, so I had an element of protection. Through his sporting prowess, Braden also had alliances all the way to the very top, the seventh-formers, those who ruled all, so that added another layer of security. While there was some racially prejudiced teasing at times, the Maori and Pasifika students were not a group to be toyed with, so as a 10-year-old brown skin in the school, I had some of the toughest and biggest guys keeping an eye on me too. In the early 1980s the school was still quite traditional and the pecking order required that students followed rank. In most instances that was good for me, but my personality was starting to emerge as I grew up, and that included a dislike for unnecessary authority and rules.

Around that time, my passion for bicycling began too. Mum had taken us on some day rides to the city that had opened new horizons for me. I had always thought a car was needed to get into town. I started to ride my BMX bike everywhere and spent hours at the local track at Tahunanui Beach. My bicycle became my passport to freedom – it was my own vehicle and I was in total control – every bicycle ride was an adventure and I loved it.

As a toddler I spent time in Samoa, where my Samoan grandfather was a minister of the church in the village of Faleasiu. In New Zealand our family were not regular church attendees but Braden and I had to go to Sunday school during our primary school years. I didn't mind it because Dad, perhaps feeling a bit guilty for making us go, used to stop at the dairy after picking us up and let us choose a chocolate bar. We often used to stay overnight at Nana and Granddad's while our parents were away or so they could have some time together. We enjoyed the spoiling we'd get and always looked forward to going there. We had befriended the local kids in that neighbourhood so we had a whole other social group to play with too.

One day I was sneaking some cookies out of Nana's pantry, which I must admit wasn't an easy feat. It demanded great skill and superb timing; Nana's supersonic hearing was tuned to the chink of the pottery lid on the jar. On one of my cookie raids, I took the time to probe a little deeper into the pantry. High on a shelf I spotted a small golden box that shone invitingly so I took it down and examined it carefully. I tilted the lid to discover real cigarettes, not the Spaceman candy ones I had pretended to smoke for years. I didn't know Nana smoked. This was the closest I'd been to an authentic cigarette and it was terribly exciting. I put the box back where I found it, minus one of its contents. Hoping Nana didn't count them, I cupped the cigarette in my hand and casually went back to my room to study it some more. My adventurous streak was taking over – I wanted to try this thing and soon. I needed a light. Surreptitiously pocketing some of Granddad's matches from the tallboy cabinet by the garage door, I burrowed underneath the grapefruit tree and lit the cigarette. Although I didn't know how to inhale, I just puffed away, but at the time I was legitimately smoking so I was thrilled. Unlike many kids who get turned off from that point, I was into it – I thought it was marvellous and I wanted to learn this new skill and show it off to my mates. I decided not to tell Braden, as I wasn't sure I could trust him on this discovery, and besides, here was a chance for me to be better at something than he was for a change.

For the next few months my new hobby was supported by taxing Nana's secret stash. Later I discovered where she kept her master supply, the carton, so I was able to occasionally tax a full packet. The golden box of Benson & Hedges was classy, but I didn't want to smoke the same cigarettes as my Nana for too long. I needed to form a relationship with my own brand. While buying lollies I had studied the vast and colourful array of packets proudly displayed over the top of the shop counter. The one that sparked my interest and habit was North Pole. I felt a connection with the words as they represented exploration. With trembling nerves I entered the local dairy, picked out some bubblegum packets and muttered in my deepest voice, 'Packet of North Pole, please.'

'They for your Nana?'

'Yes, sir.'

I was amazed at how easy it was to buy a packet of smokes; I was 11 years old, cruising the streets on my bike with my very own packet of North Pole. To borrow a more modern expression, I was 'the man'.

I can remember being surprised that the cigarettes themselves were pure white, not the traditional yellow filter I was accustomed to. I was even more surprised to find when I lit up my first one that they had a minty flavour, but I figured it was all part of the North Pole experience. It wasn't until a few months later when I bumped into some other kids smoking at the beach and they pointed out my smokes were menthol and designed for old ladies and made men sterile, that I realised it was no wonder I'd had no trouble buying them. I decided I needed a new brand and to find out what sterile meant quick smart.

With Braden and I regularly riding our bikes off the steep Tahuna Hills, Mum insisted we buy a family home on the flat, which would be safer for biking and also on the school bus route. We moved to the suburb of Stoke, closer to Mum's kindergarten and handy to the timber mill Dad was working at. He'd given away following a career in quantity surveying and opted for more physical and practical work, and probably less responsibility. By now we had started taking long summer holidays camping in Golden Bay. I thoroughly enjoyed these trips, relishing the freedom and open space. We could bicycle all day, swim, dive for paua, and light bonfires on the beach at night. They were special times – eat when you're hungry, sleep when you're tired style.

There was another sub-group of mates from different towns that came together at the camp each year. The first few years we went fishing for eels, played in the sand and kicked balls about. But as we got older our interests changed, more towards girls, smoking and drinking. A few of us discovered that the communal fridges in the camping ground contained beer, and by carefully calculating a tax rate, we could amass a decent collection of bottles and cans without alerting anyone to their diminishing stocks. Together with a cigarette around the campfire, these drinks would round off a good day for us young teenagers. By now, Braden had discovered that I was smoking and he was keen to be part of the action too.

To get smokes, we'd developed some sophisticated shoplifting techniques, with two or three of us distracting the shop attendants while one of us, often me, would gather the goods, typically cigarettes and occasionally by the carton. One day I was particularly adventurous and instead of grabbing the Rothmans I was instructed to get, I snatched a carton of Lucky Strike as well. The boys went wild with praise – I had scored a unique and rare brand and authentic US filterless Mafioso-looking durries at that. As we lay in the park smoking ourselves senseless, we proudly named them 'lung bleeders' because they were so hard to inhale without coughing like a poofter.

This may sound funny, but even though I was regularly shoplifting or nicking stuff, smoking, and drinking whatever alcohol I could get my hands on, I was a good kid. I did my homework, ate my greens and did the jobs Mum and Dad asked me to do, most of the time. I had a few TV programmes I liked to watch, such as *The Dukes of Hazzard*, *The A-Team*, *Battlestar Galactica* and *Diff'rent Strokes*. I had a VIC-20 computer and loved to read comics. I had a Sony Walkman that played Bon Jovi and Twisted Sister tapes. Bizarrely, I had a soap collection, of all things, and what is even more concerning is that it was really big with hundreds of pieces of soap; my dad must have been really worried about that. With our neighbour's permission, I converted her abandoned chicken coop into my den, using it to store my cigarettes and rolling tobacco and various other items I'd stolen. I spent a lot of time making the hut secure and comfortable, lining it with carpet and covering the walls with pictures of naked women. I wasn't particularly interested in them – I had them more because it seemed the right thing to do. Unlike a few of my mates who were obsessed with porn, masturbation and sexuality, I didn't have the same fascination and was in no hurry to have a girlfriend. I knew I'd have a girlfriend one day but that day could be years away. I wanted to play sport, ride my bike and smoke. Not that much has changed, I guess, except I don't smoke any more.

Form 2 (or Year 8 in today's lingo) was a big year for me. I turned 12 and later in the school year something significant happened – school camp. Nelson College owned a wilderness lodge in the Matakitaki Valley, a remote area a few hours' drive from the school, and ran an exceptional outdoor education programme there that would allow the senior students to head into the back country in groups of five, unsupervised, for three, four or even five days at a time. During the Form 2 year, a tame version of the senior programme was delivered and it totally enthralled me. For a week in the hills, we built fires, slept in tents, cooked our own meals, drank from streams, crossed rivers, and climbed mountains navigating with map and compass. I took to this environment like a grinning pig in shit. The best schoolwork I ever did for the year was reporting on the Mataki Lodge camp. I was fully engaged in this subject – outdoor pursuits and wilderness experiences – and wanted more. But it wasn't quite the type of thing my parents were doing – not at that level anyway. I'd have to wait until my next Mataki visit in the fifth form, or Year 11, three years away.

In the meantime I busied myself with school life, soccer, and hanging out with my mates, riding our bikes around Isel Park, playing 'Spacies' (arcade games) at the Avon Dairy and going into town on Friday night, to Spaceworld and Wizards. I developed an interest in music and saved up for a ghetto blaster (stereo), one with a graphic equaliser and double cassette ports. I had no idea what a graphic equaliser did (I still don't), but apparently it was an important feature to have. A couple of my mates were break dancers, so I'd spend hours with them on the streets while they squirmed and writhed around on a piece of cardboard. We formed a gang for a short while, the Stoke Street Kids, and would go out at night and tag 'SSK' around the place; none of us wanted to sniff glue, so we just drank and smoked. But it was sort of pointless marking out our turf because there were no other gangs, so we decided to dissolve SSK; and although we did discuss splitting up and forming a rival gang, we decided that was pointless too – we were stupid, but not that stupid. Uncle Eddie, Dad's brother, lived in Wellington where Braden and I, sometimes with a mate in tow, would travel to stay with him, often to go and see live bands. Eddie lived in the city so we were within walking distance of the video game parlours and McDonald's, everything we needed.

My mates and I used to get up to all sorts of mischief – nothing too serious, graffiti and some other pointless vandalism, as well as a phase of prank calling. Our favourite was having turns informing people that we were from KFC, and that if they could squawk like a chicken they could win a year's supply of free takeaways. One day we called up the school staff and had members of staff clucking and crowing over the phone for hours, much to our amusement. We were about to stop when we dared our mate Kane to phone the deputy principal. Kane went through the entire briefing and when he asked Mr McKenzie to do his best chicken impersonation, Mr McKenzie said, 'Kane, have you got nothing better to do with your weekend?' We were summoned to his office on the Monday, the word getting around the staffroom about who was behind the free chicken competition.

I was doing okay at school. I excelled in English and was quite good at art. I liked geography, hated languages, and struggled at maths. I was put into an alternative maths class, and when Mum asked me what that was I told her it was advanced maths, that I was a mathematical genius. I thought at the time she believed me but looking back I suspect she thought I was a lying little shit. She never intervened though; she prioritised independence. As kids we never saw much of Dad. He worked long hours and in the weekends we played our sport and he played his golf.

Sometimes he'd go to watch Braden play sport but he rarely came to my games, which suited me just fine as he only criticised everything.

By the time I was 15 nothing much had changed in what I did but the ante had been upped. I wasn't in any real trouble because I never got caught. Fashion was now a factor and having the cool gear was very important. In my social group we all wore basketball boots even though none of us played the game. Jeans and a canvas belt, Pony hoodie and sometimes a tee shirt over top. A real oddity for a while were black blazers purchased from thrift stores; we'd then get them screen printed with our favourite band on them, and I had Dire Straits.

I had a job delivering pamphlets, junk mail, which would take me about three hours every fortnight. I could do it on my bike with a satchel on my shoulder, and just needed to resupply a few times from home. The pay was low but I used to make it worth my time by taking coins from any milk money that was out at people's gates (this was still the good old days when milk came in glass bottles and there was home delivery). I'd give them a pamphlet and take a coin, seemed reasonable. I used to stop at the Nayland Road dairy and spend my riches, often chatting with the girls from the family that owned it, one of whom was Jodie. Amazingly, it took some years for my stratagem to be discovered. Some professor on the route concluded that the same day they received their junk mail, they'd not receive their milk.

Braden was playing regular live gigs with his band (Blue Light discos organised by the police) and even his band practices became gigs in their own right, an audience of drinkers and smokers. Our parents had busted him as a smoker. He didn't care. He was a rock star so he needed an element of bad. He didn't expose me though so I remained secret about it. He ran into a few problems with alcohol resulting in some drunk and disorderly behaviour, once again facing Mum and Dad. I was starting to acquire the air of an angel, innocent despite the fact I was often as or even more guilty. Braden was always quite protective and often took the heat. We'd both got to the stage (or age) where we had access to marijuana (one of my mates used to get it from his mother), so we were smoking that as well.

Sixteen was another milestone – more independence and more mischief. Being young for my school year, most of my friends were up to a year older. This meant they had driver's licences, some had their own cars, they could legally buy cigarettes, and some could pass for 18-year-olds and easily buy alcohol. If that failed we'd wait outside the liquor shop for a dodgy-looking character to come by and get them to buy us what we wanted, for a small fee. We'd also discovered that tomato plant leaves, when dried and burnt, smelt close enough to marijuana to be sold as that to easily fooled juniors – if we felt they were getting suspicious we'd lace the bags with a small amount of the real thing – until one day a customer was caught by his teacher who then came looking for us. 'It's just tomato leaves – honest, Sir.' We had to repay the kid, and although tests luckily bore out our claim it drew the curtain on that particular income stream.

I was going to a few parties that lasted all night, and they were often very wild. It was like they followed a script: somebody's parents would go away so a few friends would come around for drinks; a few hours later the music was pumping, carloads more teenagers would turn up, including a few gatecrashers; there would be plenty of alcohol and dope; inevitably a couple would have a domestic drama, a fight would break out, the liquor cabinet would be raided, sex would take place on the parents' bed and the noise would flare up until someone would yell, 'The pigs are here!' The police would arrive to a rapidly diminishing party and a young teenager who had just realised that they had done something really stupid, standing in the middle of a vandalised house.

Fundamentally, I had sound (or at least some) morals and values. Sure, I was breaking a few rules, but more in a Robin Hood type of way. I wasn't a bad boy, but I saw some bad out there. I witnessed mindless violence, deliberate vandalism, blatant thieving and some extremely unethical and immoral behaviour. I didn't like some of the things I saw but felt quite powerless to do anything about it. It reinforced for me, though, what was important and what I didn't want to be like. There wasn't a shortage of losers around and I sure as hell wasn't going to be one of them.

CHAPTER THREE

NASTY FIGHT

There was a bully on our school bus, a tough guy who commandeered the same seat, or any other seat he wanted. As he came down the aisle one day I just knew he was going to evict me from my seat. By now I had developed a strong dislike for being told what to do.

'Move, I'm sitting here,' he ordered, towering over me.

'Fuck off, I was here first, you'll have to stand.'

I'd been in a few fights by now, mainly due to racial jokes. Fights are not as glamorous as they look in the movies. Being punched in the face hurts a lot and stuns you with shock. I took a big blow to the head and the blood quickly followed, but there was no way I was going to move. By now my brother had arrived on the scene and the bully sensed he was outnumbered. He backed away, still feeling strong because I was covered in blood, but I'd won some respect along with a sore jaw. The bully left me alone after that.

Another activity I got up to with my mates was 'doin' cars'. This involved sneaking out at night and wandering the streets breaking into vehicles, by either simple techniques with wire or just trying the doors to find one unlocked, which back in the 1980s was quite often the case. We would target money, loose coins mainly, music cassettes, or anything else of interest or value. On a good night we'd make about 20 bucks each but the appeal was more for the excitement than the rewards. One night I found a professional archery set with a quiver of arrows. After firing a few around the neighbourhood I took it back to my hut. I later traded it for some marijuana but the guy lived about 5 km away and biking around with a bow and arrows would look a bit suspicious so I had to wait for the cover of darkness to make the deal. On two occasions we found cars with keys in them so we treated ourselves to a drive – we didn't 'steal' cars, we just 'relocated' them.

Over summer, I was actually earning legitimate money picking berries. I was a fast picker and could sustain long hours of hard work no problem if I knew that the more I picked the more I'd earn. We were paid on bucket weight so I always topped my buckets up with a bit of water to increase the total. Most teenagers got bored and started berry fights, ending up losing their jobs, but I worked like hell and made as much money as I could.

Looking back, I had twisted ideas about things – perhaps all teenagers do. I spun in two social circles. One involved stealing, crime, drugs, video games and getting pissed. I wasn't a bad-arse but I aspired to be one. I was training my body to tolerate alcohol and had decided I needed to drink daily or at least regularly to achieve this state. I was well aware that being able to 'handle your piss' was a very important skill one must possess, elevating one's coolness to epic proportions. Braden had established a neighbourhood hangout in the shed at the bottom of our property. We named it 'The Shed' – for want of something more creative. All our mates hung out there and often slept over. It had a big stereo, TV and video player. It was complete with a dozen or so mattresses, a few couches, beer fridge and dartboard. Braden also had his music equipment, guitars and drum kit. There was always a beer and smoke to be enjoyed in the shed while listening to a favourite record. We used to gather there weekly to watch *Miami Vice*. The rule was that when Sonny Crockett, one of the lead characters, was smoking we would have to as well. Given he had a cigarette on the go almost every minute of every episode, we'd consume a few packets between us in the hour. Over time we also watched the entire James Bond collection.

Being committed to adapting my body to smoking and drinking, it suited me just fine. Mum always kept a cask of wine in the fridge so some days I'd just knock back a wine to make sure my system was processing alcohol of some sort. Around that time tattoos started to come into the mix, often from homemade guns using a small electric motor and a drawing compass. I ended up with a yin-yang symbol, even though at the time I thought it was the Town & Country Surf logo. I'm just grateful I got something timeless – some guys got Motley Crue or Iron Maiden tattoos, and I'm highly doubtful a 75-year-old will still be listening to the Crue.

The other circle I was spinning in was the outdoors one. In the fifth form I was able to join the school's Mataki leadership programme – the 'boot camp' style course that trained students to lead groups on sixth- and seventh-form trips. That year I spent two weeks at Mataki Lodge and it was hugely rewarding. I started to spend more weekends in the hills tramping and less time in town getting drunk and being a dickhead. One factor in moving away from the nowhere lifestyle was the arrival of my younger sister Zariana. Having a new life in the house changed my perspective. It highlighted that I had a life ahead that offered many great and wonderful things, if I could get my shit together. I wanted to achieve some significant things I could be proud of, and clambering out my window at 2 a.m. dressed in black, sneaking around in the shadows was not going to be one of them. It had to stop. Another big eye-opening moment was when one of my tramping partners entered and completed the Maungatapu triathlon. From memory, the race included a 25 km mountain run, 12 km kayak and 55 km road cycle over two decent mountain saddles, taking most people about seven hours to complete. I was fascinated. I started to wonder if I could do something like that.

In the sixth form and 16 years old I was spending most of my free time in the mountains tramping and in the rivers trout fishing. I had a motorbike that enabled me to reach the trail ends and also had mates with cars that wanted to venture out. I quickly developed strong bushcraft skills and spent six weeks leading groups at Mataki Lodge that year. I was into pushing boundaries and probing deeper into uncharted areas that the school groups traditionally went to. The only subject at school I cared about was outdoor education. I started running to improve my fitness for hiking but I still drank, smoke and went on stealing sprees with my other mates. Around that time street kids were common and we emulated them a little. The difference was that they sniffed glue and slept under bridges. I went home sniffing a hearty meal, hot shower and warm bed.

Part of the reason I focused on becoming a better person was to try and hook a better girl. I knew the good girls were not going to want to date some miniature gangster, not when they could date an adventurer extraordinaire. I never intended having loads of girlfriends, instead I planned to streamline the dating process, spend the time choosing wisely, and save a lot of hassle, money and time. All the girls I've ever been interested in have been females I believed I could spend my life with. I've always looked at relationships with long-term projections. I think the first girl I really became interested in was interested in me too, but she had a boyfriend at the time and it got complicated. Deep down I felt she was too good for me anyway. I still needed to become a better person, so I headed to the hills. The next girl I fell for was an exchange student from Australia. I was building up the courage to kiss her on one date, the first kiss, manoeuvring carefully towards the moment, when she very casually said, 'Hey, do ya wanna fuck?' Gotta love the Australian way! We had some fun for a brief time and then she went home, so I headed to the hills.

By the sixth form I'd had enough of school. My rebellious nature had got me involved in a few confrontations over that year and I couldn't see the point of doing another. Most of my close friends had left and their lifestyle appealed to me more than being a schoolboy – they had jobs, cars, money for smokes and could buy beer by the crateful. I came home at the end of the school year and announced to Mum, 'That's it, I'm leaving school.' Much to my surprise she said, 'If that's what you want to do, that's your choice.' In general terms, I had expansive freedom growing up, which I think was just as well, because if Mum and Dad had tried to pin me down or put too many limits on me, they would have had a war on their plate – I'm sure Mum knew that. I didn't know it at the time but, looking back, I was a kid who needed room and space to explore.

So in 1988 at 16 years old, I moved out of home, tried working in forestry and on the docks unloading fishing boats, before settling to work in dispatch on an apple orchard. The forestry job only lasted a week because I was placed in a gang of skinheads and we clashed a little on some issues – I don't think the boss was convinced that the cut above my eye on the first day resulted from hitting myself with my loppers. That year my parents took us three kids to Australia to the World Expo. Although I'd travelled over the Pacific to Samoa a few times, it felt like Australia was my first overseas trip, and it was terribly exciting. The plan was to do a road trip from Sydney to Brisbane, visiting some family, being tourists and going to the Expo. Though what it really was for me and Braden was a road trip drinking XXXX beer and smoking cones. The drinking age in Australia at that time was two years below that in New Zealand, so we only had to pass as 18-year-olds, not 20-year-olds, and as it was very relaxed over there anyway, I assume they saw these two Kiwi lads cruising about and thought we must be of age. Despite throwing up out of the car window a few times, due to a few too many shots, the trip was superfun and planted a travel seed for me. I was right into the freedom and exploration of travel, ever-changing landscapes and situations, and planned to do a lot more.

In summary, at 16 I'd been in love twice, left school, left home, got a job, rolled my own cigarettes, rode a motorbike, drank beer and escaped into the mountains whenever I could. I had acquired a taste for a few spirits along the way, particularly Southern Comfort, Bacardi and rum, but everything on the top shelf held my interest. I thought many of those drinks were simply delicious. I'd sometimes meet a mate up the river on our motorbikes, and we'd fish for trout, light a fire, cook a meal and drink a bottle of liquor.

My most memorable motorbike experience was when a mate and I headed to Mount Arthur for a tramping weekend. I had a Honda XR 200, steel tank, tired, gutless. The steep road up Graham Valley was too much for the bike with two boys, two packs and two bottles of whisky. On the steepest pitch, I got off, took my pack and told my mate to ride up and wait. What I meant was ride the 500 metres up the gorge and wait, but he understood it as ride to the top, which was about 6 km uphill. I stood gasping in disbelief as the engine faded into the distance. 'You fucking idiot!' I cursed as I hiked up the road for over an hour. I was so wild when I reached the car park that I jumped on the bike and rode it in to the hut, highly illegal. Two days later we had a small issue in getting the bike out again, so I put a sock over the licence plate and we blatted out.

The fact we were in the hills in the first place was credit to the Mataki camps we'd done. A by-product of the Mataki Lodge scheme was that annually it produced a small group of highly skilled, experienced, fit and capable young outdoor leaders. Twenty years later people would say that 16 is far too young to be responsible for others in the outdoors, but I believe that by 16, or even earlier, young people are easily capable of exploring the back country on their own, provided they have been taught the necessary skills. Going for a hike in New Zealand is literally child's play when you consider what 16-year-olds, especially in more isolated cultures, have done over the course of history.

During my final year at school an unofficial competition had started over who was doing the most epic trips, the longest, the roughest and remotest, and also the fastest – speed was important. A young man named David Moore was setting the pace with speed ascents of Nelson's surrounding hills, including a 60 km route involving solo trips up Mount Richmond (1684 m) practically non-stop. Inspired by this example, friends and myself were also penetrating deep into the parks at fast pace, often travelling by torchlight to get more miles under us, in either Mount Richmond Forest Park or North West Nelson Forest Park. We went hard, and even now, as a seasoned endurance athlete, I acknowledge that the trips I was doing as a teenager were bloody out there and still ones I'd be challenged by now.

As young boys ripping through the woods, we uncovered one of the biggest conspiracies in the sport of hiking, a huge industry that has robbed people of cash and enjoyment. The device is commonly known as a hiking boot. We'd start our trips in boots but take some soft-soled running shoes as spares for around the huts and camp. Experience soon taught us that frequently our feet would get sore and we'd end up with our running shoes on and boots tied to our packs. One day someone suggested we flag the boots away and just start in runners. Since then I very rarely wear boots, only in snow. I estimate I've spent about five hundred days of my life hiking in the mountains and on about fifty of those days I wore boots, around ten per cent. I am starting to wear boots more because they do last longer than a heavy outdoor trail shoe but I still find the shoes far more comfortable.

Those early tramping years started to change my perspective on distances. I remember hiking to some mountains on one trip and looking down at a town, and it taking me a while to figure out what it was. It was Blenheim. As a kid I'd always perceived Blenheim to be a long way away, so to hike for a few days and see it gave me a real sense of achievement. I believed what I was doing was quite extraordinary. I used to enjoy nothing more than climbing to a high point and rolling a cigarette, taking in the views and fresh air!

I enjoyed life out of school. I worked hard on the orchard in the packing shed, often working late on night shifts. I had my own room and my own shelf in the fridge in the shared workers' accommodation. I kept my shelf well stocked with beer and most days enjoyed a can with lunch. I stopped playing team sport once I left school and spent any free time exploring the rivers and trails in the parks. On occasion I'd venture into Nelson and go to a party with my mates, or drive around and around town for no real reason, drinking beer and toking on joints. I was starting to get frightened with the speed my mates were driving cars, often under the influence. I can remember some terrifying trips in cars hitting and even exceeding 100 miles per hour – crap drivers in old cars. Nightclubs had arrived on the scene and we spent some time in them, as under-age drinkers and dancers.

One night after the apple season had ended, I was squashed in the back seat of a car that was pulled over by the police. It turned out the car was overloaded – especially as there were people in the boot – and that the vehicle had been reported stolen. I didn't know this when I had just jumped in for a lift, either from the beach to town, or from town to the beach (occasionally we'd go up the Maitai Valley too – beach, town, valley, or variations thereof – they were the options, small town). As the police asked questions and collected details, the friend I was with discovered that one of the officers was his uncle, who pulled us aside and asked us what we were doing. He believed us when we said we'd only hitched a lift and that this problem wasn't really anything to do with us. He gave us a warning, and told us to go home and do something decent with our lives. It was a close call and it got me thinking. There were better things out there to do than this bullshit. I was far happier wandering around the mountains but I also had ties to this teenage business of alcohol and cars and stuff. That night, with a few drinks in me, I remember sitting on the footpath outside my home crying. I was confused and upset. I wasn't happy with this scene. I needed to action some change.

CHAPTER FOUR

NEW FUTURE

Part of my problem as a teenager was that I had no interest in a career or any inkling of what I wanted to do. I was happy to get a job but there was a gap between seasonal work and I didn't know what I wanted to do long-term. I had absolutely no clue, no career goals or even a direction. I had a list of tramping trips I wanted to do and had made some plans for a couple of 10-day missions, but before I embarked I needed to sign up for the unemployment benefit, or 'the dole' as it's commonly known. At the interview with the caseworker they asked the normal questions about what I'd been doing, what I wanted to do and what I was interested in. I said I didn't really mind what work I did in the short term and that my main interest was exploring the wilderness and adventures. By the end of the meeting I had myself a small income and some information about a course offered at Whenua Iti Outdoor Pursuits Centre.

It was a 12-week explorers' course targeting disadvantaged people in the community. The criteria meant the students had to be either unemployed, low education, in trouble with the law, have low self-esteem/confidence, minimal life skills, or dealing with drug or alcohol issues. While you didn't have to tick all the boxes, some of the students did, and I met enough, or most of the criteria, to get a spot. The course was advertised as a personal development programme involving abseiling, caving, kayaking, rafting, rock climbing, running, tramping and windsurfing. This was my ultimate dream and, as I got paid more to do the course than be unemployed, life was starting to roll. I relocated to Riverside Community, a colourful and convenient accommodation provider along the road from the centre.

On the first day, I met the centre founder, director and main tutor Hazel Nash along with the 11 other students I was to do the course with. It was an eclectic group, ranging in age between 16 and 26, a few naughty lads, a couple of geeks, some with psycho problems, a group of drug/alcohol rehab guys, one female and me. We went through the standard introductions and trust exercises associated with such courses, with the aims, objectives and rules spelt out to us loudly and clearly. There is no doubt the course was perfectly timed for me; I was destined to take lessons from it and for it to be a major corner on my life's road. Fitness was a key component with regular running woven into the programme. The tutors would often drop us off 5 to 10 km before we'd get to an activity location and we'd foot the final bit. I already had one of the higher levels of fitness in the group and enjoyed the feelings of strength and stamina.

Early into the course I decided I would stop smoking. While we weren't allowed alcohol on the course or at the accommodation, I kept a few beers and a hip flask of Southern Comfort handy for a quiet snifter at the end of the day. A drug and alcohol counsellor talked to us about abuse, problem drinking and alcoholism, and said alcoholics tend to drink alone, don't know when to stop and often drink daily. As the workshop went along, I realised I had many of the signs of becoming an alcoholic and that frightened me somewhat. I knew that in drunken states I was a bloody idiot too. I nearly got booted off the course at the beginning when I suggested to a few of the guys that we hitch into Motueka one night and get some drinks. They shot me down and threatened to report me should I suggest such a thing again. I opted to stay off the drink for the rest of the course and to this day have not touched alcohol again. I know I wasn't an alcoholic and probably would never have been but, given my personality (inability to moderate), it's probably a good thing and it's saved me time, money, and a shitload of embarrassment and regret.

The course went by fast and I thrived on the daily challenges, the adventures and the learning. I liked the team environment, the risk and the danger. I was in my groove, having heard my calling. I made a decision then and there to become an outdoor tutor, and not just any outdoor tutor – I was going to be an *excellent* outdoor tutor. I found some mentors within the group too. One guy in particular, Enyaw, was very insightful, and we'd often sit up late chatting about life and philosophy. We discussed all sorts of things – alcoholism was a hot topic, running, fast cars, people, women, tarot cards, theories of creation and the universe. After getting to know him well over a few months I asked him the origin of his name. Expecting some exotic back story, I was left a tad speechless when he told me it was 'Wayne' spelt backwards, and because he didn't really like that name, he just reversed it. Jeez, Wayne . . .

The course held multiple discoveries for me. I learnt all sorts of technical skills, more about teamwork and communication, and a lot about myself. In one feedback session called the 'Hot Seat', where one student at a time sat on a red cushion in the middle of a circle while the rest of us offered them constructive feedback, Hazel told me she thought I was 'judgemental' and that I needed to look at that. I didn't know what she meant but I made a mental note not to be judgemental any more. Because I was so in my element in the outdoors, I shone brightly as a bit of a star student, and as a result began to see that I was highly capable, with more talents than I'd realised. I observed the daily life of the outdoor instructors who worked at the centre with fascination, confirming for me that that's where I was heading. In one workshop a tutor said to us: 'Discover what you enjoy doing the most, and then find someone to pay you to do it.' That became my mantra.

I learnt that outdoor instructors and guides could work all over New Zealand and the world, that Kiwis were famous for adventure exploits, and that we led the world in adventure tourism. There was even a dedicated magazine aptly named *NZ Adventure* that documented this wonder world that I was being immersed in. To say I was inspired does not do this period of my life justice; the truth is I was enlightened. I was in awe of the tutors. They would report in after the weekend with tales of climbing Mt Cook, running marathons, rafting remote rivers, and hiking into areas with no trails and huts. Now 17 years old, I knew with 100 per cent certainty the path my life was going to take and I hadn't a minute to waste. From then on, every waking moment was dedicated to becoming an accomplished adventurer and that momentum still carries me, although for different reasons these days.

My adventure-racing foundation was being built strongly; I was learning a vast range of skills plus redefining my perceptions of what was possible. On one trip, a 65 km trek through some rugged country, the Wangapeka, we reached the midway point of the four-day hike when one of the students developed a severe toothache. We had one tutor, Martha, and one trainee tutor, Andrew, along with the 12 students. After much discussion, it was decided that Andrew and I would escort the student with the toothache back to the beginning of the track where we could use the public phone to have him picked up and taken to the nearest dental clinic. Andrew and I would then cover the return ground fast and catch up with the party before the end of the trip. With roughly 30 km of hiking ahead of us, Andrew soon realised that once we'd dropped the student off it was going to be just the pair of us on a mission to cover 60 km or so to regroup with our team. Knowing the speed I could move at, he opted to settle into a hut and let me go alone with the student. That suited me fine. By the end of the day we reached the car park and I waited around until the student was collected. Then I set off back up the track into the fast-closing darkness. I was comfortable hiking at night under torchlight.

I walked 30 km that night and arrived back at the hut early morning, got the fire going and cooked Andrew and I some breakfast, and we then got back on the track and hiked another 30 km to join the others late that night. I had basically hiked 90 km non-stop and had been awake nearly 40 hours. I guess what was intriguing to the others was that I wasn't tired or fatigued. I sat around drinking tea and chatting, and would have been happy to keep going.

Another hugely significant moment took place when we were returning from a day of windsurfing in Golden Bay, driving over Takaka Hill in 'Thunder Guts', an old green Bedford van. Long before health and safety regulations, all 12 students were sitting in the back on beanbags and scraps of foam, amid circulating fumes and deafening engine noise. As we climbed the hill, which is really more like a mountain, the tutor told us about an endurance triathlon. 'You see that mountain range over there, they run over it, a marathon, then they kayak across the lake up there, run down to the valley, then cycle over this hill,' he said. Some of the students were amazed and spoke about this as if it was mission impossible. 'I could do that, easy,' I told them. It got a round of laughs. Later back at the centre when we were cleaning up, the tutor, JT, pulled me aside. In summary, he told me that I was full of talk, that the people who did that race deserved higher respect, and that if such a thing was 'easy' for me, then I should be doing it. I was really upset, watering eyes upset. Deep down I heard what he was saying. I tended to talk things up. I decided that day that I was going to do the race, which was only a few months away, and I was going to prove to the tutor I had more substance than he'd given me credit for (although I suspect he knew I could do it, probably easily).

By the end of the course my passion, interest and general obsession with being an outdoor instructor was clearly obvious so I was offered the chance to remain at the centre as a trainee tutor. By the end of the second course Hazel suggested that to cement a career in outdoor education I should go to Otago University and complete a degree in physical education which at the time was the closest qualification to the field. For that to happen, though, I had to complete secondary school and gain University Entrance. If I wanted to be smart about my goal, I had to go back to school.

However, before 1989 was up, I had my first endurance triathlon to complete. My brother and a friend agreed to be my support crew and with Dad's brown Toyota Crown and a borrowed kayak, we headed off to the big event. On our road trip, we cruised the streets of Motueka and found ourselves in the health-food store. Probably afraid we were about to steal something, the shopkeeper asked, 'Can I help you, boys?'

Chest puffed out, I replied, 'I'm racing in the North West Nelson Endurance Triathlon tomorrow, and I'm looking for energy food.' We got ushered over and in a quiet discussion got shown some green pills from under the counter. It felt like we'd entered the world of performance-enhancing drugs and banned substances.

'Do you boys know what the strongest animal is?' he asked.

'A lion?'

'No, guess again.'

'A gorilla?'

'No, no, no, it's a whale, and do you know what whales eat?'

'Fish?'

'No, seaweed, and this is the pill form, it's called spirulina,' he said as he held the pills up to the light.

Armed with a jar of whale food, I felt invincible, which in hindsight was somewhat foolish, given whales are massive lumbering swimmers that tend to make headlines mainly when they're either hunted or beached.

I was only 17 and embarking on a race that would take me all day. It went well for me. I ran through the mountains and kayaked the lake, ran down the valley and mounted my bike. By now I'd been racing for over six hours and handling it fine. I was about midfield. Halfway up the hill I started to struggle, the heat of the day sapping my strength, and I ran out of drinking water. Luckily, my support crew caught up and pulled alongside.

'Boy, am I glad to see you guys – I need some water.'

They drifted back a bit and then came alongside again. 'Um, we don't have any water, we can find some, but we've got beer.'

'What! No water? I can't stomach beer!'

'How about some of the whale pills?'

'Sure, pass them here.'

They drove off in search of water while I tried, with a dry mouth, to eat spirulina tablets – not wise. I finished the race in just over eight hours, flashing a big grin and a green tongue.

At the finish line a number of people came up to congratulate me on my effort. I thought it was quite strange, but these days if I saw a 17-year-old complete such a race, I'd congratulate them too. It was quality positive reinforcement for me and I soaked it up. Someone even mentioned that I should do the Coast to Coast – now there's an idea. But first I needed to re-enrol in school.

CHAPTER FIVE

NAYLAND FRIENDS

In 1990 I enrolled at Nayland College and moved back home. I was still 17 years old but I felt many years beyond that. I didn't want to return to Nelson College as I'd had a few run-ins with staff and bent a few of the school rules towards the end of my final year and I wasn't sure I would be welcomed back. The main issue was my growing resistance to authority and my lack of tact in questioning things – rebellious, you could say. The main benefits of Nayland College were that it was closer to where we lived, the senior students did not wear uniform, and I wanted a girlfriend so being a co-ed school increased the odds – half the school was girls and, from observation, there was a pretty good selection.

Over that summer I read an article in *NZ Adventure* magazine about a guy who climbed to the top of Mt Cook with his mountain bike to ride it around on the summit. Taking the bike to the top seemed a bit silly but the mountain bike itself enthralled me. I'd been riding a motorbike for a year or so and getting into the mountains was my main interest, so the whole idea of a pushbike that could be taken into these areas had my name written all over it. I made a trip into Nelson City to a bike store to find out more about these new bikes.

The first place I visited didn't appear to stock any of these revolutionary bicycles, but as I got further inside I saw a display in the far corner, four bikes superbly displayed on wood bark to give the impression of the outdoors, among some greenery and rocks for added effect. Awesome! These things were mean, the fat knobbly tyres being the big attraction. Prior to this, I'd ridden BMX bikes with a maximum value around $200. The cheapest mountain bike on display was $1,000. You could buy a good second-hand car for $500 back then – a Datsun 180B, Toyota Corolla, or even a Ford Anglia.

A gentleman approached to ask if I needed help. I explained to him that I wanted to get a mountain bike but saving $1,000 would take me some time, especially as I was about to start school again. He informed me that with their HP programme all I needed was a 10 per cent deposit and we could negotiate the terms, possibly up to 24 months. What the hell was HP? Wasn't it a sauce? I asked him to explain this new lingo for me. Soon afterwards I can remember saying, 'So what you're saying is, if I give you $100, I can ride this bike out of the shop today?'

That afternoon I was the proud new owner of a totally rude (I thought it was cool at the time) smoky pink Avanti Ridge Rider, and for the next two years I was paying off a bike I had long before wrecked and sold on. After no more than a minute of riding my mountain bike I officially became a passionate mountain biker and set out to perfect this new sport. From that day on, I spent about two to four hours a day riding in the forest, every day. I would even go as far as saying that by the end of the 1990s, no one knew Hira Forest better than me. I was riding every road and every firebreak at least once a week, 99 per cent of the time for fun and fitness, one per cent of the time to monitor a few marijuana plants I had growing in there.

I had also entered the Buller Marathon because that's what outdoor instructors did in their spare time. My running was going really well. At one of the Whenua Iti workshops (the context was drugs and alcohol but it could apply to most things) we'd learned that to make lasting change in your life, you need to change your playground, playmates and play toys. Being back in Nelson I needed to distance myself from my buddies whose weekends revolved around cars, parties and heavy metal music, the beach, town and valley. The main issue was the drugs and alcohol that circulated as well. That's what I ultimately wanted distance from. I needed distraction. One of my tools to achieve this separation was to go running on Friday and Saturday nights, so from about 7 p.m. to 10 p.m. on these evenings I'd lace up and hit the pavement. I often used to run around the gathering places of my friends and it provided a different perspective. I used to think I was out running to become a better person, more worthy and, although I didn't know the term back then, I was on a journey of self-improvement. Experts would probably say I was just running away from problems and I'd agree 100 per cent. I reckon you can run from just about anything – I'm still running!

My new school life began with vigour and born-again enthusiasm. The year away from school had taught me how many great opportunities there were and how many I'd wasted. I was going to maximise this year, that's for sure. It was particularly pleasing to discover half a dozen mountain bikes in the stands on my first day. They had their own special parking area so I racked mine there too. I looked forward to meeting the other mountain bikers and by later that week we'd connected and planned some rides together. Finishing school at 3 p.m. and still having six hours of daylight in the summer meant a small group of us were clocking up mega kilometres each week.

Because I'd played some representative soccer in my age group, I already knew some of the guys at school, one being Deane Parker, who'd been the goalkeeper in the team. It turned out he was one of the mountain bikers and we were in a lot of the same classes so we hung out. Deane was a valuable source of information about the girls in the school and was able to offer useful advice. I'd earmarked a few potentials and discussed these with him. One lunchtime, we were sitting at our usual spot near the gym and cafeteria when a girl walked by whom I recognised from a brief meeting of a friend of a friend a few months earlier.

'Who's that?' I asked Deane.

'You like her? That's Jodie MacDonald, sixth-former, not bad, pretty cool, good runner, has a mountain bike, parents own the dairy down the road, got a boyfriend though,' he said.

Yes, I remembered her from the dairy, that's right. I wasn't worried that she had a boyfriend. I was ex-Nelson College, I had mates who were bad bastards, I'd been in the workforce, I had rafted wild rivers, abseiled into deep dark caves, run a marathon for fun, and I wasn't afraid of anyone, especially a sixth-form Nayland boy. I decided at that moment Jodie was the girl I was going to chase.

Early on in the school year a newsletter was circulated asking students what events, if any, they wanted to enter in the school swimming sports. Although at Nelson College I hadn't gone in even one swimming event the entire time I was there, at Nayland I decided to make up for that and promptly entered every event, about 15 altogether. Then I went and saw the head of PE and told him that I'd entered all the events including the diving competition but I didn't know how to dive. I had a week to learn so we headed to the pool for some lessons. After a few head splitters, belly flops and even some back landings, I could finally go from the end of the high diving board into the pool in a movement that vaguely resembled a dive. The swimming sports came around and the day became a test of endurance, completing events one after another. On occasions, they had to delay the start of some races to allow me time to exit the pool at one end and be back on the starting blocks for the next. After a couple of early podium spots I then came last in every event. I think some students were thankful for my presence because I removed any chance of them being last. Appreciative of my continuous exertion, students, staff and spectators cheered on my Forrest Gump-style efforts.

The day concluded with the diving competition with everyone gathering around the square pool. I had to execute three dives and I was psyched to nail them well, mainly because Jodie was in the diving competition too. I did the first and second dives well, but for my final dive the judges announced it had to be a somersault.

'What? I didn't know that – I can't do them,' I called down.

The head judge repeated the rules and they quietly joked amongst themselves.

One thing I've always been good at is making splashes so I thought 'Stuff it', took a running leap and angled off towards the judges, crashing close by in a bomb that sent a wall of water all over them and the judging table. That's what I think of your somersault rule!

The school year went by quickly, with all my spare time spent either working or mountain biking. Weekends were devoted to mountain-bike races and a crew of us even organised our own race series, for which we'd make up race posters to circulate throughout the bike stores.

I had indicated to Jodie that I was interested in her but she was pretty aloof, or playing hard to get. Well aware she had a boyfriend at the time, I did roll on up uninvited to a party I knew she was at, knocked on the door and asked to speak to her. She emerged awkwardly and asked me what on earth I wanted, turning up like this and creating a scene, scandalous. I told her I really liked her and that I thought we should start going out with each other. She told me I'd best leave, which I did. I'd said what I needed to say and knew it was just a matter of time – she'd come around.

I had a number of jobs that year to fund my mountain-biking addiction. Dad had generously loaned me $2,000 to buy a proper race bike so I had to work regularly to repay him. I had a number of seasonal jobs: one was an after-school job picking and bagging apples for a local store; another was a night job packing kiwifruit. I didn't mind the work, it was quite social and a number of school friends were doing the same thing, a couple of them mountain bikers too. The best job I had, though, was riding rickshaws in Nelson City in the weekends, mainly Friday and Saturday nights.

Greg Fraine was a local bike-shop owner and had represented New Zealand as an Olympic cyclist. He was always supportive of the younger riders and had imported a dozen or so rickshaw bikes from somewhere in Asia. The plan was to offer them as a novel taxi service to get around town. We would pay Greg a commission on what we earned. The late-night rickshaw work primarily involved taking drunken partygoers from one bar or club to the next. They tipped generously and often wanted us to race other rickshaws. I was part of a core group of about six operators and we would stage sensational races across town, ensuring the racing was close and exciting. We could make a few hundred dollars some nights. The bikes, though, proved a nightmare for Greg and required hours of servicing after each weekend, mainly rebuilding the rear wheels. But it was super-fun times, good training and we all paid for our racing mountain bikes.

I became aware of something then that enabled me to make a career out of being an athlete. Many of my friends were fit and skilled mountain-bike riders. We had good bikes and we all rode them plenty. We'd race regularly in events and we'd often race each other in training. But I was winning the majority of the races – in fact, I was rarely beaten. One thing I was acutely aware of was that I rode more than anyone else. I was always doing add-ons to our rides. We'd go riding and once we'd split up to return home, I'd nearly always go home the long way, taking in some extra climbs. Some days I'd even ride alone before we met for our group ride. As a young emerging athlete, I become convinced that in order to be the best, I simply needed to ride longer and further than everyone else, and for many years, I think that was all it came down to. I was yet to learn that copious amounts of training do not directly correlate with success, and that athletes who do train massive volumes in fact run the risk of burnout, boredom and losing the spark that fired them up from the get go.

After running the Buller Marathon in 3:15, I was keen to run under three hours because I'd learned that to be a member of the sub-3:00 club was a landmark in the sport. I had done some math and had a plan. I could cruise 10 km in 40 minutes, so I figured if I ran at four minutes per km all day, I'd breeze home to a 2:45 to 2:50 time – piece of cake. And if only I'd had cake for breakfast instead of Coco Pops I may have done that.

I reached the 10 km mark so close to 40 minutes it was uncanny. I went through 20 km at 1:20 on the dot, fleet-footed. As I ran towards the 30 km and 2:00 hour marks, media started to gather around me, cars driving alongside with photographers hanging out the window, cameras snapping away. 'That's right folks, I'm the man and we all know it,' I said to myself, confidence boosted. These reporters had done their homework; headline reads 'Teenager smashes the 3:00-hour barrier'. Supporters on the street sides were clapping. Then the media car makes an announcement over the loudspeaker: 'Ladies and gentleman, here we have the women's race leader . . .' I hadn't realised, but just behind me was a woman leading a small group of runners; she'd caught up and was pacing off me for a while. We ran like that through the 30 km point and I was spot on with both my timing and pacing, 2:00 hours to the second.

The lead woman started to prise a gap between us, running away and taking the media with her. I accepted the final 10 km was going to be way harder; my legs were exhausted and the effort to run well was increasingly difficult. The occasional runner would glide by, whispering encouragement but quietly pleased they'd made up a place. I concentrated on small goals – running well to the next corner, keeping up with this guy until the end of the straight, running hard for five minutes then having a little respite.

At about 37 km the road came up and smashed into me, bang. That must be the wall everyone talks about. No, I'd actually stumbled and fallen; I was lying on the road. I jumped up and kept running, slowly. Tortuously, distance and time entered another dimension; one minute felt like 10, 10 minutes felt like hours. I was dizzy, depleted, hazily endeavouring to calculate the distance remaining and the time I had worked so hard for to break 3:00 hours. I had 'hunger knock' – the effect of hard exercise without sufficient nutrition. It hit suddenly, forcing me to a slow and painful stagger towards the end. Let the grovelling begin. But smacked by fatigue and loss of energy, I still had hope, and although I didn't have much time remaining, I didn't have far left to run either. I entered the sports stadium with a little over a minute to go, the adrenalin kicked in, and the crowd cheered me on knowing I was likely to be the last person to run sub-3:00 that day and I sprinted trancelike to the finish line – 2:59:49.

Stuff that for a joke, mountain biking is my sport.

CHAPTER SIX
NOW FASTEST

Inspired by Fresh-Up television advertisements of adventure athletes running along alpine ridges wearing backpacks with skis attached and kayaking down white-water rapids, I decided I wanted to be part of this action. I didn't yet have the skills required for that race, so I was drawn to the Coast to Coast multisport race, a similar thing, and New Zealand's most famous adventure-sporting event with a truly iconic course, from one side of the country to the other. Before my final schooling year was completed, I started in the springtime to prepare for the 1991 event. My biking and running was going well, I'd bought a road bike and was doing some local bike races, but what I needed to work on was kayaking. This was proving quite an obstacle as I didn't own a kayak, didn't have the money to buy a kayak and didn't have a car to move a kayak around to water where I could paddle it.

Deane and Simon were my close school mates and we spent mountains of time mountain biking, discussing mountain biking, girls (especially girls who mountain biked), and anything to do with outdoor sport. As well as being a handy biker, Simon was a surfer and knowledgeable on water sports, and he told me about a guy who made kayaks just down the road from school. Simon also knew a bit about how boats were built and said that if we could borrow a mould we could make a kayak easy enough and very cheaply. It sounded like a good idea, so one lunchtime the three of us hopped on our bikes and cycled down to Sisson Kayaks, where the factory workers were sitting around in the sun on their lunch break when we rolled up.

'How's it going boys – what can we do for you?'

'I'm going to do the Coast to Coast but I don't have a kayak,' I said, quite matter of fact. 'Is it possible to borrow a mould so we can make one?'

Red-faced and clearly offended, Graham Sisson, the company owner, let rip with a tirade of abuse and we quickly scarpered back to school. 'What a lunatic', 'what an arsehole', 'what a wanker' we swore as we rode off.

Plan B was to see if I could hire a kayak. We made some enquiries and I arranged to hire a kayak from the Nelson Canoe Club for a paddle out on the harbour. The kayaks were stored in a locked container at the port and after dropping off my ten dollars for a day's hire I was instructed where the key was hidden at the lock-up. Another friend, Adam, was training for multisport as well, so he and I biked down and went for a kayak, both thinking the same thing. Now that we knew where the key was kept, what was to stop us from going kayaking all the time? This was going to be the best ten dollars ever spent. For months we'd regularly go kayaking, sometimes even taking other friends out. We'd often bump into a guy Barry who was the fastest paddler in town, but because he saw us at the shed regularly he probably assumed we'd either paid our fees or were members.

One day we were returning from a paddle when the person in charge of hire was at the shed. He demanded to know what was going on and we lied that we'd tried to contact him but couldn't, so decided to paddle and make contact later that day. He accepted that as a reasonable answer but warned us not to do it again. We biked off relieved but knowing that would be the end of our free kayaks. Looking back on it now, I'm not sure why I didn't just join the club, but for some reason that never occurred to me. Later that night I got a phone call from the club president who gave me a stern lecture and said if we were found using the kayak shed again the police would be called. It turned out the hire guy had bumped into Barry and told him about the two schoolboys who'd been caught using kayaks. 'Those two?' said Barry. 'They've been out three times a week for the past three months.'

The Coast to Coast was now only a month away and I still didn't have a kayak. Thankfully, a cycling friend heard about my dilemma and offered me his Sisson Delaware for the race. I now had all the gear I needed and was happily training away, not really having any idea of how to train properly, but keeping active and staying fit. I was cycling 40 km a day to pick berries and fruit for a job, plus running and biking solidly through the weekends. I wasn't getting in much kayaking but did what I could. A good mate from Nelson College who had originally inspired me into endurance challenges, Mike Hogan, was also doing the two-day Coast to Coast and I was doing more training than he was so figured that had to be a good thing. The race itself would start at Kumara Beach with a 3 km run to collect our road bikes and cycle 55 km towards Arthur's Pass, dropping our bikes and transferring to a 26 km mountain-running stage up the Deception riverbed, over Goat Pass and down the Mingha Valley to Klondyke Corner where the race would stop overnight. This was all new ground for me, not having been to these parts of the South Island.

Simon and Deane had agreed to be my support crew. We'd seen the event on TV and knew enough about it to be really, really excited. Simon had just spent $300 on a Toyota Corona and we reckoned that'd be the ideal vehicle for the job. It looked classy with the kayak on the roof and a Klein Quantum road bike on the rear rack. With the latest Talking Heads cassette loaded into the tape player, we headed west to Kumara Junction for registration, the event banquet at the community hall and the briefing from the eccentric race founder Robin Judkins, who was infamous for outrageous outbursts of swearing and abuse. Me and the boys were having a blast, it was better than we could have hoped – here we were at the Coast to Coast, wow, the real deal, the big time. My mate Mike, a talented musician, was taking a less serious approach by now, and had set out to make his Coast to Coast a guitar-playing, beer-sipping, multisport road trip. As the sun set over the horizon of the Tasman Sea, we said bye to Mike who was sitting on the bonnet of his car outside the pub, jug handy, strumming away and singing to a group of people gathered around.

Back at our car, Simon was starting to get quite stressed about the fact it wouldn't start, despite the fact we'd opened the bonnet and had a good stare at the engine and randomly pushed and pulled a few things. A passing mechanic stopped and took a look. (Hurray!) 'It's not going anywhere boys, she's toast.' (Oh no!) By now it was dark and everyone else had gone back to their accommodation to rest up. We discussed our options and the first and best one I could think of was to ring Mum. She was currently on the West Coast with Dad and my sister visiting friends, and I managed to get in contact. 'Our car's broken down – I need you to be my support crew.' She was a few hours away in Westport and would get here about 1 a.m., so we made ourselves comfortable in the car and hatched a plan. Deane would jump in the car with Mum and Dad, keeping his support crew role, while Simon would stay with his car and get it fixed, hopefully in time to catch up with us during the race. Somewhere in the early hours our help arrived and we transferred all my gear to Mum's car, and fitted racks, bike and kayak. It was loaded to the roof, bulging at the sides, sagging at the rear. Then I managed a few hours' sleep before getting ready for the 6 a.m. start.

We arrived at the bike transition area which was approximately 3 km from the beach. The plan was to drop my bike and the others would drive the 55 km up the valley while I'd walk to the start line with the other 500 or so competitors. My bike was locked to the rack and we couldn't find the key. A few hours earlier when we'd transferred all the gear over, the bike lock key was placed somewhere in the car. In a mild panic we scrabbled around in the dark for the key, finally found it, racked my bike, said our goodbyes and good lucks and I jogged down to the beach, making it with just a few minutes to spare. There was a small contingent from Nelson and we grouped together for support and a photo.

Despite all the delays and lack of sleep I was fully charged up. I couldn't have been more excited. I was on the start line of the bloody Coast to Coast about to undertake the biggest physical challenge of my life. My main goal was to finish; my second goal was to beat Mike. He had done one more endurance multisport race than me, and started his career in the sport six months before I had – hugely significant advantages in my view. First up, though, I wanted to finish. Ahead of me I had to run, cycle and run through the Alps – epic! Savouring every moment and absorbing everything around me, I had the enthusiasm of a puppy off on its first outing. The ocean lapping at our heels, Judkins booming through the loudspeaker, the countdown, the starting horn, 'Gooooo!': I was off and running up the sand, then clambering over rocks onto the road near the front runners, trotting along with a massive grin on my face and a bit surprised that the pace wasn't as fast as I'd expected.

Pacing, these guys are all pacing, smart. I started pacing too but I had to keep slowing down to hold my position back in the pack. Now 2 km into the race and I was in the front group – I hadn't sped up, others had just faded back. I found my bike and started riding, again surprised the pace wasn't faster. I was in a group of about 20 riders speeding up the road just as it was coming light. We whistled through Kumara township, passing Simon and his car roadside. About 10 km into the stage the pace slowed and we were caught by a group of another 30 or so. The bigger bunch settled down with about as many team riders as individuals. The scenery was magic as the road weaved its way up the Taramakau Valley, lined by native forest and the occasional farm wedged into the bush, and helicopters buzzed us from time to time which I thought was friggin brilliant. I noticed Mike wasn't in the bunch. As we neared two hours of riding I knew we must be getting close to the transition area and start of the mountain run. The pace had picked up and the tension in the bunch had escalated, which in turn made me even more adrenalin amped.

The valley was narrowing and we were starting to get glimpses of some very big mountains. The finish of the stage was soon after the railway crossing, where I'd been warned that all hell would break loose. Sure enough, we crossed the railway lines accompanied by jostling, shouting and yelling. Then some dozen riders broke from the pack gunning for the line about 1 km ahead. I bridged over to them and sat comfortably on the back, with a good gap over the bunch of 40 riders behind us. The transition was smooth and shortly after we were crossing the river and heading up the Deception Valley.

This is the most vivid memory I have of the race. I was running along narrow forest trails with the lead group and looking down at my race bib in disbelief that I was really in the Coast to Coast. It must have been quite a funny sight, a group of men aged 30 to 45, focused, concentrating, and tagging along at the back an 18-year-old looking at his race bib and smiling from ear to ear. But it didn't take me long to start wondering why they were going so slowly. I felt great, fresh and strong. Where I was clearly a lot faster was crossing the river. Early on in the run section there are five river crossings and after each one I'd find myself in the front so I'd ease up and retake my place at the rear of the group. After 40 minutes or so of doing this I decided not to stop and carried on running. I figured there must only be 20 km to go and I was feeling so good I knew I could sustain a higher pace.

I quickly dropped the group and carried on up the riverbed. From what I could tell, I was now leading the race and this only fuelled my appetite for the adventure. But then something really odd happened: I caught up to a group of runners. How could this be? As I got closer, I discovered they were mostly runners from the group I'd not long departed from. So I repeated the process, bounding past again at the next river crossing and tearing off up the riverbed. Some five minutes later I started to catch runners again, split from the bunch this time, but still from the group I had started with. I was about to repeat the manoeuvre when one of them, Doug Lomax (who I was to discover was a Coast to Coast legend), put out his hand and stopped me running past. Doug asked me if I'd done the run before. I told him I hadn't so he suggested I stay with him and he'd let me know when it was good to go ahead. He explained that there were many hidden paths that save significant time and unless I knew about them I wouldn't have an 'ice cube's chance in hell' of being near the front by the pass. It seemed like sound advice and I sensed I could trust him.

After a while Doug asked me what I was eating.

'Nothing,' I told him. 'I didn't bring any food, I'm just drinking water.' He was shocked and proceeded to dig out some barley sugars from his bag.

'Here, eat these, they'll give you energy.'

I didn't feel like I needed any energy but I was happy to eat them – quite a good idea, I thought, carrying lollies on a run. As we got close to the pass some of the other runners started to pull away but Doug told me to stick with him.

'They don't know the right way,' he whispered.

By now I'd lost track of where we were in the field – it seemed like there were runners all over the show, ducking into small tunnels in the forest and spreading out. Doug assured me that I would be free to run on soon enough. As the pass came into view he asked me how I was feeling. I told him I felt really good so he told me to take off.

'You'll be fine from here out,' he encouraged. 'Go for it, son!'

I bolted like a rodeo bull, tearing over the pass and off down the Mingha Valley, finally set free. I could see a few runners ahead of me – Doug had said that a few team runners had got away but not to worry about them. I just ran the best I could with the comfort in my mind that whatever was to happen I had exceeded my expectations. I knew I was in the top five or so and that Mike wasn't in front of me.

Reaching the last river crossing and the final 3 km along the highway, a large crowd had gathered to welcome the runners off the mountain. Exaggerating the effort needed at the crossing, I splashed water everywhere and really turned on a show. Then someone yelled out, 'It's the first individual!' The crowd went wild (a few claps). My first instinct was 'Wow, the first individual', looking all around, and then someone called out to me that *I* was the first individual. 'Who, me?' I called back. Those two words became the media headline for the day.

Kicking out at blinding speed and crossing the finish line in first place, my run time set a new record for individual two-day runners, although in the grand scheme of the race, it was not a particularly fast time. Doug finished fourth that day and I think both of us have always wondered what time I could have run had I known the way. Not many race leaders have had to jog half of the distance before they were able to race. Robin Judkins greeted me warmly but with undeniable surprise. I wasn't one of the pre-race picks by any stretch. Completely hyped up, I looked and felt as fresh as if I'd just popped down to the river to splash a bit of water on my face. The media wanted to know who I was, I was getting photos taken and other competitors were coming over and shaking my hand. For a young chap seeking approval, it doesn't get much better, and I believe this experience alone set the tone for what would be another 20 years of winning races. It taught me that anything is possible and not to set limitations, to just go out and give it everything and see what happens. 'Always be open to possibility' was the motto I adopted and would use in teams I captained and athletes I coached from that day forward.

After the initial excitement I noticed my support crew were not there. A race official asked me if I even had a support crew! I explained we'd had a few issues, which the media understandably pounced on – the story was getting better by the minute. An announcement was put out over the PA system asking for my crew while the medical team took care of me. Relaxing on a stretcher in the ambulance, sipping a recovery drink, with regular visits from the media entourage, I didn't mind. I was a fucking superstar and loving it. Meanwhile, in the Arthur's Pass tea-rooms Mum was on to her second cup of tea and reading a magazine while Deane respectfully tried to suggest they should go to the finish line.

'Look, Deane,' she replied. 'They say the runners take between three and a half to eight hours to complete the run. The only way we'll be late is if Nathan is the first runner. Besides, the sandflies down there will be ghastly.'

Dad was milling around when he overheard some people saying, 'The leader of the race is a "Maori" teenager from Nelson – he finished ages ago but his support crew aren't there.'

Soon afterwards we were reunited. They were overwhelmed by my achievement but equally disappointed to have missed it. We set up camp and enjoyed an evening relaxing while a few hundred people stopped by to see what sort of kayak I was using the next day. Mike ended day one in 208th – like me, he'd had a very late night too. While I knew I had a slim chance of winning, I was going to try anyway, although we agreed in our camp that a top ten finish would be a marvellous outcome.

However, the river paddle didn't start well when I ploughed into the first easily avoidable rock I could find. I tipped out, swam to shore and discovered a crack in the kayak. I didn't have anything to repair it with so I just paddled on, having to stop a few times as the day went on to empty the water out. Being my first time down the Waimakariri River, I was really tested, in terms of both mental tenacity and paddling endurance. I couldn't believe how far it was, and while spectacular it just went on and on, which I found utterly boring. It was also demoralising being constantly passed. I reached a point where I officially hated kayaking. Finally, I could see the bridge that marked the end of the stage and my road bike: thank you Lord for the ride I am about to receive. I figured that I was out of the top ten now but a strong ride could see me make up time.

I was so pleased to be out of the coffin-like kayak and on my bicycle that I rode the final 70 km sitting on the front of a group of riders, hammering all the way to Sumner Beach. Given the way day two started, in numerical order in groups of ten, it's difficult to know where exactly you are overall, but soon after finishing I discovered – with a mixture of satisfaction and disappointment – that I had placed eleventh. At the awards ceremony I got a standing ovation when I collected the trophy for the mountain run; and Graham Sisson came up to me afterwards and told me to pay him another visit at his factory, he'd have a kayak for me. My good mate Mike soldiered home in 239th place – out of all the competitors who completed the crossing, no other would have sung as many songs and drunk as much beer as he did en route. He was a champion, too, in my book.

Back home in Nelson, news of my Coast to Coast mountain run scored a half-page spread in the local paper and I was interviewed on the radio. It felt good and was motivation to keep striving. The following week Robin Judkins called to apologise because he'd given me the mountain run trophy when it should have actually gone to a team runner who'd gone faster – I was the fastest individual runner but it'd slipped Robin that team runners were eligible. It didn't worry me, I'd had the glory. I vowed to go back to the Coast to Coast again in a year's time but better prepared. It didn't quite work out as I planned though. Despite initial intentions of a race-winning bid, I was drawn to mountain biking far more as a sport and passion. All I wanted to do was ride my bike.

My other goal while living at home for the year was to work and save some money to go to university. Braden was clocking up a few years at Otago and it looked like good fun, plus I wanted to move towards a career. I decided to visit him in Dunedin and to meet with the Physical Education school. Mike kindly lent me his car to travel down in. I stayed at Braden's flat and one night there was a wicked party at which everyone got devilishly loose. I woke in the morning to discover Mike's car had been covered in artistic graffiti. It looked quite good but it wasn't my car. I was nervous about Mike's reaction when I returned it but I needn't have worried, he didn't give a damn. He truly was a laid-back character. Actually he was quite lucky even to get the car back as Braden had decided to travel home to Nelson with me. It was late at night, he was driving, we were engrossed in conversation, went over a railway level crossing, and suddenly an almighty horn blast gave us a hell of a fright. We immediately noticed a train to our left travelling in the opposite direction, and then looked back over our shoulders to see the flashing red warning lights.

'Did you just drive in front of a train?' I asked.

'Yeah, it seems that way.'

'Are you wasted?' He had developed an appetite for mushrooms in Dunedin, the mind-altering type, not the gravy or risotto type.

'No, I'm straight, honest.'

It was a close call but we made it back safely.

There was plenty of seasonal work around and I had good contacts. Apple picking was my best way to earn money – as a contract picker I could earn over a thousand dollars some weeks, which at that time was a shitload of money for a young man. It'd require some 10- to 12-hour days but I wanted to make money and the job was physical, which suited me. Another advantage for my bank account was that there were a couple of other nimble-fingered pickers at the orchard I worked on so it was competitive, trying to out-pick each other for the most bins tallied, which most days I'd win.

Spare time was spent mountain biking, hanging out in the bike shop, or working on my bike. I was dominating the cross-country racing scene. My belief in the main reason I was winning so many races was that I was riding more than everyone

I was competing against just got stronger. Many of my school mates were into riding, but for every hour they trained, I'd do two. A big difference was that most of my friends rarely rode on their own – for them, biking was a social activity based around rides. For me, riding was riding, it was all time on the saddle regardless. The fact that I was comfortable spending many hours a day on my own – in fact, I liked it – differentiated me from my peers. I enjoyed the complete freedom and time alone with my thoughts. Not relying on people to train with meant I could do more and have more control over the type of training I wanted to do, what I wanted to achieve. I did join social rides but nearly always I'd do my own training before or afterwards. The quote 'Champions are people who perfect what others consider boring or monotonous' sums me up. I'm happy to do the same thing over and over and over again, if it'll make me better.

I had taken up trout fishing a few years earlier but had made a conscious effort to make the most of getting a licence over summer and get to the rivers. I enjoyed the environment as much as the sport and getting some dinner was a pleasant bonus. My ideal was to get to the remote wilderness rivers when I could, especially the Karamea and its tributaries. I had spent the summer working with a guy who was a keen fisherman so we planned a week-long trip into the Tasman Wilderness Area in search of trophy fish. The target was the Beautiful and Roaring Lion rivers, but they were at least two days' hiking from the nearest road end, so we fished the Leslie and Karamea rivers as we headed towards our ultimate destination.

The Karamea is a big river that can be crossed easily in a few places, although due to earthquake slips it has many lakes that typically lead to rapids. After leaving Karamea Bend, we started to spot some magnificent fish, but as we fished down-river we realised we'd potentially made an error in that we'd stayed on the left bank for too long, and a bluff we could see downstream would halt our progress. In front of us was a huge rapid and above that was a deep lake that went back upstream a few kilometres. It'd be about a 6 km round trip to get to the opposite side of the river that we were looking at just 50 metres away. There was an island in the middle splitting the rapid and I thought it could be possible to cross, at least to the island.

My mate wasn't so sure so I said I'd scope it out. I went to the top of the rapid and lined up my route, using the downstream current to help me cross, and the exposed boulders as sanctuaries. I got onto the island okay but was surprised at the power and depth of the water – had I lost my footing, I would have been tumbled down the rapid a long way. I shot over the island to see that the other channel was bigger, swifter and menacing. I wasn't keen. I signalled to my mate that I was coming back, but I couldn't find an obvious line on the return trip and started to get nervous. I had to try something and I didn't want to delay for too long because as time went on, the more I didn't like my predicament. In the end, I committed and went for it. I clung to a boulder and then leapt to the safety of the next one but didn't make it – I was washed off my feet and swept away. I tried to stand a few times but it was hopeless. I was getting dunked and disappearing underwater. Eventually, I desperately grasped hold of a rock, surrounded by white water. My friend had run down the riverbank after me but was powerless to help at that stage.

The water was cold and I knew I needed to keep moving. I could just stand so I tried again to reach the safety of the shore, and this time I nearly got to the side when my foot got stuck between two rocks. The force of the water was so immense, it felt like my leg was going to snap off below the knee, and it freaked me out. For a short while I had to use all my strength to push my leg against the force of the water to free my foot. When it finally came free I was swept off my feet again and washed down the rapid, this time to the bottom, smashing into rocks on the way. By the time I was clear of the rapid I was in deep water well over my head and floating down the river in the current. I attempted to swim to shore but I was utterly exhausted. I felt myself go under a couple of times, swallowing water and, knowing I was close to drowning, using all my strength I glared at the land and swam. I made it, crawling out of the water and collapsing on the stones. Throughout all this, I should add, I'd had my pack on.

My friend arrived. He was scared too. I was in a state of shock and shivering uncontrollably. He got me into dry clothes and got us moving, backtracking up the valley. Once I was warmed up I was okay. I ate some food and we went to the hut. It was a very close call. That night I had nightmares of drowning, and for the rest of the trip I was extremely nervous near the river, especially any rapids, the noise of the white water making me tense. I reckon that incident marked me for life – as a result I've always been extremely cautious as a white-water kayaker and rafter. A few years later, I kayaked that rapid I swam in my tramping gear. It was called the Garibaldi.

Before the year was out, though, I found myself on another trip into the Karamea, but lower down. I was invited by friends in the rafting industry, Don Allardice and Todd Jago, on a reconnaissance to check it out as a potential commercial trip. To their knowledge, it had been rafted a few years earlier but it was difficult to source information. Don had kayaked it but needed to find out how a raft would cope getting down. The river is choked with large difficult rapids, up to Grade 6 on some flows. As we flew up in the helicopter we rounded a bend and a loud 'Holy Shit!' bellowed in our headphones. In front of us was a huge cascade of turbulent white water fighting its way through strewn boulders, some as big as a bus, nearly half a kilometre in length. Unbeknown to me, that was a new rapid, which hadn't been there when Don had paddled the river a few months earlier. The name stuck.

On another memorable fishing trip, my mate broke his rod on the second day. On the third day, he borrowed mine and broke that too. The trip was linking rivers between Murchison and Motueka and we were now in the middle with no rods, when we'd budgeted on fish for meals. For three days we hiked out on milk powder and dehydrated peas trying, without success, to catch eels.

Back home I was still chasing Jodie to go out with me. We'd got to know each other by now and loosely kept in touch. She was nearly always dating somebody but she wasn't keeping boyfriends for long. I never gave up, though. I was confident we'd get together – it was just a matter of time.

On one occasion I knew she was at a party and that she wouldn't be allowed out after midnight. So I waited outside her house, stalker style, and intercepted her when her boyfriend dropped her off. She didn't mind. We chatted for a bit and I told her I was waiting for her whenever she was ready. Dating her was a long-term project. I'd said my piece so it was time to be patient. My work and bike riding kept me well occupied in the meantime. After apples, I picked kiwifruit and then the pruning season began.

In July I went to a party with some mates and Jodie was there, as I knew she would be because one of her best friends was dating the guy whose party it was. At some point during the night Jodie invited me to go outside and chat. Here we go. She told me she was single and asked if I was still interested in her. I told her I was, we hugged and kissed, and it's been that way ever since. Perseverance paid off.

When springtime neared I needed to start preparing for the Coast to Coast. There was a major race on back then called the Mountains to Sea, from Mount Ruapehu in the central North Island to Whanganui on the coast. It was a three-day multisport race but the most appealing part for me was the gargantuan amount of kayaking it contained, a total of 125 km. Entering it forced me to paddle train. Accordingly, my first real date with Jodie was a day's sea kayaking. One of my tutors at Whenua Iti, Ian Trafford, owned a sea-kayaking company in the Abel Tasman National Park and was happy for me to use his kayaks. I took Jodie up the park for the day. Adventure trips became regular for us – hiking, mountain biking, exploring for the day, and spending quality time learning about each other. It was quite unique for a teenage couple but it set a strong foundation for our future relationship.

Training in the Abel Tasman was the easiest way for me to do long paddles, plus my mate Todd was training to be a sea-kayak guide so I'd join him on paddles too.

I went up and did the Mountains to Sea race but came away disappointed. After my Coast to Coast success I'd become someone to watch – I was now a 'name' in the sport and with that came a level of expectation. I was aware of this and felt the pressure to perform, but I was still very much a novice, and the truth was that I hadn't trained well enough for the multi-discipline race. I completely obliterated the field on the bike, struggled on the run and got smoked in the kayak. I think I finished in tenth place, which in all fairness was a highly creditable result, but not at all what I had hoped for.

My last summer job before going to university was picking berry fruit. That was good income, tasty nutrition and a physical outdoor job. As summer neared, though, I got a better offer. Ian's sea-kayak company was growing rapidly and he needed more staff. I was one of very few people who could kayak, knew all the names of the beaches in the park and was available. It was a big deal for me working as an outdoor guide. It was confirmation that I had what it took to work in the outdoor industry. I was on my way.

CHAPTER SEVEN
NEXT FREEDOM

My relationship with Jodie was going really well. It was easy and we had a mature outlook. In many respects, we were planning our future. After a summer of sea-kayak guiding and mountain-bike racing, we headed south to Otago University. She was keen to maximise the university experience and signed up to the Arana halls of residence. I couldn't think of anything worse than sleeping in a dormitory and eating fat-infused meals in a communal dining hall. Even though I was only 19, I couldn't see myself fitting in with a load of young people straight out of home. Accustomed to my independence and freedom, I went flatting.

Two mates of mine from Nelson were at Otago – Jonny who'd done his first year already and Rod who was signed up for the same course as me, Physical Education and associated papers. Jonny found a flat at the back of the city: like most student hovels, a poorly insulated 1920s timber house on a steep, shaded section. It was ideal. We were looked upon at the time as 'sport billies'. Our flat was home to mountain and road bikes, kayaks, skis, and climbing and tramping gear. We ate healthy food and it was extremely rare to see a drop of alcohol in the place, even though we lived directly behind the Speight's brewery.

On the way to Dunedin I'd done the Coast to Coast two-day race again which had ended up being a disappointment on many levels due to my inexperience. After the success of the previous year, I assumed I'd be able to lead through the mountains on the run again easily, and that the kayak stage was where I needed to focus my efforts to chase a win. The sea-kayak guiding formed part of my training by taking clients on longer trips in the Abel Tasman, loading my boat with stuff I'd be unlikely to need, and doing more and harder paddling throughout the day. I spent a lot of time on the Motueka River in both a white-water and racing kayak with pleasing results – I was transforming into a kayaker. Jodie wanted to come to the race, Dad was keen to be support crew again and my brother agreed to pop over from Christchurch, where he was now studying, to lend a hand.

We gathered in Kumara for the normal proceedings and race briefing. As the race drew nearer, I started to feel the pressure of expectation. Twelve months earlier I'd not only surprised myself by leading after day one, I'd rocked the multisport community who were now keenly anticipating what I could produce a year later. There was some simple maths involved: I could run and bike strongly, I'd set a record time over Goat Pass, and I was fast becoming an accomplished mountain-bike racer with some respectable results on the road bike to boot. Now I could kayak too. But my kayaking level had only gone from beginner to intermediate, not beginner to advanced, as some people seemed to expect. I still had a long way to go.

The day preceding the event is somewhat of an expo – the 'show and tell' of multisport. Athletes check each other out, looking for signs of how much training has been done and what equipment was used. Because of my 1991 success, people were curious to know what I'd done since and specifically what sort of kayak I was paddling. While I'd been training in an advanced kayak lent to me by Graham Sisson, I was going faster down rivers in an intermediate kayak he also lent me, so I opted to race in that. I was well aware, though, that I was being written off as a contender because I didn't have the narrowest and sleekest boat on the roof of the car. I pledged then and there that I would become one of the best paddlers the sport had seen, but it wasn't going to happen overnight.

Not being able to manage the pressure and keep perspective, I didn't sleep well the night before the race. I was awake for most of it and even got up and went for a walk along the beach around 2 a.m. I was building the race up to something much bigger than it was. It was vital that I succeeded – I had sponsors, people who believed in me and had invested in me. Anything less than winning would be letting a whole lot of people down. I suspect part of me wanted to prove that last year wasn't a fluke. I wanted to confirm to myself and the world that I was a talented athlete. Looking back, I was far more focused on the result than the process. Had I not been worried about the outcome but concentrated on racing as best as I could, I would have gone significantly better plus enjoyed it more as well.

On the race morning I didn't feel well. I was tired and anxious. I tried to relax and eat my breakfast but just felt ill. I racked my bike and said my goodbyes to my support crew – I'd see them up the valley in about three hours. Wandering the 3 km to the beach chatting with other competitors, I knew deep down that I wasn't going to do anything extraordinary. It was a great morning, clear skies and warm temperature, but Robin Judkins warned of a fast-approaching storm.

The West Coast of the South Island is renowned for rapidly moving frontal systems bringing high winds and dumping heavy rain on the western side of the Southern Alps. The rivers can rise at astonishing speed. I've seen streams that are ankle-deep trickles become raging floods in just a few hours. People using the back country on the Coast are often delayed waiting for river levels to subside. One of these storms was on its way, so we were warned to make haste and expect cold temperatures in the high country, especially going through Goat Pass, which is above the forest, with only knee-high tussock grass to protect athletes from the weather at that stage of the run.

The first run and cycle stage went to plan. I felt good on the bike and happy riding in the lead group. I wasn't really aware of the competition but I noticed that there were some very fit-looking guys rolling along in the bunch. As the group sped up in the final few kilometres, everyone eager to get to the front so they would have an easier job of connecting with their support crew amid the chaos, my cycling legs and experience meant I could easily time a surge to be at the front at the right time, which I did. My brother grabbed my bike and Jodie helped me change shoes, Dad passed me my bag and I was off, exiting transition with a couple of other runners.

Through the first river crossing and onto the vague bush trails, I felt the complete opposite to last year at this exact point when I was filled with boundless energy and had a spring in my step. Today I felt flat, heavy-legged and tired. There was no way I would be able to maintain the speed I was running and I slowly drifted back from the leading group of half a dozen guys, containing individual and team runners. As the route got steeper and more taxing, I struggled to keep an efficient pace, and every so often another runner would catch and pass me. I was eating and drinking well but simply had no gas in the tank. My plan was to limit the damage, and hopefully lose no more than 10 to 15 minutes, as I was confident day two would serve me well, paddling and cycling. As I crossed Goat Pass I was shocked to hear I was in about twentieth place and about 20 minutes off the leader.

The weather had well and truly moved in and the rain was making the descent greasy, somewhat out of control. Slogging my way down the Mingha Valley in the pouring rain, I wasn't having a whole lot of fun but still managed to stay positive – the race was far from over. Even with only an hour of rain the rivers were starting to discolour and it was obvious they were rising fast. My tramping background gave me plenty of confidence and I crossed them without issue, reaching the highway for the final 3 km to the finish line of day one. The rain was pelting down hard and I was completely soaked through, but running steadily to the end. I was in twenty-fourth place, taking five hours and 33 minutes, a massive 21 minutes slower than the year before.

Once I got changed into dry gear I chatted with my support crew. They were cheerful but we all knew that something wasn't right and that from a racing perspective I wasn't in any great position to win. I'd need a miracle on day two, which probably wasn't going to happen given that last year I posted the sixty-fourth fastest kayak time. Confident that I was going to paddle faster, I accepted the situation quickly and decided that a top 10 overall placing would be a redeeming goal.

By now the weather had completely let loose with driving sheet rain and high wind. We started hearing reports of runners stranded and even stuck on diminishing islands as the flooding rampaged. A number of helicopters were working full-time shuttling people over the swollen rivers. For safety reasons, Robin needed to get people off the mountain-run stage as they weren't equipped for a night out in such conditions. With swift work from the staff they were able to clear the course before dark, everyone home safe with a tale to tell as they warmed up with a hot drink.

That night the rain never eased, flooding the campsite where over 500 people were staying and saturating everything the water could get its hands on. A whisper went around the camp that the 67 km kayak stage was cancelled and that we'd be cycling direct to Christchurch, about 140 km. While I wasn't all that keen to paddle a swollen river, the idea of cycling in the rain for four-plus hours didn't excite me much either. But that's what we ended up doing.

My ride went okay but I spent most of the time on my own. The event starts athletes off in numerical order in groups of ten. Most of the guys in my group weren't cyclists, so immediately off the start line our 10-person group became three or four. We worked together as best we could, hoping to bridge over to some other strong cyclists, which never happened. In those days, 140 km was a long bike race for me, so by the time I reached the finish line I was well and truly over it – in general terms, I thought it sucked. I ended up in twenty-first place, which kind of sucked too. I did feel a little better when I heard that the one-day racers didn't even get to do the mountain run, and had to cycle to Otira, run over Arthur's Pass on the highway, then cycle to Christchurch – that would have sucked extra big time.

It didn't take me long after the race to decide that multisport was something I could come back to later in life. Most of the people racing multisport were 10 years older than me and I was more interested in mountain-bike racing now anyway. After the post-event formalities Jodie and I continued south to Dunedin to start university. I knew I'd be back at the Coast to Coast at some stage, as a contender in the one-day event.

CHAPTER EIGHT
NOW FREEZING

Due to being disorganised about enrolling at Otago University for 1992, I missed out on starting the degree I wanted to do, Physical Education. However, I met with the Dean who was a Coast to Coaster too and really keen to have me in the school because I was an emerging athlete. He designed a year of study for me that would hopefully mean I could still complete the PE degree in four years. That suited me fine as I was interested in developing my racing as much as I was planning a career. It didn't take long to slip into a routine: lectures, study and training. Jodie stayed at my flat most of the time, making her room in the hall of residence somewhat redundant. The racing scene was very competitive so I was getting solid racing, managing to win most of the mountain-bike races in Otago that year. The road-cycling scene was very strong and served as brilliant training plus there were other events going on to take part in. The sporting scene in general was very strong.

Still wanting to improve my multisport racing and especially my kayaking, I joined the Otago University Canoe Club (OUCC), which proved to be an excellent thing for developing my boating skills but a terrible thing for my study. The OUCC was essentially an outdoor sporting club offering excellent paddling adventures around the lower South Island but also rock climbing, hiking, skiing and mountaineering trips. Every weekend I was either racing bikes or off on a mission with the OUCC, kayaking in Queenstown or rock climbing in Wanaka and, once the ski season began, I was hitting the slopes. My student loan provided a steady income to build up my artillery of outdoor sporting equipment with – I was spending as much at the wilderness shop as the university book store.

Jodie was easily distracted by the adventure possibilities too. She had won the New Zealand women's downhill mountain-biking title that summer in Nelson and was building up to the World Championships held in Canada in the spring. Dad had lost his licence for a year, driving home from the golf course one afternoon after a few beers, but the upside for me was that I could use his car for the duration, a Subaru 4×4 ute with a canopy and roof racks. Jodie and I frequently toured around Central Otago exploring, with bikes, kayaks, our tent and hiking gear – life was great.

Flatting life was fun as well. All keen mountain bikers, with Rod and I competing in cross-country races, we got up to our fair share of mischief (mainly Jonny and I). It was a hard time for mountain biking in the early 1990s. When the sport was young, we'd been able to ride anywhere, including national parks, as there were no laws against it. But as the sport grew in numbers, controls started to be put in place. The council had gone to quite an effort to close off many of the great rides, such as Mount Cargill, Pineapple Track and others, erecting some elaborate signs and issuing fines to bikers intent on riding the trails. One night, Jonny and I decided to reopen all the trails on behalf of the mountain-biking community. From midnight to about 5 a.m., we removed all the 'no mountain biking' signs throughout the city and stacked them under our flat (for all I know, they're still there, if they haven't been used as firewood by later tenants). For a few glorious months riders were treated to open trails before the new signs went back up, but this time we left them – we'd made our point. It didn't stop our entertainment in collecting signs though, and by the end of the year we had enough to manage a large roading project, or sell pies, real estate or newspapers.

Being on tight budgets and student rations, we discovered that the walk-in chiller at the Mornington supermarket was an invitation to load up a backpack with as much dairy product as possible – meaning our flat often had a full range of cheeses, salami and yoghurt. In retrospect, I feel bad about some of our antics, but at the time it was just another form of adventure and exploring. We started to experiment with nutrition a lot that year. Midway through we trialled a 'reverse eating' plan, which was exactly as it sounds. We'd wake in the morning and have a full dinner, protein and carbohydrates; lunch was about the same as normal but we'd have cereal and fruit for our evening meal. After a few months we didn't notice any real difference other than that we went to bed hungry most nights. We were training two to four hours a day so our calorie demand was fairly high. We trialled a few other things but in the end found a normal diet gave good consistent results, even though at times buying healthy food was not always easy on a student bank balance. However, that did mark the beginning of a continuing personal quest to find the ultimate nutrition.

For the next few decades I experimented with every sports diet theory I came across and finally settled on some conclusions of my own. What I learnt is that there is a lag time of about ten years from the cutting edge of high-performance sports nutrition filtering through to everyday people. Frequently I'm excitedly told about some new nutrition idea that I have researched and tried about a decade earlier.

Humans are nutritionally flexible and that needs to be celebrated – it's also critical to our survival. The planet could not sustain us all eating the same diet. At any given moment in time, there is a finite amount of food, the global food store. And it's not much – if the planet stopped producing and growing food we'd run out in a matter of months (it's generally believed to be about six weeks). We'd deplete stores even faster if the whole world adopted a specific diet. For example, if overnight the world went vegetarian, we'd eat all the vegetables in about four weeks and the time needed to grow more wouldn't be enough to combat starvation. Going raw and vegan would be even more severe. The same can be said for primal and paleo type diets – if we all simultaneously decided to have a high animal protein diet, seven billion people would gobble up all the animals in a matter of weeks. Reluctantly, we'd need to start digging for potatoes.

Keeping people fed is a major political agenda. Many countries these days rely on importing food to feed their population; without importation, they'd starve. Australia is a good example – it's believed they can produce their own food to feed about 15 million, but they need to trade minerals for meals to feed a population of 25 million. All diets only work if small percentages adopt them – not everyone can be the same, the planet needs that variety, in taste and geographical foods (eating local). There is little sense in having a diet regime where the bulk of what you eat is shipped from the other side of the planet. Non-meat-eaters can criticise their non-vegetarian brothers all they wish, but to do so is hypocrisy. The ape's intelligence evolved when it started to catch big animals – had the ape been satisfied with berries, there'd be no iPhones.

What I have learned is that every few years someone writes a book about some revolutionary diet – gain energy, lose weight, be healthier. It all sounds good. There will be some quirky theory and some delicious recipes, endorsed by a few famous people who credit their youthful looks and astronomical success to it. A book that simply agrees with the common knowledge won't sell – it needs to have a hook. For instance, I could write a book telling people that – provided they did a few other things as well – they'd feel better if they ate their daily food in alphabetical order: 'Start your day with an apple, then a banana, a carrot, date, egg . . .' Because here's the catch: it's the other stuff that makes the difference. All these books and theories and eating plans promote lifestyle change as well – drink more water, get more sleep and exercise, and the golden piece of advice, avoid heavily processed foods, especially those containing preservatives and sugar.

The answer actually lies in lifestyle and what you *don't* eat. If you eat natural food, drink plenty of water, get quality sleep and exercise, and reduce the junk food, you'll reap the benefits, it's that simple. To be healthier, we need to reduce the intake of processed food. We can't do it overnight or we'd starve, but we do need to phase it out, to demand healthy food and choices. The food manufacturers will produce healthy food if that is what sells. So people don't need to stress about whether they should be vegetarian, vegan, raw, primal, paleo, or any other label that is dreamed up. What they need to focus on is reducing the crap they eat and making lifestyle changes. It's very simple. The real issue we face as a planet regarding food is wastage. We waste over 25 per cent of the food we produce.

I'm not a fanatical eater anyway – I celebrate that our bodies have adapted to eating a wide range of foods. I aim to eat healthy, wholesome food most of the time, in combination with smart lifestyle choices. I'm also mindful that too many athletes retire and balloon – bad eating habits can put weight on fast. As a teenage athlete I'd come home from training, drink a bottle of milk and eat a loaf of bread. It wasn't uncommon for me to sit down in the evenings with a cup of tea and eat a packet of biscuits, a block of chocolate, or a tub of ice cream. Mum had a story about me getting home from training one day and eating a kilogram of bacon, in sandwiches. Calories vaporised when I was young and doing the big miles, but as I get older, especially after 40, treats seem to go almost instantly to my waistline. If I want to trim up, though, it's simple – I reduce sugar and wheat products.

As a young athlete at university, I didn't need to worry about overeating – appeasing my hunger was the challenge. I did consider getting a part-time job but I was doing okay on the money I was receiving without suffering from malnutrition. The previous summer I'd grown a couple of healthy marijuana plants in the Kaiteriteri Forest and had a cake tin full of dried weed. Because of my sport, I very rarely used it myself, almost never, so selling the occasional $25 bag to friends kept fuel in the Subaru. I vowed once I sold my stock that'd be the end of it, which it was. The final bit was used in Jodie's 'Getting kicked out of Arana party'.

About midyear, Jodie and I decided it was pointless her staying at the hall and paying fees. But if she left she'd still have to pay thousands of dollars for the rest of the year. However, the fine print said that if a student was expelled from the hall, then no further payments were required. As well as being a talented group of outdoor sportspeople, the OUCC were also an incredibly wild bunch of socialites, so we decided to throw a party in Jodie's room, with the theme being 'Help Jodie get kicked out of Arana'. The OUCC rose to the occasion.

We had a few ground rules – everyone had to be sober and no damage could be done to the hall. About 30 people crammed into Jodie's room for the briefing at the 10 p.m. party launch. The first thing we did was burn all the dope I had left – we didn't smoke any, just flared it up for effect. Everyone then doused themselves in beer and pretended they were completely pissed. We pumped the music and opened the door. An instant party exploded into the corridor. Everyone had put in a big effort to help Jodie get kicked out. One of the highlights was our mate who had a chainsaw going – without the chain – running about pretending to decapitate people (a chainsaw going in a corridor is a very scary thing). The shopping trolley derby was also a popular event, thanks to the team that got the trolleys there from town. The blow-up doll who hung herself in the corridor was bad taste but added to the cause, while the team that abseiled off the roof and into Jodie's window was a valiant contribution although it did get them in trouble with the proctor. We called the police ourselves to report drugs and misuse of a chainsaw. Most of the other students hid from the chaos but a few joined in the fun.

It wasn't long before the sub-warden turned up, visibly shocked and demanding an end to the mayhem. They were given mouthfuls of obscenities so off they went to get the warden who stormed in and ordered Jodie to stop the party. Pretending to be drunk, she brushed him off until he uttered the magic words: 'You are expelled from the hall!' The warden must have been very confused at this point, as the music was immediately turned off, everyone stopped partying, quickly tidied up and left, soberly and amicably. Task complete, Jodie moved into our flat and didn't have to pay any more hall fees.

As 1992 went on, I got less interested in study. While I enjoyed many of the papers, especially the education ones, the more I learned about physical education the less I wanted a career in it. I wanted to work in outdoor education and there seemed little point in doing anything other than becoming highly skilled at outdoor sport. Midway through the ski season Jodie took off to Canada for the Mountain Bike World Championships, her highlight getting fourth in the dual slalom racing with the stars of the sport. I had qualified for the national team myself but opted not to race – I didn't have much money and knew I had no chance of a top result on a global scale. With her away for a month, I joined up with a few friends from Australia and we went on a South Island ski trip. Our goal was to ski every black run in the South Island, which we did, skiing 16 fields in three weeks. The hardest run was Plake's Mistake at Craigieburn. By the end of that trip I decided I'd done enough skiing and bought a snowboard, which was a relatively new sport in New Zealand at the time.

It was a significant year in my relationship with Jodie too. On one trip away, to Moke Lake, just out of Queenstown, we lay in our tent chatting and she told me that she wasn't sure if our relationship was for her. We'd had a disagreement over a trust issue. A year earlier when we first started dating, she had gone to the US on a family holiday returning via Hawaii where she'd had a small romance with a guy, no big deal. On returning to New Zealand she'd told her best friend Jackie about it, who happened to be dating one of my best mates Deane. As you can imagine, the news reached me, which I didn't care about, despite Deane suggesting I dump her. Lying in our tent a year later, Jodie decided to confess. To her surprise, I told her I'd known all along. Ironically, she found it difficult to grasp that I had known but not said anything, implying that if we were keeping secrets from each other how could we expect to have a healthy relationship – all of sudden *I* was the one in the wrong. That led to her asking if we had a relationship worth continuing. Perhaps somewhat ahead of my years, I shared my view. Together we would face adversity and challenge, otherwise whenever we hit a problem and started to question our decision to be together, we may as well have been doomed from the start. I suggested we make a pact to be together for life, or forget about it. I'd happily get married if that helped. For a couple of teenagers we left that campsite with a serious commitment to each other.

As the year ended, I dropped my studies and put all my energy into whitewater kayaking, working towards my instructor certification. I had a job lined up sea-kayak guiding in the Abel Tasman again and moved into a flat with a mate in Marahau and had a busy summer, guiding and mountain-bike racing. I was consistently in the top five male cross-country racers nationally and was dominating all local races. I was enjoying the outdoors lifestyle. I'd spend the day paddling around the waters of Abel Tasman National Park and would go biking after work most days. I was starting to learn that doing things I liked, being active in nature, was a much more pleasurable way to live.

Based on that, Jodie and I decided not to return to university in 1993. She had got good results after her first year but was unsure if her courses were suitable. Her dreams of becoming a rich and powerful businesswoman were quickly diminishing and the lure of a life in the outdoors was becoming increasingly appealing. After the summer season of mountain-bike racing we moved to Wanaka for the ski season. We'd both had successful racing seasons with Jodie winning the national downhill title again. I'd had a good season to finish fourth in the country. Equipped with skis and snowboards, we headed for Wanaka.

Knowing we had little chance of finding work, especially given the fact we weren't actually looking for it, we signed up for the 'Government-Funded Ski Team' (Social Welfare). It took us a while to find somewhere to live but we landed the dream accommodation. Because of my rising sporting acclaim I'd started to build a network of people around the country. A mate I'd met in multisport lived in Wanaka and I discovered that his father managed the local hotel. Keen to help us out, he agreed to rent us a room for the whole season for one hundred dollars a week, which the Government-Funded Ski Team underwrote. We had a number of friends who were ski bums and we quickly became the envy. They were paying more rent to live in cold sheds, with limited hot water and poor-quality living. In contrast, we had unlimited hot water and a bath, central heating, TV and access to a kitchen, and we walked out of our room into downtown. It was luxury for us and I managed to snowboard about sixty days at Treble Cone. I was also biking and running most days, getting in a great base for the following mountain-bike season. Jodie and I were discussing a season bike racing in the US.

Prior to settling in Wanaka, we'd done a sea-kayak trip to Stewart Island with a bunch of other guides. We'd had a good time exploring and paddled through some severe weather. While we couldn't paddle around the island, I intended to return one day to give it another try – it was, and still is, the ultimate New Zealand sea-kayak trip. We had both read the nutrition book *Fit for Life* and adopted many of its principles, largely choosing vegetarian eating that year. As a cross-country racer I was always watching my weight which tended to sit around 80 kg – which was on the heavy side for the sport – but I had a good power-to-weight ratio so could race competitively. I tended to be better suited to the courses that had more gradual climbs and flatter sections, and had plenty of endurance so would always finish strongly.

As the ski season wrapped up I began to plan the summer. Jodie and I liked Wanaka and I'd met a guy who co-owned a river-kayaking company there, running daily trips down the Matukituki. When he heard I was a sea-kayak guide and training instructor, he offered me a job. Jodie was also offered work. One day the mountain was shut due to rain so the company owners and I decided to pop over the hill to Queenstown and paddle the flooded Kawarau River. I'd paddled the Dog Leg numerous times so knew what I was getting into. Once at the put-in we were all surprised at how high the river was, joking that it would be a fast trip. The section is technically not very difficult, about Grade 3, but what makes it a challenge is that the flooding creates huge crashing river waves and hydraulics. The trip was a blast until the last part of the final rapid.

Not being able to see anything more than white water and not knowing the river intimately, I accidentally dropped into a hole, a retentive river feature, which held me there. Upside down in the cold water, I rolled back up to discover I was still in the hole. I was flipped over again and rolled back up. This process was repeated a few times. By now I'd been in the hole for about fifteen seconds and wasn't having a good time. Over I went again. This time I decided to stay upside down hoping I would get flushed out by the green water exiting the hole deeper down. This worked but I remember fighting with the river to keep hold of my paddle. Upside down and moving downstream, I knew I was out of the hole but for some weird reason I couldn't roll up. Momentarily confused, I exited the kayak – which in kayaking is known as 'having a swim' – and back breathing air again I understood what was going on. My right shoulder was in immense pain and I couldn't move it. It was dislocated – one of kayaking's more feared injuries, partly due to the pain but mainly due to the ongoing problems it can create.

I managed to get to the riverbank but had lost my kayak and paddle, which one of the guys recovered. Now freezing cold and in the most pain I'd ever felt, they tried to comfort me. I'd swum to the wrong side of the river – had I gone to the right bank we could have got in the car and gone straight to hospital. On the left bank we were a bit stranded and it was apparent there was no way I was getting back in a kayak to cross the river. Curled over supporting my arm, there was only one position I could keep it where I wasn't screaming in agony. Luckily, the bleakness of the situation lifted when a commercial raft turned up and asked if we needed help. The guide moved the boatload of Japanese clients around and I was carried across. The raft trip, transfer to car, and journey to Queenstown by road put me through a decent amount of suffering, rendering me somewhat delirious. Once in the hospital the anaesthetic was complete joy – ahhh. I woke up a little later with what felt like deep bruising in my shoulder. It was time to get a coffee.

Later that week I contacted Mick Hopkinson, regarded as New Zealand's kayak guru. He'd been an instructor to me and I wanted his advice. He suggested that I didn't paddle a river for six months, but spend time rebuilding strength, and then learning to paddle better. Sea kayaking would be okay provided I was sensible. This advice meant I couldn't work for the river company so I decided to return to the Abel Tasman. Jodie got a job guiding also. However, when I started working I soon discovered that the pain in my shoulder was simply too much. I couldn't lift kayaks either and my boss and I decided that I couldn't guide that summer. At first I was annoyed but when I went to register for the unemployment benefit, I was told I would instead receive a sickness benefit, given I'd had a job lined up but couldn't do it because of injury. The other bonus was that it was at nearly my full pay – far more than the unemployment benefit. What a score! The situation got even better as I could ride my bike fine, so that summer I was training full-time – mountain biking and cycling – riding 500 to 800 km per week. I had my strongest season racing road bikes ever, competing in tours and events with the elite of New Zealand cycling.

My most memorable moment on the road bike was in a major New Zealand tour where I was a lead-out man for a sprinter. On the final day we headed into some hills and the sprinter knew he was going to be dropped, so he told me to do my own thing on the stage, to go for it. I found myself in a breakaway group of five riders after attacks had been mounted on the climb. In the group were three Olympians – Brian Fowler, Chris Nicholson and Graeme Miller. By then I had moved to number three in the national mountain-bike rankings. Graeme was a hero of mine on the road and I was blown away to be in a break with such company, and was handling it just fine, respectfully sitting on the back while Brian was setting the pace. Chris was a friend, so it felt good to know he was there. We sped up the mountain. By rights, I should have been the first to be dropped, but as Brian increased the speed, I could see it was Graeme who was buckling the most and he started to struggle to maintain contact with Chris's wheel. Then a gap began to open and soon enough a bike length. I knew I needed to pass Graeme and occupy that space otherwise I too would lose contact, but it took me a few seconds to muster the courage to go around him. I did but it was done out of respect – he was a legend. I finished the stage with the breakaway.

Had I committed myself to road cycling at that time I suspect I could have reached a fairly high level, but mountain biking still squealed my wheels the most.

CHAPTER NINE
NAUGHTY FUNDING

Because of my shoulder injury, juggling funds and sport, Jodie and I decided to put racing in the US on hold for a year. The International Olympic Committee (IOC) had announced that mountain biking would be a demonstration sport at the 1996 Games in Atlanta, and New Zealand's top two male cross-country riders would likely get to ride. Making it as one of the top two was a realistic goal. I was the number one rider in the South Island and there were about three or four North Island riders that were competition. The current champion, Jon Hume, was clearly a cut above and guaranteed an Olympic place, leaving the rest of us to battle for the other spot. My plan was to race the World Cup and US NORBA (National Off-Road Bicycle Association) series in 1995 to get my world ranking higher and become the second Kiwi rider, which would then set me up for a strong chance of making the Olympic team in the 1995/96 season.

An additional reason to spend another year in New Zealand was that Whenua Iti Outdoor Pursuits Centre, in conjunction with Nelson Polytech, were offering a full-time course in outdoor leadership in 1994. Jodie and I were both planning careers in outdoor education and this was the first programme that was specific to the industry. We promptly signed up and moved in with my parents and my younger sister. The course was terrific, with a mixture of outdoor skills training along with workshops in human behaviour, communication, teamwork, that kind of stuff – soft skills, we called them. There were 18 students and everyone was really engaged and committed. We'd spend three days a week doing outdoor activity and two days in the classroom. Every weekend Jodie and I would be out in the wild doing expeditions, climbing and paddling.

When the course started I explained to Social Welfare that I was doing a full-time course now and getting a student allowance and that the sickness benefit could stop. However, about a month into the course I noticed that my bank account seemed to have too much money. I was still receiving the sickness benefit. I visited Social Welfare to explain but was surprised when they said they'd stop future payments but I should just keep the overpayment. This all happened again a few weeks later when the payments were still going in. And again I got the same response. When the payments still kept coming I told Jodie we should just keep the money and if we needed to repay it one day we'd have it ready. But by midyear I decided we should just spend it, so for the rest of the year Jodie and I became somewhat of an enigma to our classmates, as we had all this additional unexplained funding. We'd go snowboarding at Mount Hutt for a weekend, buy new outdoor equipment on a whim, and eat at restaurants. When the course ended late that year, I popped into Social Welfare and told them I had a job sea-kayak guiding and that I didn't need the sickness benefit any more. They congratulated me on finding a job and the money stopped the next week. I do feel a little bad about that, as it totalled around $15,000, but it really helped my study and I've paid some hefty tax in recent years so I reckon me and the government must be about even now.

The course in outdoor leadership promoted inward reflection, so I started to think more about myself and how I contributed to the world, including making the decision to stop thieving, primarily shoplifting, which had become slightly addictive. Interestingly, in sport, the rules of engagement have always been sacred to me, so to intentionally break a rule has always been out of the question – push the limits, yes, but to deceive people, to knowingly cheat, never. We had some of the country's top instructors working with us and were doing some amazing adventure trips. Hiking and bushcraft were core skills that crossed over to all areas. The course had focused on rock climbing, kayaking and caving, plus a white-water rafting component. By now I had done plenty of rafting and had bought a commercial raft with a few mates. I was offered a job raft guiding the following summer but was put off it by the amount of driving involved, although I helped out from time to time. I opted to do another sea-kayak guiding season instead.

Perhaps the highlight of the year was when Jodie and I got invited to China by our bike sponsor at the time, Diamondback Bicycles. When they learned of Olympic mountain biking, the company decided to get as many bikes as possible on the start line of the inaugural event and formed the Diamondback Racing (DBR) World Team. If they could sponsor the top riders from all major nations, they could end up with a huge percentage of their bikes in Atlanta. With the manufacturing based in China, they flew in all the DBR riders from around the world and put us through a series of races over two weeks. Different riders were sent to various parts of China and then all the riders, about fifty, gathered in Beijing for the final event.

It was a taste of being a pro athlete – five-star hotels, all expenses paid, full bike service, massage and VIP treatment. It was a superb trip and we performed highly which was a bonus, with a few podium placings in the early racing. Best of all, though, we got to meet the top riders, many of them ranked in the top 20 in the world. Travelling through China in 1994 was a big eye-opener for us. We were sent to Chengdu in Sichuan Province, where the poverty, people, food, and seeming lack of rules in contrast to a strong military presence, all made for a life-changing trip. It was really the first time we'd been in the middle of a continent also which was interesting – old mountains, big rivers, stable weather.

The tour ended with all the riders being taken to the premier Peking Duck restaurant in Beijing. We sat around huge tables, listening to Chinese dignitaries yelling their speeches, toasting rice wine, and then the glistening roasted ducks were wheeled out on trolleys and the skin and fat delicately carved off leaving the flesh of the duck exposed. They looked delicious. But we were all nonplussed when they put the plates of skin and fat on the tables and wheeled the ducks away. It seems that by Chinese standards that was the best bit – lucky us. Meeting the management of the DBR World Team and the top riders also meant that the following year, when we were based out of the US, racing on the World Cup and NORBA circuits, we'd have support from our sponsor.

Jodie celebrated her twenty-first that year on the Clarence River as part of our final trip with the course – five days paddling and rafting our way from the mountains to the sea. Another sea-kayaking season went by and we both raced mountain bikes over summer, travelling around on the six-race national circuit. Jodie was winning back-to-back national downhill titles and I was improving about one place a year, both of us making the New Zealand team each season. Socially, it was the same crowd every few weeks, just racing at a different location, and we have fond memories of the road trips, the events, and being part of that movement when the sport was still very much in its infancy.

At the end of summer in 1995 we headed off on a four-month bike-racing trip. Jodie was still the women's downhill national champion and I was ranked number two in men's cross-country. Our first stop was Australia for a World Cup cross-country. I was racing well but the World Cup was a whole new level. In a field of about 200 riders, a top 50 result was going to be an achievement. We arrived in Cairns a week before the event and spent most of the time training on the course. As it was only a cross-country race, Jodie focused on her training for her first US downhill race the following month. The venue for the cross-country was about 20 km from the city where the riders were all staying. Most days we'd ride out and train on the course for a few hours and then ride back to town in a regular headwind. Word got around that at four o'clock the sugar-cane tractors and trailer units would be on the road at 30 km/h, ideal for cyclists to sit behind drafting, getting shelter from the wind. By the end of the week, there would be a large group of riders all lying on the grass by the highway waiting for the convoy to trundle past.

The race didn't go well for me. Typically a slow starter and not conditioned to the extreme heat, I found myself almost dead last soon into it. As I started to make my way up the field I noticed riders were getting off their bikes and running through the forest to rejoin the track, missing out some large sections of the course. While this was cheating, technically it was the fault of the course markers, failing to ribbon off the trail in places which allowed riders to cut corners. Out of principle, I refused to do it, but it cost me plenty of places, finishing sixty-second in the end. We spent a few more days training there before flying out to the US.

San Francisco is the birthplace of mountain biking and there were a number of major races in the region which prompted us to head there and set ourselves up for the road trip. Our plan was to buy a van that was capable of transporting three bikes inside it as well as having room to sleep in. Our contact there, Rich Sangalli, whom I met when he was doing some bike racing in New Zealand, helped us get a Ford E-Series Econoline. It was big and black with tinted windows and we bought it off a biker – the rear window had a Harley-Davidson sticker on it and another one that said 'Ace of Dice'. The biker guy suggested we take that one off. I figured it could provide us some security so I left it on.

We spent an awesome week training with Rich in the Bay Area and then got on the road, equipped with a cooker, food, bed and our bikes. Our first race was in Sacramento. We took our time travelling through the Calistoga valley, driving a few hours each day then finding some trails to go riding on. It was magic – hot sunny weather, packed-dirt single-track riding, new trails each day, ride, relax, ride, relax – about as good as life could get. A few days into the trip we pulled over on the roadside for a picnic lunch but nearly choked on our sandwiches when a motorcycle gang pulled up and surrounded us.

'Compare!' said the leader, holding his fist in the air.

We didn't know what to say.

'Compare!' he repeated.

'Sorry, mate – I'm not sure what you mean,' I replied.

He asked if we were bikers and we nodded approvingly, but quickly pointed out when we realised our mistake that we were 'mountain' bikers. He looked at the sticker on the back of the van so I quickly told him we'd just bought it. Then he suggested we take the sticker off the back window and they continued on their way. I took the sticker off.

Travelling in the US back then was quite an experience. It felt like we were in a television programme because most of the TV we'd watched growing up as kids was from there. We had fun and laughs with people trying to understand Jodie too. Her authentic Kiwi accent often meant locals thought she was speaking a foreign language. One day a man asked her where she was from, and she told him she was from New Zealand.

'Where did you say you're from'?

'New Zealand,' she replied.

'Where? I can't understand you.'

'N-e-w Z-e-a-l-a-n-d!' she said slowly.

'Oh, Iceland, no wonder I can't understand you. I don't speak Icelandic.'

The mountain biking was superb and each day we were riding in different areas. We discovered we could make quite good prize money at the state championships, so we chased those races when we could. By the end of the year we were state champions in Washington, Montana and Idaho in our respective events. My favourite rides were in Utah. We raced in eight states with the highlight of the riding and racing being in Colorado. With races there and many others in California, we drove across the Mojave Desert three times. After two crossings Jodie said she wouldn't do it again, so for our third crossing I waited until she was asleep, then got behind the wheel and drove all night to Mammoth Mountain in California.

Early on in the trip we bumped into a group of Kiwi lads, four riders from Rotorua. We knew them at home but had had no idea they were doing the same thing, a mountain-bike-racing road trip of the US. They ended up being on a very similar schedule to us so we travelled in convoy for much of the trip, training together and sharing meals. We learned that parking overnight in 24-hour supermarket car parks was not illegal so we did that quite often. It was quite handy, as a few times I'd wake in the early hours of the morning hungry or thirsty so I'd just get up and go into the supermarket. One night, around 2 a.m., me and one of the Kiwi lads went into the supermarket but couldn't find any staff. We started rolling rock melons down an aisle and later put some bottles up as skittles. Still no staff came, so after a drink and snack we returned to our vans.

One of the bigger surprises I had was when I was lining up for a race in Steamboat Springs. A few people in front of me was Rod, my old flatmate from university. On an impulse, he'd decided to do some bike racing in the US too. He'd spoken to my mother and figured we were in Colorado somewhere, so he headed there. After the race he loaded his stuff into our van and the three of us carried on with our road trip – bloody brilliant. However, while it was fun to have Rod there, he was vying for one of the Olympic spots as well, so it wasn't exactly ideal for us to be living, training and travelling together. I nearly got him into trouble too.

We headed to the World Cup in Mammoth Mountain a week early to train on the course. Jodie was racing the famous Reebok Eliminator on the even more famous Kamikaze Downhill Track – great names, aren't they? Rod and I were downtown one afternoon; we'd been training and were on the search for food. We pulled into a car park and I said that I wanted to get one of the official race flags once the race was over. All around town and the event village were hundreds of these flags promoting the event, and afterward it's tradition that riders take them down as souvenirs. I had a better idea – I should get one now and avoid the rush come Sunday. So I took one down off the streetlight pole, put it by the van, and then we went to town. When I came back to the van there was a police car parked there.

We walked over and were met by an officer who asked us if we knew anything about the flag beside the van. While I had committed quite a few crimes to date, if anyone asks me a straight question, I'll give them a straight answer. I told him I was entered in the World Cup race and that I was planning to take the flag back to New Zealand, and that it would be displayed with pride at my local bike shop. I then learned that if you give an American a uniform they go power crazy. Before I knew it I was face down on the ground, handcuffed and dragged to the police car. 'Um, I think you're getting me mixed up with a serial killer.' Down at the station I was fingerprinted, photographed and interviewed. It was completely over the top, when I could have simply put the flag back.

Anyway, the officer in charge came along and we had a chat. He was far more understanding and could see I wasn't a serious threat to US safety. He explained that they were expecting some trouble with the mountain bikers as thousands were in town for the race. The Union Cycliste Internationale (UCI) were prepared to deal with any riders who got into trouble as an alternative to the police system, so I had a choice of going to court the following week or UCI handling my incident. I knew if UCI handled it, I'd be suspended from the race, so I chose the court option. I had a good ride to finish forty-second and was the second Kiwi rider (from five), making it a successful race. On Monday I went to court. When the judge asked me what would happen in New Zealand for this crime, I told him nothing would happen, and he laughed, gave me a US$70 fine and told me to behave myself whilst in the US. Little did I know that this trivial incident would become a major problem further down the track.

Jodie rode amazingly to make it into the final 16 women in the Kamikaze, which got her into the Eliminator, which was a crazy head-to-head race, two people on course, winner advances. All riders were clocking over 100 km/h, so she put a 58-tooth chain ring on her bike to pedal the wide-open sections. Jodie was bumped out but it was a huge achievement to make the final cut, as she was the only amateur rider to have made it into the Eliminator. After a month or so, I told Rod it was time to do our own thing. He was fine with that – we'd had some good times and I had saved him from being arrested. After four months of racing and sightseeing we returned to San Francisco, sold our van and went to REI (Recreational Equipment Inc.), spent all the money on sporting gear, then flew back to New Zealand.

We both had jobs sea-kayak guiding so we needed to find a place to live. Mum suggested that instead of paying rent we should buy a house. I didn't have a cent to my name and it seemed like a very serious thing to do, but she assured me it was quite easy. Jodie was interested so we went and spoke to a mortgage broker. In 1995 buying a house was quite easy – we bought our first home for $105,000 with no deposit, just a guarantee from my parents. It was the ideal location for us, right at the trail head for the mountain-biking tracks in our home town.

During that summer, however, it started to look unlikely that the Olympic dream would eventuate. Because of its rapid growth, the IOC decided that instead of being a demonstration sport, mountain biking would go direct to being an official medal sport. This was good news for mountain biking but wasn't great news for the riders at the time. The change meant that mountain biking would become a code of cycling and the New Zealand cycling team was already full with road and track athletes. The only way we could get into the team was if we were ranked in the top 20 in the world or if enough of our riders were ranked high enough to move the country's ranking into the top 20, neither of which were going to happen in the next 12 months. Kathy Lynch got to race the women's Olympic mountain-bike race because she was in the road cycling team already, and her world ranking in both disciplines was very high. I lost motivation after that, did one more national series, finishing on the podium and making the New Zealand team again, but decided to retire from the sport and focus on my career.

But I did finish off the year with a prodigious escapade on a bicycle. The Kennett Brothers were widely known in the New Zealand biking scene, having pioneered much of the mountain biking among other legendary exploits. I'd raced against all three of the biking trio at various stages of my career and had huge respect for them, both as riders and people. I got a call from Simon asking me if I would be interested in riding on their triple bike with the aim of trying to break the record for the round Lake Taupo Cycle Challenge, New Zealand's largest cycling event. It sounded fun, so I agreed to meet them in Taupo.

They'd readied the bike and had mounted a motorcycle fairing on it for extra aerodynamics. They reckoned they could go over 100 km/h on it. After some testing at the Wellington velodrome they had decided to remove the disc brakes as they created wind drag, and instead put a regular cantilever mountain-bike brake on. However, a test ride proved that because the front rider was so far from the rear wheel, the stretch in the cable meant that the brake hardly worked. The solution was to put the rear brake on the handlebars of the third rider, so a normal-length cable could be used. I was glad I was on the back. We went for a short ride before the event started, giving me a chance to test the brake. The difficulty was that I couldn't see forward – in order to see past two riders I needed to lean over so far that it caused the bike to become unstable. Therefore we developed a system where if Simon wanted me to apply rear brake he simply called out 'brake on' and 'brake off'. It appeared to work well enough.

The race began. Sadly we got a puncture in the opening kilometre and had to wait for about 5000 riders to go past before the mechanical support arrived with the high-pressure pump we needed to inflate the wheel again. Back on the bike, we spent the entire ride, about 100 miles, passing single riders like they were spectators on the side of the road. We could ride at 70 km/h on the straights at times. The real exhilaration, though, was the big descents. Careening down a hill nearing 100 km/h, the noise of the wind in my ears meant I couldn't hear clearly what Simon was saying, whether it was 'brake on' or 'brake off'. Approaching a corner at high speed went something like this:

Simon: 'Brake on.'

Me: 'What?'

Simon: 'Brake on!'

Me: 'Okay.' I'd apply the brake.

Simon: 'Brake off.'

Me: 'What?'

Jonathan: 'He said "Brake off".'

Me: 'Oh, okay.'

How we managed to get down in one piece was nothing short of a miracle.

Despite a valiant chase we didn't manage to catch the front riders, so while our actual riding time was fast, our event time, including the stoppage near the start, was nothing noteworthy.

CHAPTER TEN

NELSON FOUNDATION

Living in Nelson and working in Marahau was excellent training, I was cycling 70 km to work and back again each day. The 700 km per week commute translated to some great results at the end of my bike-racing career. I loved working as a kayak guide and was more than happy to spend the day touring around the park. It wasn't always easy – some days I'd have difficult-to-please clients and other days the weather could turn bad, adding to the challenge of keeping people happy and safe. Towards the end of the 1995/96 season, my boss, Hugh Canard, who perhaps thought my 140 km daily cycling commute was a little ridiculous, suggested we go into business together and start a small sea-kayak company that was based in Nelson but still operated in the Abel Tasman by transporting the clients over each day. Offering a transport service to the kayak trip would save me about five hours of cycling a day. As well as making logistical sense, the business presented a new challenge. The sea-kayak season was typically about seven months long so we decided to buy a four-wheel-drive 13-seater van that could be used for transport to Rainbow ski field over winter.

The winter of 1996 was spent setting up the company. Jodie and I were also working as outdoor instructors at Whenua Iti Outdoor Pursuits Centre when they needed us. Jodie was still downhill racing – she'd gone to the World Champs again and was chasing another national title, which she won later that season. I had done six seasons of guiding by then and Jodie had done four, so collectively we knew all we needed to know about the industry, plus we had Hugh on board. Our company, Kiwi Kayaks, was a small business offering low-priced sea-kayak day trips. We'd collect the clients from their accommodation in Nelson and drop them off again afterward. It was a long day, but because we only ran one trip per day, we'd guide just three to four days a week and do marketing and promotion the rest of the time. The company was an immediate success and we ran trips daily over the 1996/97 summer.

Because it was a small business it was never going to generate huge profits, but it provided us with an income and taught us valuable lessons. After the first season, I was nominated for the 1997 Pacific Business Awards and won the Small Business of the Year award. We celebrated by taking a holiday in Samoa with my father who had invested a small amount of capital in the company. Braden decided to join us. This was my first trip back as an adult and it was Jodie's first time there. We spent several weeks touring about, with Dad filling the role as tour guide. Whilst there, I decided to get a Samoan tattoo – a decorative arm band. It was important for me to get it in Samoa as it had more cultural significance plus I could get it done by traditional methods. Dad thought it was a fine idea. I worked with a local tattooist to develop a design and told him I wanted one that represented courage, so he blended some of the artwork that was traditionally used for the warriors. All my Samoan relatives thought it was wonderful. By contrast, when I showed it to Mum back in New Zealand, she was outraged and disgusted. It highlighted the connotations tattoos have in different cultures as well as some of the cultural differences within my own family.

The 1997 ski season was about to begin and our van was contracted to supply transport. As a driver, I had a season pass, so I would take a load of people up to the mountain, snowboard all day and then return to Nelson. Some days, if the conditions weren't great, I'd spend the morning instructing the beginners that I'd taken to the field. The ski season merged into the kayak season, so the transition from snowboard to sea kayak was just a matter of days. Meanwhile, Jodie was doing her final year of mountain-bike racing. One more national title and she'd be happy to retire. From my experience racing for a season in the US, I'd picked up some good ideas about how the races could be better managed, so I decided to organise a round of the New Zealand national series.

Most mountain-bike events in New Zealand tended to be in the remote forestry areas known only to the riders, whereas in the US they tried to run the events as close as possible to the people – in city parks or areas with good access for both riders and spectators. There's an iconic hill in Nelson called the Centre of New Zealand (so-named for obvious reasons) which overlooks the city with a shared trail system for hikers and bikers. The local council were willing to close some of the trails for a weekend so the event could take place. It was a huge success with hundreds of spectators enjoying the racing in an exciting atmosphere and exposing more people to the sport. In fact, it was so successful I agreed to run it again the following summer. Dad was a winner that weekend, too, as he took along his barbecue to sell a few sausages and made enough to pay his golf fees for the upcoming year.

That winter I was also working for Whenua Iti again. I had always had a strong connection to the centre and was regularly in and out of the place, doing some part-time work or borrowing outdoor gear. My main job was a contract the centre had with Nelson College helping run the Matakitaki Outdoor Education Programme, which I had been through myself and knew very well, teaching bushcraft, river crossing and navigation. From Monday to Friday we'd have 30 to 40 students at the lodge and we'd do hiking-based outdoor programmes. By the end of that winter I'd learned an incredible amount about navigation myself, spending day after day in the mountains teaching map and compass work, establishing a superb foundation for being an adventure-racing navigator later on. By the time summer rolled around I was back to sea-kayak guiding and running the business.

This period of my life was really fun. I had a lifestyle sea-kayak company that provided Jodie and I with a comfortable income for most of the year. We had our own home and from time to time had friends renting rooms to help pay the mortgage. I was spending most of my free time white-water kayaking, mountain biking and, every so often heading to the hills for a hiking trip, typically exploring the remote and rugged corners of the local parks. My main focus was building my career in outdoor education, so what I needed to keep doing was developing my skills and experience, which simply meant continually going on adventure trips. While I didn't have a specific goal at the time, the outdoor industry offered plenty of opportunity so I had a strong faith that provided I kept heading in that general direction, things would work out. If I just opted to do the things I was passionate about and do them well, everything would fall into place.

A good example of that happened that year when the Ministry of Foreign Affairs and Trade offered me a job setting up a sea-kayaking company at Marovo Lagoon in the Solomon Islands. My experience in setting up Kiwi Kayaks plus the fact I was of Samoan descent made me an ideal candidate. I was sold immediately even before I knew it'd be a paid job, so when I learned that the pay rate per day was about the same as that for a week's guiding in New Zealand, I couldn't sign the paperwork fast enough. It turned out to be a very special experience.

With over a thousand islands, Marovo Lagoon is the longest saltwater lagoon in the world and quite possibly one of the top five sea-kayak destinations. The marine life is rich, the waterways idyllic, and it had been made a World Heritage Site shortly before I arrived there. Ministry of Foreign Affairs and Trade workers like myself were tasked with setting up sustainable business for the local people, to lessen the appeal of selling their forests to Malaysian logging companies. Because they used canoes and boats as their main form of transport, a sea-kayak company was a natural fit. My main task was to train the guides to an international standard. I was given ten or so potential guides with the aim of putting them through a month of intensive training and hopefully emerging with some senior guides to take charge of the company and some regular guides to work for it.

From the capital of Honiara I flew to Seghe, on New Georgia Island, then travelled by boat through Marovo Lagoon to a seaside village and was shown to my home for the next few weeks. It was a comfortable bungalow on poles over the water, all made with natural materials, quaint and homely. After breakfast the next day, I met with the trainee guides. About twelve people showed up, mainly men but a few women as well. Although most had never paddled a kayak before, they had all grown up paddling canoes so their water confidence and basic paddle skills were high – even higher than mine in some respects. After introducing them to a fibreglass sea kayak, explaining all the features of the boat, I asked for a volunteer to learn how to Eskimo roll. One of the guys hopped in and about twenty minutes later was rolling the kayak confidently, tipping upside down and righting himself with the paddle whilst staying inside it. Having watched the lesson keenly, the next student, a guy called Lulu, got in and rolled the kayak perfectly. It was a testament to their boat and paddling prowess when, one after another, they all just jumped into the kayak and rolled it first time. It was simply a paddle stroke they had neither needed nor seen before.

After a few days of basic paddling and rescue techniques, the group soon whittled down to six as some of the students had other village duties and some just failed to turn up again, but we had a great team so we stayed with that. For the next month we'd paddle every day, planning trips, training guides and setting up the company. We'd do a lot of fishing, catching tuna most days and snorkelling for crayfish, which for religious reasons they couldn't eat (but if we were on a remote island with no one else around, the crayfish were a delicacy).

On my days off I'd go exploring. One day I headed off on a 60 km paddle to the south-western or exposed side of the island, when 5 km from shore in a building sea of wind and swell, I noticed that the bow of the kayak was dipping. It was getting deeper and deeper into the water and I could see that very soon it'd be pointing to the ocean floor. Trying to figure out what the problem was, I decided that the front hatch cover, which was a fairly primitive screw-down system, mustn't be sealed properly and over a few hours water had seeped in. Now it was so low to the sea level that more water was spilling in. A long way from shore and in very remote waters, no one really knew where I was and the kayak was sinking. Somehow, I needed to get the water out of the bow. I had a pump so I planned to get out of the kayak, swim to the bow and pump the water out, hoping I could do it before a big wave filled the front compartment with water, making it worse. At least the water was warm. Paddling into the wind, I was just about to climb overboard when a shark fin surfaced next to me. Oh my god.

I had been warned that the area I was paddling to was 'shark infested' but it seemed to me that people say this everywhere in the world. Meanwhile, the problem was getting worse by the minute. If I didn't act fast I'd be seriously screwed. My only option was to John Wayne cowboy style down the kayak, sitting on the deck with a leg each side, feet in the water. The shark had gone but swimming still wasn't an option. It was a difficult balancing act, so I took my time. Straddling the kayak like a horse, I got down to the hatch as the boat bounced around in the waves, which were about 1.5 metres high. Timing was critical, so when the time was right I took the hatch cover off and started furiously pumping the water out. This was the most risky part – with the hatch open, things could go from bad to worse really bloody fast. With most of the water out of the front compartment I resealed the hatch, shimmied back to the cockpit and paddled to the nearest land as fast as I could, completely exhausted.

After sleeping on the beach for a few hours, I made sure the kayak was dry and safe and then completed the trip, arriving back at the lodge a little after dark. It had been an epic day on the sea and the guide team were quite impressed I'd done the trip. I didn't tell them about the drama but did point out to them the poor craftsmanship around the hatch, explaining how it leaked and filled up the front compartment. They had a fleet of quality kayaks being handcrafted by local timber boat builders and everything was in place to start taking multi-day guided tours. The main package was a seven-day trip from the south-east to the north-west, paddling with tailwinds about 20 km per day between eco-lodges, along the shores of Vangunu Island, paradise preserved.

The food was very basic but exceptionally good – fresh fish, tropical fruit and vegetables. There were some really fascinating World War II wreckages scattered around the lagoon, which I knew would be of interest to some clients as well. The lagoon was decades behind the modern world – in terms of mystique and mystery, it was almost centuries behind. One night we were boating around the lagoon and high on the mountainside we could see a fire burning. They told me it was devil priests or witch doctors. I came away from that trip having made some close friends and with a firm belief that it was set to become a top 10 global sea-kayak destination. Sadly, political unrest began around the 1997 elections and tourism numbers dropped heavily. The projects I had been involved with establishing were all set to launch but people were being advised not to travel there. The hard part for the local people at the lagoon was that they were completely removed from the troubles in the capital city and on some of the other islands. Everything went on hold.

In 1998 I was asked if I could return to Marovo and get the guides excited about the project again. A year had passed and they hadn't run any trips. While going back would have been a fun trip for me, I felt there was little more I could teach them and it would have served of little benefit to them. I suggested that it'd be far more productive if the senior guides came out to New Zealand and I showed them the sea-kayaking industry here and what they could expect for the future in Marovo Lagoon if kayaking became a major attraction, which I believed it could. I proposed a two-week trip where they would spend a week in the Abel Tasman observing other guides, and then a selection of other trips – Cable Bay, the Marlborough Sounds and Kapiti Island.

Hosting them was a huge amount of fun as they experienced so many things for the first time, particularly modern technology. When I stopped at a fuel station one day to clean the company van with an industrial vacuum cleaner, they all insisted on having a go and the van had never had such a thorough clean. They'd never been to a movie before either, so one night I treated them to *The Matrix*. They thoroughly enjoyed it, even though they struggled to determine what was reality and what were special effects. They may have thought there were some very different, highly skilled and extremely powerful humans living somewhere else on the earth. I was surprised they weren't interested in sports cars or some of the other machinery of the western world, but that all changed when we arrived at Abel Tasman National Park and they saw some of the water taxis. When a boat pulled up with twin 300 hp Evinrude motors they were absolutely blown away. They'd grown up with boats powered with smaller 15 hp outboards so when they boarded the water taxis they all wanted their photos taken next to the motors. Witnessing the Abel Tasman sea-kayak industry at peak season, with hundreds of kayaks out on the water each day and approximately 100 staff employed, gave them a vision to aim for. Unfortunately, the political situation deteriorated further and the Marovo project got shelved again and has not been operational, not at least in the way it was intended. I believe there is an Australian sea-kayaking company running trips there now. It's a truly remarkable destination for sea kayakers and I intend to return there some time.

CHAPTER ELEVEN

NO FEAR

Life was ticking along nicely but by the end of 1997 I felt the need to get into some training and adventure. It was time to return to the Coast to Coast, this time for the 'Longest Day', what most consider the premier race. Whenever someone asks if you've done the Coast to Coast, an air of disappointment usually follows when you say you've only done the two-day race – same event, same course, but one race takes two days and other only one, a long day.

We weren't earning excesses of money and Jodie was getting frustrated by my unremitting hunger – I was eating a whole box of cereal for breakfast and still looking around the kitchen for whatever could be consumed. She suggested I write to Hubbards to see if they could help me out. I crafted a letter to Dick Hubbard explaining what I was doing and that I was inhaling his cereals by the box. He kindly wrote back saying he'd supply me all the breakfast food I needed for my training, and each month large cartons of the stuff would arrive. It was a significant saving, especially as I'm happy to eat cereal for dinner.

My kayak skills were sharp, my cycling ability was bordering on elite level by New Zealand standards, so I needed to get my mountain running back in shape. I spent the summer training with some good friends who were also racing the Coast to Coast. Mike Webb was my main training partner and he was very knowledgeable about both the race and the athletes. We'd run, bike and paddle for hours, both of us eyeing up a top 10 result, the difference perhaps being that Mike saw top 10 as a big achievement, whereas I thought being outside of the top five would be close to a fail. Around that time, Steve Gurney was clocking up multiple wins, while Andy MacBeth and Mark Elliott were both giving him some close racing. As always, there were a solid group of athletes all aiming for the podium.

February 1998 rolled around and I lined up on the beach with the other Longest Day competitors, feeling very relaxed and confident. Gurney was a legend in multi-sport and especially in this race, but because I had consistently beaten him in mountain-bike races, I considered him beatable in the Coast to Coast as well. But it wasn't going to be in 1998, at least not by me. My goal was to have a strong race and see where I was in relation to the field. I wanted a result that I could use as a benchmark to have a serious attempt in 1999, so I needed to know where I stood.

The first cycle was easy. I cruised along in the bunch pleasantly surprised that the pace was much slower than I had expected. While I was sure I'd be fine to race up to 12 hours at a high intensity, I still wanted to be sensible and pace wisely. It was uncharted ground and very rarely did anyone have a first Longest Day they were happy with. Most people underperformed in their debut. Once onto the run a few runners bolted – Mark Elliott and another rising athlete in the sport, George Christison. I knew both were better runners than me as I'd raced them a few months earlier in another endurance triathlon, where George won, Mark was second and I was third. Now they were bolting up the riverbed and the pace they were setting would destroy my legs so I sat back in the pack of about six and made my way up the valley comfortably. Gurney was in the group so I figured that was a good sign. Slowly the group whittled down until it was just Gurney and me going over Goat Pass. I got a bit of a shock when he dropped me going down the valley – I'd always considered myself a good trail runner and particularly a fast descender, but he put a few minutes on me in the final 10 km of the stage – although he did know the course intimately. I came off the mountain run in fourth place and happily got on my road bike for the short dash to the river and kayak stage.

As I was getting into the kayak I could see Steve disappearing downstream in pursuit of Mark and George. My kayaking was at a new level since I last did the race some six years earlier, so the enjoyment was far better. I was getting unofficial time splits every so often that I was making time up on the next competitor although I didn't know who it was, but racing for a podium placing was motivating so I kept at it. Off the river, I was informed that Steve was leading and Mark was in second. I was about ten minutes back from George who was a strong rider plus there was only 70 km to go, less than two hours' riding. I had nothing to lose so I set my sights on catching George. It was no news to me, though, that George was a tough racer and he wasn't going to forfeit third place that easily. Both of us were getting time splits from our support crews as an intense battle formed. With 10 km remaining I'd closed the gap to a minute but George was hanging on tight. I kept digging deep and finally, with less than 3 km to go, I managed to bridge up to him. I could see he was exhausted, draped over his bike like a towel and desperately trying to find more strength. At heart I was still a bike racer and knew then that I had it. I powered past him and on to the finish, taking third place by just over a minute.

I was really happy. I had finished 22 minutes behind Steve but that didn't faze me. I knew right then that I could cut 10 minutes off the first cycle, save at least that again on the run, and still improve my kayaking. I figured in twelve months' time I could win the race. Jodie had hoped we'd go cycle touring around Europe for the winter so she wasn't so excited about my plan to train for 10 months for the next Coast to Coast. She said she would go to Europe with or without me. As much as I wanted to be with Jodie and cycle the Continent, I also wanted to give the Coast to Coast one totally committed attempt. Because we'd both dedicated years to competitive sport, Jodie wanted to move on, to establish ourselves more securely financially and ultimately have a family in a few years' time. As far as she was concerned, racing the Coast to Coast was pure recreation. So she got herself sorted and hopped on a plane to London, her plan to cycle tour around the United Kingdom and then Europe. My training buddy Mike Webb happened to be cycle touring in similar places at the same time so they planned to meet up for parts of the trip.

With Jodie away, I needed just enough work to survive on and be able to train 20 to 30 hours a week. So I became a youth recreation worker at Nelson City Council for three half-days and one full day per week. It was the perfect job. Most of it was organising sports and games with the students doing a life skills and employment training course. I had a budget for some activities which I usually spent playing paintball or taking the students four-wheel motorbike riding. Quite simply, I was paid to have fun and still devote all the time I needed to training and racing. My brother and cousin moved in so we had a real bachelors' pad going, regularly worshipping the Sony PlayStation until the early hours of the morning. The dedicated focus of my training was paying dividends. As the summer racing season approached, I was going around the country on a race record-breaking rampage, setting new records for stages and events.

I've always been a bit of a loner. I'm comfortable on my own and happy to spend hours a day training by myself. I value the peace and quiet and the opportunity to think without disruption. For that reason, I rarely seek out training companions. Some level of social contact is needed so perhaps 20 per cent of the time I train with others but, not being into crowds either, normally with just one other person at a time. But with Jodie away riding her bike and buying baguettes, I was left to pay the mortgage. It was the leanest budget I'd been on since being a school kid.

Some weeks I was reduced to counting up all the loose coins I could find and being cheerful that I had enough to buy a chocolate bar – excellent, a spare 85 cents. I was managing to pick up some casual work as a white-water kayak instructor and did the occasional sea-kayak guiding trip, which was cash in hand.

The time apart from Jodie made me appreciate and value our relationship. We'd been together for seven years, in which time we'd travelled, bought a home, run a business and shared all sorts of experiences. We were both naive teenagers when we started dating and we'd spent all our twenties together. We had largely been shaped by the same experiences and influences. Deciding I'd ask her to marry me when she returned, I got a local carver to make an engagement necklace – having worked in the outdoor industry, we'd both heard of too many ring-related injuries.

I picked Jodie up in Christchurch and we planned to spend a few days travelling back to Nelson where I was doing a multisport race. Along the Kaikoura coast we stopped for a picnic by the sea and I asked her to marry me. Thankfully, although a little surprised, she agreed to the deal. She had returned with an idea too. She had done an Outward Bound course a few years earlier and had always thought it'd be a great place to work. For an outdoor instructor, completing an Outward Bound contract was something of a qualification in itself, a seal of approval in outdoor education. The three-year term was in many ways a three-year Outward Bound course for the instructor too, as the job tended to present constant challenge. Jodie had done the math and figured we should sell our kayak company and both work at Outward Bound. We'd be able to put one salary directly onto our mortgage and after three years we'd be in a stable situation to start a family. It sounded good to me so we filled in the application forms.

Towards the end of the year, there was a week-long selection course and both Jodie and I were accepted onto it. That was no surprise as we had both been working as outdoor guides and instructors and held valuable qualifications. The selection course at the time was in some ways a mini-Outward Bound course, condensed into five days. Fourteen people were on the course and we were told that of the successful applicants, four would start immediately and the others would have start dates stretched over the following 12 months, if they were offered a job at all. The staff running the course kept telling us to relax and be ourselves, to have some fun, but I was surprised by how competitive many of the prospective applicants were. Some of them were so desperate to impress that it all seemed a bit over the top.

Consequently, I couldn't help playing up a little, 'taking the piss', much to Jodie's disgust. While others strutted their stuff, making themselves out as gurus, I made out I was a complete novice and knew nothing about the outdoors, falling out of my kayak and pretending not to know how a compass worked. I figured the selection staff would see through it because, using the New Zealand Outdoor Instructors Association qualifications as a measure, I was a highly qualified candidate. A few weeks later we each received letters from Outward Bound. Jodie was offered a job but I wasn't – obviously the panel didn't get my joke. I didn't care, but Jodie was livid. Because we'd already decided we'd only go to Outward Bound if we both got jobs, she claimed I'd ruined our chances of a career opportunity, steady income and change of scenery. Typically, it takes me somewhere between 10 and 20 minutes to accept bad news and move on. It takes Jodie a week or two, so we had a few challenging moments in that period. She replied to Outward Bound thanking them for the offer but saying she wouldn't be able to take the job because I didn't get one, as it wasn't an option for us as a couple engaged to be married.

I was enjoying training for the 1999 Coast to Coast, and I have many classic memories of the trips to Arthur's Pass to train on the course. At the end of spring I met my mate Simon for a training run. The weather had been really bad and we knew there would be some snow on Goat Pass but we decided to go anyway, figuring it'd be a fun adventure. Jodie dropped us off at the start and then went to a friend's bach in the village. Simon and I said we were happy to run back there after we'd crossed the mountain.

Starting later than we should have, we trotted up the valley, bracing ourselves each time we had to ford the frigid waters. It was much slower going than normal with higher water and a generally colder temperature than we were used to during summer. About two thirds of the way up we started to hit patches of snow, and within a few kilometres of the pass we were in deep snow, plugging our way upwards. The route was almost invisible in parts and despite the fact I'd been through the run countless times, I couldn't recognise some places at all, even taking a wrong valley for a short while. We were damn cold, with the snow cutting into our bare legs, and I started to wonder if we'd get out in daylight. Finally we made it to the pass, where there was a hut, and we discussed staying overnight, but the lure of a hot meal by the fire and a good bed won over. Back out in the elements, we waded through deep snow and started the descent. Darkness fell upon us when we still had an hour to go before reaching the highway. Thankfully, we were out on the open riverbed now and there was enough moonlight to illuminate the path, but we continuously ran into boulders and fallen trees we couldn't see. The bruise count on our legs grew astronomical. Eventually, we got to the point where we knew we'd reach the road and could relax, knowing the mission would soon be complete. Once on the road we joyously jogged to the village. Jodie had the fire raging and a hot meal waiting. She'd just started to worry about us.

That night it poured and the river flooded. We went to the start of the Coast to Coast paddle stage and stared at the huge brown torrent ripping past. Simon said there was no way he was going to paddle, although I was tempted. The river was by far the biggest I'd seen it, but I knew the gorge well and couldn't really see what the problem would be with the volume of water. There was nearly a gale-force tailwind so I was really keen to see how long it'd take, and what it would look like. Jodie has always trusted my judgement in such matters, and even though the river was clearly in flood, she was okay when I said I was putting on. Once on the water, I was rocketing along like never before. Training trips would normally range between 3.5 to 4.5 hours depending on flow. As I sped down the river I knew it was going to be a lightning-fast trip, provided I could stay in my kayak. Rounding into the gorge, though, I wasn't convinced I'd made a good call. The pressure waves were enormous, but thankfully there was enough room to avoid most of the frightening stuff. On two occasions the wind was so strong I was blasted across the surface of the water to the opposite bank, clinging to stay upright. After an hour of extreme paddling through the gorge it started to mellow out for the final section. I made it to the end, pumped up and on a high. It'd taken me 2.5 hours. I found out later the river was flowing at 1200 cumecs (cubic metres per second).

The sea-kayak season had begun so Jodie stepped up as income earner for us while I put the final touches to my training. I was racing locally three to four times a week and smashing every race I took part in – I couldn't have been happier with my form. The media had also picked up on the fact I'd raised my game to a whole new level and were anticipating an exciting tussle between Steve Gurney and me – dubbing it 'the King versus the Prince'. By comparing race times, I worked out I was paddling, biking and running faster than him. Bring it on, was all I could say. Regretfully, the weekend before the race Jodie insisted I went out to dinner at the beach with her and some friends. It was a cold night and while I enjoyed the company I was freezing cold for most of the evening, waking up that night with a red throbbing ear and discomfort. The next day I was given antibiotics for an ear infection and spent a few days really ill before heading down to the West Coast for the race. It seemed I'd pushed myself over the edge, an easy thing to do when you reach peak fitness. That said, a few days out from the race, I felt my strength come back and I was eager to get cracking. I had an amazing support crew complete with a media person, massage therapist, bike mechanic, my gym instructor, Jodie and my family.

The Longest Day race had developed a set of unofficial rules. The foremost golden rule was *never* ride the first cycle hard, the belief being that the race was so tough and long that people needed to conserve their energy for the first few hours. I'd studied the history of Ironman and how guys like Mark Allen and Dave Scott were racing harder every year, continually dispelling myths around how Ironman should and could be raced. Accordingly, I didn't believe the Coast to Coast needed to start with a bunch training ride. A few others had tried to go hard on the first ride and failed but none of them had been cyclists of my pedigree. Unbeknown to all but myself, in 1999 I was going to race from start to finish. I was going to time trial the course. It was a risk, but to beat Steve I needed to risk something. So I rolled the dice.

Setting the pace on the opening run, I was the first person to start cycling, and attacked up the road at a speed I knew no other multisporter could match or be brave enough to try, and sure enough I was off on my own, hoping that in the darkness my escape would go unnoticed. As the sun came up and the media cars started to get on the course I got information I had built up over five minutes on the chase group. Well aware that I was fit and fast, Steve wasn't going to take any risks so rallied with some other guys to reduce my lead to three minutes by the end of the cycle. I didn't care, though, as the pace had been quick and I knew they had all ridden harder than they would have liked.

Once onto the run I felt good and set to work, again extending my lead. Closing in on Goat Pass, I learned that I'd been six minutes ahead of Steve at Doreen Creek, but that wasn't good news. I'd studied Steve's previous run times and while my pace was hot, it seemed Steve was running better than ever. Once over the top and into the descent I started to feel myself fade so I slowed for a while to replenish food and drink. With less than 5 km to go on the run I'm not sure why but I glanced over my shoulder and saw Steve about 1 km behind, or less. This was not good. I knew I needed a decent margin on him before the kayak. The ride to the kayak was over quickly and I transitioned onto the river. I guessed I would have added time to the gap back to Steve but it was inevitable he would catch me somewhere downriver. I respected his ability to paddle the river well and he knew how to race the course – he had won it numerous times, after all. The race was halfway through.

I figured if I could just stay in front for another hour or two and put in a strong paddle myself, then I could exit the boat within 10 minutes of Steve – a gap I believed I could close on the final road-cycling stage. I was kayaking well and knew how to take fast lines through the rapids so it wasn't going to be easy for either of us. But about a third of the way into the paddle I started to get some lower back pain. I'd never had that before and it really started to have an impact on how much power I could get into the paddle. I suspect it was a result of racing hard for eight hours over three disciplines. Steve caught me before the halfway mark and we chatted for a bit. He asked me if I was okay as it was quite clear something wasn't right. I told him my back was playing up and joked that'd I see him later on the bike. While it had taken him a long time to catch me, it was surprising how fast he got away from me afterwards, and try as I might I couldn't keep him in sight. My immediate goal was to limit the damage.

Passing Woodstock, I was told the gap was seven minutes, and by the time I exited the kayak it was closer to ten. I was really pleased to be on my bike and the change of discipline felt like a new day. It wasn't long before I was humming along the Canterbury Plains, my bike computer reading between 40 and 50 km/h. My support crew started to feed me time splits – I was gaining back about one minute every 5 km. This was looking good. If all went to plan I might see Steve about the same place I passed George a year earlier. I certainly couldn't go any faster anyway. Reaching the outskirts of the city with 30 km remaining, the time gap was down to four minutes. Then things started to dismantle. First up, I hit the headwind, which seemed to come from nowhere. Then the road got flat, when prior to that it had had a very gradual descent. The extra energy required to ride on the flat into a headwind knocked me back big time. I took on some food and drink, hoping that would help. My speed dropped down closer to 30 km/h. My legs felt so heavy I couldn't push the big chain ring, so I had to change down gears, and my speed dropped more. In short, I was rooted and my race was over. Steve, to his credit, powered on to victory. He was a master of that course and executed a well-planned race. I limped home to take second place some 16 minutes behind.

Looking back, Steve had everything under control, while I was inexperienced and still very much an amateur by comparison. Despite not winning, though, I was really happy. My ultimate goal that day had been to race hard and not have any regrets. I felt that I'd got myself into terrific condition to race for victory and in many other years my race time would have been enough to win. I'd taken a big risk with my strategy and, while it didn't pay off, I came fairly close. I led the entire race for nearly nine hours and still managed second. At the finish line, people came up to me offering congratulations and condolences, many of them saying, 'You'll win it next year.' Kind as that was, I wasn't going back. Jodie and I had a deal – it was time to close the door on the Coast to Coast and move on. Training for it demands huge sacrifices over Christmas, New Year and summer. During the sunshine season my mates were all off white-water kayaking, rock climbing, windsurfing and hiking while I'd been cycling, flat-water paddling and mountain running. I wanted more freedom to adventure and less structured training.

The morning after the Coast to Coast I woke up with stiff legs so I got on my road bike and went for an easy 90-minute spin before breakfast. After a hot shower

I felt much better. That afternoon we attended the awards and I couldn't believe how sore and crippled Steve seemed – he could hardly walk or even stand up straight. He looked shit. I knew then that he knew how to push himself to a place I didn't even know existed. I was humbled and deeply intrigued to learn where that place was and what it was like. The following Monday I won the kayak club race at home and on the Tuesday I won the A-grade cycle race. On Wednesday, Steve came to Nelson, we met for lunch and went for a swim at the beach, and he was still incredibly sore and stiff. Yes, he had pushed himself far more than I knew how to. He suggested we team up for the Southern Traverse adventure race taking place in Nelson later that year.

CHAPTER TWELVE
NEXUS FORMULA

Outward Bound came back with job offers for both of us in 1999. They understood we were a package deal and they really wanted Jodie so they got me as well. It was a winter start date so we promptly put Kiwi Kayaks on the market. I seriously considered keeping it and employing staff to operate and manage it but by now I'd spent nine years working in the industry and wanted a change. Besides, I was certain the industry was on a collision course for a collapse and decline. I'd seen it grow into a major operation with 13 companies and paddling in the park in summer had lost its appeal for me due to the crowds of people. When I first started guiding and we got to a beach with someone else on it, we'd move on to the next one – we didn't need to share beaches. Nine years on and some days we couldn't land on a beach because it was covered with kayaks. One trip I sat floating on the water with my clients waiting for another party to leave so we had room to land. I was sure word would get out that the Abel Tasman was a madhouse and people would stop visiting.

So I was happy to sell and nearly sold it to the first interested party but the guy had a heart attack while we were paddling. We were out in a double kayak and I was in the back chatting to him about the business. Next thing, he was clutching his heart and then he passed out, collapsing on the deck, arms draped into the ocean. I raced to shore, assessed him and called a water taxi, and within minutes he was on his way to hospital. He survived but needless to say didn't buy the company. We did sell it soon after – the buyers later sold it for over a million dollars, more than ten times what they paid for it. The industry grew to astronomical levels and to this day is thriving. We probably should have kept it.

Autumn arrived so it was time to head to Anakiwa, the Outward Bound site in the Marlborough Sounds. Jodie and I had three-year contracts ending in December

2001. We rented out our house and made the move. It was then that the reality sank in for me. I'd been a semi-professional athlete for the best part of five years. I had just established myself as one of the top multisport athletes in the country and I was walking away from it. I was about to start the first full-time job I'd ever had, which at 27 years old, I was quite proud of. As we drove down the dead-end road into Anakiwa, Jodie recalls me saying, 'What the hell I am doing here?'

I got off to a good start all the same, and was soon out at sea with Jodie and two other instructors who we were observing, learning the ropes, so to speak. I had taken a fishing rod, so while we were sitting on anchor at the end of the day I asked the instructors if they fancied fish for tea. 'Yep,' they replied. 'A salmon would be nice.' I stepped onto the back deck of the launch, cast the rod and started to wind it in. Bang, I had a fish on which I played to the boat, landing it on the deck, a healthy-sized salmon. It was really quite incredible. Gone for less than a minute, I returned inside with the fish to wide-eyed amazement.

The first four months was staff induction where we got to know where everything was kept, how things worked and what the job entailed. Month five we were officially instructing staff and leading groups. At the time, the core business was the 'Classic Course', a 22-day programme for people aged 18 to 27. In each group, or watch as they are known, are 14 students. The programme is divided up into three-day schemes: sailing, kayaking, rope and rock, hiking, solo and community service. Added to that were a few spare days instructors could use to cater for the group's needs. 'Creative Day' was one option, using art and drama as mediums for personal growth – not a popular choice of mine – and there was also 'Marathon Day' which involved running, a very popular choice of mine.

I arrived in a period where Outward Bound had a contract with Work and Income NZ (WINZ) to provide courses for long-term unemployed youth. Some of the young people were fully into the course and the opportunity it presented but many of them were not. These were challenging courses for the organisation and many of the staff as the youth were normally either uneducated, lacked skills to get a job, were heavy drug or alcohol users, involved in crime, or quite simply didn't want to work. Some of them were very immature and some were just downright stupid, going through life making dumb choices. Many of them aspired to be gangsters and troublemakers, so consequently they had criminal convictions and ongoing issues with the law. But behind the smokescreen – tobacco or pot – most of them were very talented and special young people. I knew this because they weren't any different from many of my old friends. At Outward Bound, though, they were wreaking havoc, and some of the courses were pretty lawless and out of control. The police were frequently called in as a result of theft, fighting or drug use.

Very few of the staff had the skills, patience or understanding, or in some cases the desire, to work with this sector, which was fair play as these courses could be starkly different to instructing a regular course that they'd be trained to run. The WINZ contract was, however, very valuable income to the school so changes were made to keep the courses going, plus they were contributing to community well-being by creating an opportunity for these youth to turn a corner. The first change instituted was that the Catalyst Course, as it was named, was to be offset with the regular Outward Bound (or Classic) courses. When the boat arrived at the start of each course and about 150 students walked down the jetty, 10 to 20 Catalyst students would be immediately whisked away either by truck or boat, and segregated from the Classic Course.

My first few watches as an instructor were great, delivering the Classic Course, which was easy and fun, but I was drawn to the Catalyst students, many of them being Maori and Pasifika. I would quickly create a positive connection with them and get to know them quite well even though I wasn't their instructor. Noting this, the school director asked if I wanted to work on the Catalyst Course. Traditionally, newer instructors didn't work on those programmes, but no one else was wanting to either. To most of the other instructors the Catalyst Course was stressful hard work and to be avoided where possible. I had a different view. To me the Classic Course was more pressure. They were in essence paying clients. Many of them had worked hard to save money to fund their Outward Bound course. They were a customer with expectations, and it reminded me of the adventure tourism industry, where people purchase an experience so with that comes pressure to deliver – expectations.

The Catalyst students, by contrast, didn't pay. Most of them didn't even want to be there. Many of them had no idea what the course was about, and their level of expectation was extremely low. This allowed more flexibility and freedom. My challenge as an instructor was to create a shift in the student, to help them move from one place to another, forward and progressively. The Classic Course students often came from affluent homes, were usually highly educated, their outlook broadened by travel, and with good personal and social awareness. Facilitating change in these people could be a huge challenge. Conversely, creating change in a Catalyst student was a guarantee, provided they weren't booted off the course or didn't quit.

One day Jodie and I had a day off so we kayaked into Picton for lunch. We'd been on different schedules so hadn't seen much of each other. She was loving life at Outward Bound, fully engaged in a job that combined working with people and outdoor adventure. The location was incredible – the Marlborough Sounds and surrounding forest parks was a spectacular office, that couldn't be denied. It was a feel-good job – so much positive change was taking place with the students and her personal learning as an instructor. The staffing team was a very special group of people, inspiring and easy to hang out with. Jodie was happy. I, on the other hand, was enjoying the job for the same reasons but I felt that I wasn't completely charging – somewhere deep down I knew something was missing. By the time we reached Picton we'd identified that I missed training and racing. I decided to explore Steve's suggestion of doing the Southern Traverse, which was now just a few months away.

When I got back to Outward Bound I went straight to the school director, Gaike Knottenbelt, and had a chat. Gaike was always approachable and asked me what he could do to help. I said I wanted some time off in November to do the Southern Traverse, that I needed something else in my life and that that would fill the gap. If I could do the race, I was sure that would satisfy my desire to compete which should allow me to complete my Outward Bound contract without interruption. He agreed, so I quickly got in contact with Steve, who was still keen to race and suggested we ask Kathy Lynch, adding that she'd probably be more receptive to getting invited by me than him, as they had a history of clashing. I called Kathy who said she'd been thinking of entering, and that she should be able to get a sponsor, so we nearly had a team. All we needed was another team-mate to make up our foursome. I got into some more specific training and immediately started to feel better.

Instructing involved some long days, rising at 5 a.m. and sometimes working until midnight. Spending days hiking, kayaking, climbing, snowboarding and sailing was all good conditioning so I kept quite fit just by doing the job. On days off I'd normally clock up some hours mountain biking. I also got out for regular night runs – it wasn't uncommon for me to work all day with my students, have an evening meeting with them, and then head out trail running for a few hours. One night I was out running, about 20 km from the school, when an ex-instructor drove past. It was around 11 p.m. and he asked me what I was doing. I told him I was training for the Southern Traverse. With good intentions, he warned me that being an Outward Bound instructor was an extremely demanding job and that I should use all my free time resting and recovering. Jogging next to his car, I politely listened and reassured him I'd take it on board, the whole time thinking, 'Get real, being an Outward Bound instructor is a holiday – I couldn't think of a better job to be doing while training for an adventure race.'

Steve, Kathy and I bounced a few names around for the fourth team member and we finally settled on Aaron Prince. I didn't know him but I knew of his parents, both accomplished multisport and adventure racers. At 18 years old Aaron was a talented navigator and skilled in mountain biking and kayaking. In November we met in Nelson for the race. I felt a mixture of excitement and nervousness. This was going to be my first multi-day adventure race – I ticked all the boxes that suggested I should get through the race fine, but until you've done an expedition-length adventure race, you never know for sure. Typical courses were about 500 km and the winning time around 100 hours, and this race wasn't intended to be any different. About forty teams gathered for the race, most of them from New Zealand and a few from overseas.

Adventure racing was then and still is a fairly young sport. It began in New Zealand in 1989 when a French event management team ran a race called the Grand Traverse. Kiwi teams took the top three placings. As a keen young outdoor kid I followed the race with great interest – teams of five people hiking, kayaking, rafting and biking for days and days sounded awesome to me. The Grand Traverse was really called the Raid Gauloises after the French tobacco company, but New Zealand wouldn't allow the tobacco advertising. It went back to being the Raid and moved to Costa Rica the following year. A Kiwi athlete and event organiser, Geoff Hunt, then decided New Zealand could sustain an annual event and the Southern Traverse was born in 1991. I'd closely followed the Southern Traverse since its beginning and knew one day I'd be a competitor when the time was right, which turned out to be 1999.

Adventure racing works like this: the team must stay together for the entire race, it's not a relay where they tag in and out, and teams are typically four-person and mixed gender. For the first decade or so of the sport's development each team would have a support crew that moved the team's gear around the course to resupply them and swap equipment at discipline changes. The later races tended to be unsupported which means the organisation moves the teams' equipment. The race course is a series of checkpoints (CPs), sometimes referred to as control points or passport controls (PCs). Teams must navigate their way to the checkpoints in numerical order, mostly using just a map and compass, but some races allow GPS as often the maps are not of good enough quality – in Abu Dhabi deserts, for instance, they can't map the sand dunes because they constantly move, so we navigate with satellite photos and GPS. In China and some other countries, detailed maps are only available to the military, so again, GPS is used. Race routes are normally between 300 and 1000 kilometres, often dictated by terrain – 300 km in the Swiss Alps will likely be significantly harder racing than 700 km on the outback plains of Australia. The winning times are commonly targeted at 100 hours, around four to five days. There are nearly always unforeseeable factors that can make races a whole lot shorter or longer, normally the latter. There are usually about eight to ten stages, with on average two sports per day, meaning 24 hours.

All adventure sports can be included in adventure racing – the core codes are hiking, mountain biking and kayaking, but really anything that is human-powered, and doesn't have a motor, can be included. Races I have done have included, in alphabetical order: abseiling, canoeing, caving, climbing, glacier travel (ice axes, crampons, ropes), horse riding (I guess that has a motor of sorts), inline skating, kick biking (scooters), orienteering, snorkelling, swimming, Tyrolean zip-lines, white-water rafting and tobogganing. In November 1999 I was about to get into it, in a big way.

Up to that point, New Zealand was considered the number one adventure-racing nation and still is – Kiwi teams and athletes have won most of the races. Much of their success was due to sensible pacing. The early adventure racers were mountaineers and back-country skiers, conditioned to long days in the hills, and many of them had done the Coast to Coast a few times so knew how to kayak and cycle, quickly if they wished. The first legends of the sport in the pioneering 'John Howard' era typically won races around the planet by starting slow and steadily getting through the course while the rest of the teams collapsed and fell apart. This method of racing was starting to be seen as the winning formula until Kathy Lynch came along.

In the days preceding the 1999 Southern Traverse, Aaron and I listened to Kathy and Steve debating strategy. Steve wanted to start slow, sleep regularly and finish strong. It made perfect sense to me. Kathy couldn't see why we should spend four days doing a three-day race. She wanted to race fast with minimal sleep and thought starting slow was a complete waste of time. I think in the end Steve resigned himself to the fact we'd be racing hard from the gun.

The race started on Pohara Beach in Golden Bay, 80 double kayaks lined up with sterns touching the sand. It was warm, sunny and calm as race director Geoff Hunt gave final instructions and called a one-minute-to-start warning. We were floating on the tranquil ocean, paddles resting on the sand holding us on the start line. It was deathly silent, everyone poised for the first stroke, everyone anxious about the three, four, five, six or seven days it might take to reach the finish line. Alongside us were some of the best adventure racers in the country. This was my first one.

With just a matter of seconds before the start, Kathy said to me loudly so everyone could hear, 'Okay, Nath, paddle real hard, we don't want any of these stupid cunts getting in our way!'

Um, yeah, okay.

The first stage was to kayak the Abel Tasman National Park, about 40 km. Typically considered a five-day trip for clients and a long day trip for guides, we raced it in four hours, leading off the water. From there we transitioned to mountain bikes and climbed our way up and over the Takaka Hill, then up the long ascent to the Cobb Reservoir. If it's not already apparent, Kathy was a straight shooter and not afraid to speak her mind. Grinding away on the pedals to the Cobb Valley, Aaron was struggling – he was known for his orienteering prowess, not cycling. Kathy dropped back and asked him if he could ride any faster. He said he couldn't and Kathy expressed her thoughts.

'What? This is your fastest speed? God help us, you're not even a cyclist's arsehole, Aaron!'

I was momentarily shocked but equally impressed that it didn't worry Aaron at all, he just laughed and carried on pedalling up the road. We were going a good speed and leading the race, plus it was only the first day.

Arriving at the transition area at the reservoir we met our support crew and changed into hiking gear. The next stage was a hike in Kahurangi National Park with the route crossing the Tablelands, summiting Mount Arthur and descending Ellis Creek to meet our support crew again. It was predicted to take the fastest team 10 hours. We left just as the sun was setting and trudged up the zig-zag trail to the Peel Ridge. By now we'd been racing non-stop for nearly 12 hours, which was the longest I'd raced. This was all new territory, I was feeling great, but knew that would most likely change.

I remember high on the Mount Arthur ridge close to midnight there were expansive views over Tasman Bay with the city lights of Nelson and other towns shimmering softly. The moon was up, it was a clear calm night, and we were wandering around in the hills. At that moment I discovered I didn't want to be anywhere else, to be doing anything else. It was perfect adventure and I felt completely alive. I later termed these 'adventure-racing moments', as I discovered you could have a few of them during a race. Others would possibly call it enlightenment, a religious experience or being in the zone, or simply just something special. Such moments were so powerful for me that they justified all the effort, sacrifices and hard work that had been required to reach that point. The more of them I could experience, the better my life would be. I think it's a point where adventure and nature meet, further enhanced when challenge, risk and effort are added in. You don't have to be an adventure racer to have such moments either – you just need to get into the outdoors and challenge yourself a little and you'll have wonderful experiences as a result.

From the summit we could see the headlights of the chasing teams which we guessed were an hour or so behind. It was a long downhill off the mountains to the valley floor and we arrived at the transition area at 4 a.m. It was cold, dark and we were naturally tired. The period between 3 a.m. and 6 a.m. is commonly known in adventure racing as the witching hours, often the coldest part of the day and a time when energy in all things is at its lowest. For that reason it's the best time to sleep and Steve was strongly suggesting we took a nap, pointing out that when we woke up it would be daylight and much easier for the next stage which was mountain biking. Kathy wanted to carry on but once we arrived at the end of the stage our support crew were suggesting we take a break so we changed into dry gear and nestled into our sleeping bags for an hour. Going to sleep in a race is amazing; waking up is not so pleasant.

On waking we had a quick breakfast and got onto our bikes for over 100 km of mountain biking to St Arnaud, mainly linking forestry roads. Still holding the lead, we got on our way. The ride went well, interrupted only by a flat tyre, and again when we lost Aaron – he'd lost sight of us on a descent and missed a turn-off. For about 20 minutes it was quite concerning, as it was a race rule that we were not allowed to be separated, plus we were losing time. After the delay we got under way again but it was a valuable lesson and I was always very careful to avoid that kind of thing happening again in races.

We spent the best part of the day riding, arriving at Lake Rotoiti by mid-afternoon. It was hot and sunny heading into the next stage, a hike in Nelson Lakes National Park. Reports came through that we had a few hours' lead on the next team, so keen to maximise the daylight we transitioned quickly and headed for the hills. Night set in as we were traversing the Robert Ridge, another clear and beautiful sky to be walking under. In the headwaters of Hopeless Creek there was an abseil over a bluff and then we dropped down the track to the Travers Valley. Wandering down the valley around midnight I had my first hallucination. We'd only had an hour of sleep in the past 36 hours and all of us were having some sleepy periods, doing our best to walk efficiently through the forest. Kathy started to get excited as she could see leprechauns in the trees, screaming out with excitement for us to look at them. I was highly amused by this and after a while Kathy passed through the 'sleep monster' and was back to normal. I was feeling tired but okay, until I glanced into the forest and saw a bright-red lawnmower sitting there.

'Hey everyone, look! Check that out, a lawnmower.'

After stumbling along for a while fighting off sleepiness I too came right and got refocused on the race. We arrived at the shore of Rotoiti and started the final scale up to the St Arnaud Range, picking a spur that would lead us to Rainbow ski field. We collected our bikes from the ski field and sped down the access road to the valley floor in the dark. From there we had about 30 km to ride to Lake Rotoiti, completing a loop. On reaching the transition area the sun rose again. We'd been racing for close to 48 hours and had still only had one hour of sleep. Steve was keen to sleep again but Kathy wanted to go directly on to the next stage, 30 km of rafting down the Buller River. We were tired but Kathy pointed out that the rafting would wake us up, we could sleep later.

The first hour was technical rapids so we had a guide, my good school friend Deane, who was thrown from the raft in one rapid. We were sitting in the raft looking forward, waiting for our next instructions, when we discovered he wasn't there. We slowed up and he got back on board. Once the river got easier, Deane hopped out and I took over guiding. I'd been trained for rafting and had guided through the Granity section many times. This didn't stop Steve from wanting to be the guide though.

We decided that one person could sleep while the other three paddled. Steve was insisting I had a sleep so he could guide, and much to Kathy's displeasure I agreed and lay down in the bottom of the raft, wrapped up in our tent fly. The floating motion of the raft was quite relaxing, and I had just got comfortable and started to drift off to sleep when all hell broke loose. I woke up to Kathy screaming obscenities and the sound of air hissing from the raft. Steve had hit a metal fencing Waratah that was submerged in the current and torn a hole in the raft. By the time I got up, half the raft was sinking. The next hour was spent on the riverbank drying, repairing and inflating the raft. It wasn't Steve's fault but I was back in the guide's seat on Kathy's orders.

Exiting the raft, in true form Kathy didn't want to stop. We had a short mountain-bike ride to the start of the final hiking section and she wanted to keep pressing on, despite the fact we held a large lead by now. It was agreed we'd have an hour's sleep before the hiking stage, which was what we did. The hike started with a solid four-hour climb to Mount Owen, an area of karst country full of slots, caves and crevasses. To this point in the race Aaron had been the lead navigator but because Kathy and I had such good local knowledge, we hadn't needed to do much map-work. Emerging from the forest we were greeted by fog and rapidly increasing darkness. In front of us we had about 2 km of natural maze where the map had limited value. Aaron was going through a bad patch so we decided that the team should rest while I scouted a route through. After 30 minutes of trial-and-error probing, I found the route through the rock crevasses and we carried on. It turned out no other teams found their way through that night, and were forced to wait until daylight before they could progress.

Nearing the end of the stage we had to climb the steep wall aptly named the

Staircase. I was racing well, feeling super-strong and really pleased with my performance in my first long race. We'd been going for close to 60 hours and had only taken two hours' rest. But on the Staircase I began to struggle to hold pace and got short of breath. The team started to leave me behind, and I tried to catch up but couldn't. Totally confused about what was happening, I started to think it was the reality of the sport – that I was crashing. The strange thing was that in many ways I felt fine, I was just very weak all of a sudden. With reluctance I called out to the team and they waited for me to catch up, asking me what was wrong – I was the big strong man in the team. I said I just needed a short rest. Kathy was astute enough to see something wasn't right, so she came and took my pulse as I lay on the trail.

'Shit, Nath, your heart rate is all over the place!'

She knew immediately I was having heart palpitations and wanted to know if I'd taken some drugs. I told her to stop being ridiculous. They elevated my feet and got some warm clothing on me. After about an hour my heart rate was near resting and back to a normal rhythm. The team took all my gear and we slowly walked the remaining few hours to the end of the stage, in a sombre mood as none of us knew what would happen next. Reaching the transition area and our support crew it was wise to rest me so we went to sleep for another hour. The sun rose again and we biked off on the final stage, my heart rate back to normal. It was day three of the race as we rode towards the end. Our plan was to take it easy, finish the race in which we held a clear lead, and then get me to a doctor. Exactly 72 hours after starting, we crossed the line winning the Southern Traverse.

I was hooked, even though I was worried about what had happened to my heart. When I told my doctor about it and the race he wasn't at all surprised my heart had freaked out, but he said to let him know if it happened again.

CHAPTER THIRTEEN
NANCY FELLA

The much-talked-about year 2000 was just around the corner. The Y2K (Millennium) bug was big news and media reports of a possible global standstill were getting people worried. I wasn't perturbed about what might or might not happen, it all seemed far-fetched, but we wanted to be somewhere remote and special to welcome in the new millennium all the same. Jodie and I decided Garden Bay on D'Urville Island would be the spot – it's our favourite campsite when we sea-kayak tour there – and we invited a few friends to join us. Seven of us had a wonderful few days paddling around the island and returned to civilisation a tad disappointed chaos hadn't eventuated.

Back at Outward Bound I settled into work, satisfied with having done the Southern Traverse and planning to do it again in November later in the year. I had been asked to do a race in Ecuador and I had agreed, but it fell through when the team captain became ill. I was into my job, I had good systems set up, and I had learnt a lot about running productive and successful Catalyst programmes. Getting to know the students well early on in the course was a major benefit. I invested time in the first week talking one-on-one with them, getting their life story and finding out who they were. That helped me understand them better, but they got to know me too, meaning I became more of a friend and less of an instructor, the person in power. My big challenge was getting them to obey the rules of the course – there was the integrity of the Outward Bound course to protect but also New Zealand laws that needed to be obeyed, not forgetting health and safety regulations.

At the start of the course the only real threat you could make was that they couldn't stay on it if they broke the rules, but as many of them didn't want to be there anyway that wasn't much use. I soon learned that the first priority was get them to buy into the course, accept the terms, get excited by the adventure and the outcomes and want to do it, to believe in the value of the programme. Once they were into it, they were far more committed to playing by the rules and doing an 'Outward Bound' course. Getting the 10 to 12 students into a team was the number one task, as once they felt part of the team, they committed to a higher level. I discovered that the challenge-and-reward model needed to be shorter. With the Classic Course students you could challenge them for days without much reward, but the Catalyst students needed more frequent rewards, daily almost, which at Outward Bound meant some free time.

Some of the students had to finish the course or the consequence would be a loss of their income support, while for others it was either Outward Bound or prison. I was a strong role model – like many of them, I was big, brown, had a few tattoos and could talk their lingo. Despite the fact I lived in the wilderness and sang folk welcome songs to them when they arrived, I was streetwise enough to not be intimidated by them and they knew that, which all played in my favour. During my contract, out of the twenty or so instructors, only three or four others could really handle these students.

I ran physical courses. My students were kept active and busy. I applied some principles of training to the courses: go hard, recover, go hard again. I would always make sure each course had an epic scheme, something that pushed everything to the limit, something the students could genuinely be proud of achieving. This could be an ambitious hiking trip, sailing route, or testing kayaking on rivers. Unless we were on a hiking expedition, I would run my students every day or, should I say, my students would run with me every day. They say it takes three weeks to break or set behaviour, so Outward Bound gave people a shot at it if something was done regularly. Every morning would begin with a run and swim before breakfast. Then we'd be out on the next three-day scheme.

One of the special aspects of having the Catalyst students was that many of them wouldn't have spent much if any time in the New Zealand outdoors, and many had never been to the South Island. Most of the youth had grown up and lived almost entirely in an urban setting. It was amazing seeing them get blown away by the beauty of nature and experience the feeling of being closer to and part of the natural environment. Anyone who dedicates three solid weeks to being in the outdoors, on rivers, on the sea, sleeping on the ground, cooking fireside, gazing at the night sky, feeling the sun, wind and rain on them, will be moved – the Catalyst students even more so.

People would often ask me if the courses were beneficial, if they were life-changing for the students. I don't think you can really measure or quantify the value of such an experience, but I know for certain the experience I facilitated for those young people had an impact on them. If nothing else, they got to know that there was another life people were choosing, a life closer to nature, healthy eating and physical movement. They know it because they did it, they experienced it for themselves. What they chose to do with that knowledge was their choice. Many of the young guys started to see their heroes at home in a different way. They often looked up to older siblings and friends with gang affiliations and considered them hard-core. Once they saw into the world of outdoor adventure sport, they could see there was a whole other group of hard-core people but in a different way.

Typically the Outward Bound hiking trips are done in bush areas around the Marlborough Sounds, for practical reasons but also because it is well suited to off-track navigation. I wanted my students to climb mountains so I applied for permission to climb some of the bigger ones in the area, Mount Fishtail and Mount Richmond. I felt the Catalyst students would respond well to standing on a peak, a summit. The common outdoor education model then was to have an experience followed by a debrief discussion to extract any lesson that could be applied to life. I was always cynical of the debrief process, perhaps a reflection of my personality. I was firmly in the 'let the experience speak for itself' camp. If you climb a mountain, a real mountain, you'll be changed in some way. Nature has been my most constant teacher – the mountains, rivers and oceans have taught me countless valuable lessons. Whereas many of the other instructors were running some fairly easy activities and then spending hours debriefing them: 'So, how did you find that cruise down the river this afternoon – was the sunshine not too hot for you?' I was at the other end of the continuum, running some epic adventures with minimal debrief – if the challenge was the real thing, very little needed to be said. A cup of tea, a biscuit and some casual reflection (celebration) was more my style.

It wasn't always easy. I had a number of fights to break up, which were always quite frightening times, especially if we were in remote places. Some of the guys I had on courses were real bad buggers. I had students sneaking out at night on thieving excursions, drug and alcohol use, and a number of bullying and abuse incidents within the groups. Nothing was without consequence under my leadership. It dawned on me quite early on that one of the main reasons the students were like they were was because they'd never faced any real consequences as a result of their actions. They pretty much walked from everything. I developed a very clear model. I would explain the Outward Bound rules and conditions, which weren't many. Then together we'd add to the list to ensure we had a fun, safe and productive course. This would be the course contract. If someone broke a rule, they would get one warning. If they broke it again, there would be a consequence. It could be something as small as an additional duty, a longer run or a loss of privileges. In most cases, I had the students themselves decide on the consequences, all I did was police them. This worked well because if they resented me, I quickly pointed out it was them who'd schemed up the punishments.

For example, one group used to make a huge mess in the truck we had to transport ourselves around in. I said to them one day that the truck must stay clean from now on and they agreed. I asked them what the consequence should be if they made such a mess again and they agreed they shouldn't be able to use the truck for a while. The next day the truck was dirty again. I explained to them the truck was a privilege and they didn't deserve it, so from that point on we wouldn't use the truck, for the next few weeks we'd only do foot-based activities. I wasn't always popular but I was always respected. Sometimes the police had to be called in as laws had been broken and occasionally I'd send people home. I never liked kicking people off the course, but for me some people's actions would stray so far from what was acceptable they would be diminishing the experience for the students who were genuinely into it.

I was always highly protective of the students who were really trying and committed. One fond memory I have was during the snow scheme. We'd been snow caving in an alpine basin, and I woke the students around 4 a.m. and we climbed to a peak to watch the sunrise. In this particular group I had some extremely hard bastards, legitimate tough guys. I liked these guys on the course – they were often closer to me in age and generally got down to business. Many had done jail time so they understood the structure, and in most cases, they were very appreciative of what Outward Bound was offering them. They also did some disciplinary work with some of the other students when I wasn't about. When we summited this peak on the St Arnaud Range, I got them to sit by themselves and watch the sunrise in silence. If they wished, they could think about their lives, where they'd been, where they were then and where they were going – that was a common theme I used for reflection. We were on a snow-covered peak, under a clear sky, with the sun rising through the mountains. They all sat quietly so I let them sit. I waited for ages for some sign they'd had enough but they just sat, staring out over the landscape. About an hour later I quietly asked them to gather themselves up and I'd brief the descent route off the peak. They slowly gathered together, deathly quiet, nearly all of them had been crying, with red watery eyes. I know that all sounds a bit sensitive, but we humans are emotional beings and at certain times those emotions can rise to the surface.

Something magic had happened on that peak that morning. One guy summed it up to me when we dropped back on the climb down. He was one of the particularly loose units on the course, but maturing away from trouble. He cried and cried all the way down the mountain, telling me how much of an idiot he'd been in his life, how he'd ripped people off and caused trouble, but that the main thing he was upset about was what a poor father he had been. He didn't finish the course. A few days from the end he quit – I think the course had brought up so much emotion for him he couldn't take any more – but he was a good guy. A few days later he called to ask if he could come back and finish the course but I wasn't keen on that, as it didn't send a good message to the others about quitting.

While I had some missions with my students it was always balanced. On one course we got to the final scheme which was sea scheme, sailing in the Marlborough Sounds. The Outward Bound cutters are difficult boats to sail well and the Sounds are tricky places to sail, so sea scheme is always a good one for testing and challenging a group. On this particular course we'd had some full-on schemes already, the weather had been really bad, and I'd pushed the group quite hard and they had responded amazingly well, to the point where I didn't see any value in doing another hard scheme. I felt they needed a reward. On a sea scheme what normally happens is the students sail or row the cutter all day and camp on shore overnight. The instructors live on the support vessel, a quarter-of-a-million-dollar launch – beds, kitchen, stereo, it's real luxury in comparison. We often do some fishing, dive for paua, bake cakes, warm croissants in the engine room and generally enjoy life on board at a distance from the students.

This particular group I had was mainly Maori and Pacific Islanders. I went to the watch house that night to brief the final scheme. The plan was to sail a route to Ship Cove and back – if there was no wind they would need to row, total trip over 100 km. They could expect to be sailing or on the oars for most of the daylight hours. Having just completed a tough and exhausting three-day hike in crap weather, they were knackered. No one was excited. I told them there was another option they could choose. We could load up the launch with fishing and diving gear, good food and cruise around the Sounds for three days, get fish and chips from Picton, and they could be dropped off at the best campsites in the outer Sounds for the nights. It was the perfect way to end a hard course. They took so much pride in the launch that they completely cleaned it while we cruised the bays and would berate each other if someone so much as dropped a cookie crumb on the deck. They felt like rock stars and I reckon that was something they'll still talk about to this day. They caught plenty of fish, dived for seafood and got to see all of Queen Charlotte Sound.

In contrast, it was also my students on sea scheme a few months later that capsized the cutter off Long Island at the head of the Sound, the first capsize in 13 years. I had just got off it to have some lunch on the support boat. We were sailing in big seas with swells rolling in from Cook Strait, the wind was up and we'd gone down to storm sails, it was exciting stuff. They were sailing really well but were hit by a large gust, and amid the confusion they didn't spill enough air from the mainsail. A cutter capsize in windy conditions amid ocean swells is a bit of a disaster zone to manage and clean up but we did it and were back sailing in the same spot the next day.

Life on the launch could often be a mini-holiday for the instructors. Occasionally there would be no wind so the students would have to row for three days, which made the support boat redundant. One such time, my co-instructor and I decided to have a press-up competition, the winner being the one who logged the most press-ups in three days. To make it fair and transparent, we agreed to keep a log that was visible to the other person. The first day we just matched each other. I'd log 20, he'd log 20, I'd do another 20, he'd do another 20. By day two we had to be more discreet. He'd go to the toilet so I'd do 50. He might not notice, or get distracted by the group, so I'd quickly do another 20. The challenge was not so much doing press-ups, it was not alerting the other instructor that you'd done them. I woke up on the morning of day three to discover he'd done 250 while I'd been sleeping! I can't recall how many we did in total but it was in the thousands.

Another custom was that instructors would dine and feast like royalty while at sea. I didn't like it as you could get off the launch after three days and feel terrible, fat and bloated. One scheme I surprised my co-instructor, as it was my turn to load rations onto the launch, by announcing we were going to fruit fast for three days – the only food on board would be fresh fruit. At first he was fuming but by day three he was thanking me, we both felt great. It did start a mini 'fasting' movement until the school ended it, after some instructors were doing complete no-food fasting for the three days, which from a safety management perspective wasn't seen as sensible practice. The gluttony and indulgence resumed.

One course I was teamed with an experienced instructor called Chris Moretti. He had been an instructor some years before and was back to test the waters, to see if he was keen to do another contract. Chris and I were not a good combination, even though we both shared the view that most students just needed a good boot up the backside to be woken up to reality. He was a no-nonsense instructor who liked to use the term 'hard-core' a lot when talking with students. He also had a relaxed approach to instructing and, like me, didn't have much time for modern-day health and safety regulations – the solution to just about everything was for everyone to harden up.

On this course we had a lovely Maori lad called Herb. He was a super-nice young man and very popular with the team. Herb was a heavy guy, and he struggled with some of the activities through being overweight, but his attitude was always excellent. During a high ropes session, he fell from one of the elements (tightrope walk) and was left dangling high up above the ground (the safety system doing its job). We instructed Herb to pull himself back onto the element and carry on but he didn't have the strength to do it and after a few attempts he was finished. I climbed to him and tried to pull him back onto the element but he was too heavy for me to move him far. Herb was very good about all this, calmly awaiting rescue whilst dangling 7 metres off the ground. I set up a rescue system and Chris took Herb on belay from the ground. I was a little concerned the system wasn't set up right. The rope was attached to Herb and then went through a pulley on the safety system and down to Chris, who had the rope through a belay device. It was safe and made logical sense, but Chris was standing quite a way back from the fall line as there was a small forest directly underneath us.

I called out to Chris that I didn't like the set-up, that I wanted time to think it through before I took my knife out and cut Herb's safety lines. In true Chris form he yelled out, 'Don't be a nancy boy, just cut the lines, I've got Herb.' I could see Herb wasn't going to fall to his death but it simply didn't feel right. Herb was keen to move – hanging in the harness was risking any future he may have had of being a father one day. Reluctantly I cut the first safety line, then the second. Midway through the second cut the line snapped and Herb started going down, quite quick but no risk of being hurt. As Herb descended, Chris started getting pulled through the forest until he was below Herb, and then he started coming up as Herb went down, they collided briefly as Chris met Herb's backside, and then gravity continued Herb's descent as Chris kept coming up to where I was in the high ropes. A few seconds later Herb was lying on the ground looking up, after a slow gentle descent, while Chris was nearly up to where I was. Herb was safe. The funniest part was that with Herb acting as the anchor below, simply by lying on the ground spread-eagled staring up at us, Chris abseiled back down. Despite our whole group finding this hilarious, it was a serious safety issue and was dealt with appropriately.

CHAPTER FOURTEEN
NEPAL FRIENDSHIP

Checking my emails in the Outward Bound staffroom one day, I found an invite from a friend, Jeff Mitchell, asking if I'd be keen to race the Raid Gauloises in Tibet and Nepal in April and May 2000. It was to be a fully sponsored team comprised of four Kiwi males – Bob Foster, Neil Jones, Jeff and myself – and Louise Cooper, a South African racer who now lived in the US. I went straight to the school director. Gaike asked me what would happen if I wasn't granted the time off. I told him I'd resign, that I saw this as a chance of a lifetime and I wasn't going to miss it. Either my attitude aligned with the Outward Bound philosophy or Gaike just thought it would be a damn good thing to go and do, so I was granted leave.

The trip started with a 10-day acclimatisation trek into Langtang National Park, not far from Kathmandu. This was my first trip into the Himalayas and I was soaking it up. After a few days in Kathmandu we decided to climb quite high on the first day and start breathing thin air. The race was going to spend some time above 5000 metres so we needed to adjust to the higher elevations. Feeling great, I lugged a hefty pack and went up too high too quick – a common mistake made by the inexperienced at altitude. We got to the teahouse where we would stay the night and started to relax after 10 hours clawing our way up a steep mountain valley, with jagged ranges as far as the eye could see. Not only was I fascinated by the dramatic terrain, but by how much marijuana (including some massive plants) was growing wild right beside the trail. However, soon after we had stopped trekking I developed a headache followed by violent vomiting. As an experienced mountaineer Jeff was quick to respond. He immediately packed some gear and told the others that he and I would descend 1000 metres to the village below.

I was extremely weak and didn't want to move but he insisted. After stumbling down the mountain I was amazed at how quickly I recovered and how much better

I felt after we had dropped to 2000 metres. We ate dinner and had a solid sleep, and the next day climbed back slowly to the team, who had had a bad night. We all took things much slower and easier after that. Back in Kathmandu the team had a few days of race registration and ability testing, and then we boarded planes to Lhasa.

It was the tenth anniversary of the Raid Gauloises, regarded as the biggest adventure race on the planet, with 70 teams racing from 20 different countries. The race began on the dusty, windy plains of Tibet and finished more than 800 km later on the sun-baked Nepal/India border. We were to climb to 5150 metres, plough through snow, bike for miles on dusty and rutted roads, paddle and toboggan massive rivers, and navigate past villages and temples on long trekking stages. Although our team wasn't a realistic winning chance, we had the experience and skills to be in the race, and aimed to finish in the top five.

Simply being in the Tibetan region was a mythical experience and it was ultra-exciting getting under way in such an authentic adventure race. The monumental journey started on foot with a short trek over dusty paddocks and then climbed through a castle-shaped rocky outcrop home to a monastery. By midday we had collected our bikes and ridden 120 km closer to the Himalayas. Here we picked up two small trekking horses, loaded our gear onto them and set off into the night. But as we climbed higher and fatigue set in, I began to get acute mountain sickness again. The vomiting started and my energy levels plummeted. I'd been trying to pace myself, I'd felt great, but I'd obviously gone too hard.

The team took the gear off one of the horses and I mounted it but I didn't have the strength to balance well enough and kept falling off. We decided to stop for a sleep. It was intensely cold, about minus 10 degrees Celsius, and we were being buffeted by arid dust kicked up by a constant wind. In the early hours of the morning we nestled behind a stone wall near a village and had a few hours' sleep. Sick and weak, and happy to be lying in the relative warmth of my sleeping bag, the reality of the situation dawned on me. All I wanted to do was return to a place of comfort and easy living. It was a classic case of 'when you're safe at home you wish you were on an adventure, and when you're on an adventure you wish you were safe at home'. The hot shower, hearty meal and warm hotel bed would have to wait. I had to get focused and overcome what felt like the impossible. In denial we woke up and prepared to continue. We weren't the only team having issues though – most of them were nursing someone who was sick so we were still comfortably in the top ten.

Two locals and a couple of dogs were watching us in the darkness with intrigue. We set off and straight away I tripped and stumbled through a ditch. One of the men came to my aid and guided me back to the main trail. It felt good to have his support and it helped me balance. He kept walking with me for a while and then let go of my hand. On my own I was still slightly dizzy and not walking all that well, so he took my hand again. He and I walked together for hours, up through a saddle and onto a large plateau, the other man leading one of the horses, with their dogs trailing behind. It didn't take long for the helpful Tibetans to become part of the team, stopping when we stopped, and even pointing out the way a few times.

During the night we arrived at a checkpoint in a saddle, one of the highest points of the race, where fires blazed at a local tent camp. Exhausted athletes in full mountaineering gear lay collapsed all over the place, curled up in the foetal position to stay warm. It was a carnage zone. They weren't thinking clearly and needed to get descending. We squeezed into one of the smoke-filled tents, creating some space near the fire to get warm. The local herdsmen were jovial, clearly pleased with the entertainment the race was providing, and unable to hide their curiosity about the western women among us. After a break, and some food and drink, we put on all our gear to protect us from the biting conditions, found our two friends and continued over the pass and onwards, ever so slowly descending over the vast featureless plains. The local chaps came with us for nearly the whole day, until we could see the next transition area.

Stumbling through the mountains supported by a little man barely half my height must have been quite a sight. Through the darkest, hardest moments of the night, my Tibetan friend would pull me along, squeeze my hand and pat me on the back. I'd like to think he knew I was a strong guy but was having a difficult time. It was a very powerful example of how we can give energy to another person – I could really feel his energy giving me strength as he selflessly guided me along. Here we were, up in the Himalayas with full Gore-Tex and down technology, altimeter watches and energy gels and bars, doing what we thought was an extreme challenge, and two local men dressed in old woollen suits, and with no gear, wandered out of their stone huts and joined us for a 50 km trekking stage, then turned around and walked back home again.

The next stage was mountain biking on the China–Nepal Highway, also known as the Friendship Highway. We were still at about 5000 metres and the border was at 1750 metres so the ride was mainly descending. It truly was an amazing ride and a great saviour for me. Tibet had been the hardest physical challenge I had ever dealt with so, as I sat on my bike descending into warmer and thicker air, I kept feeling better and better – apart from being annoyed by the children who kept dashing out from behind roadside boulders and sprinting across the road in front of me. I was yelling at them to get out of the way, sometimes having to swerve to avoid hitting them, until I accepted it was just a hallucination. When we reached the border I felt like I was fully recovered and back at full power. I was ready to race.

One of the goals of the top teams was to get through the border into Nepal during opening hours, 8 a.m. to 5 p.m. If teams arrived after 5 p.m. they'd have to wait until the following morning. Despite our troubles, we were only a few hours behind the lead teams and no one in fact made it through the border. We arrived in Zhangmu late that night and booked into a hotel. After my struggle in Tibet, I was luxuriating in the comfort of having a shower and stretching out on a hotel bed following a restaurant meal. Seeing some of the elite French teams tucking into banquets and consuming large quantities of alcohol was an eye-opener – they were having a mid-race party, good for them. With the nightmare of the plateau crossing behind me, I went to sleep that night feeling much more positive. The next morning the race effectively restarted with about 20 teams waiting for the border to open.

We all sped down into Nepal feeling the heat rising quickly. The next stage was a white-water sledging section in the upper Sun Kosi River. This was a fun stage ripping down white-water rapids on a toboggan. That led into another major trekking section that headed back up to 3200 metres, and I felt confident I could handle that elevation provided I didn't overwork myself. The trek contained dark zones, meaning that during the hours of darkness we were not allowed to move, and we were instructed to arrange to stay in a teahouse along the route. Maoist activity in the west of the country had bandits marauding in the region, and although we could hear gunfire at night we never saw anything during the day.

Arriving at a hut just on dark, we were welcomed in by the family and had a superb night. Communicating in sign language, they boiled some eggs and offered us some noodle soup. They also offered us their beds and blankets – an insane level of hospitality – and wouldn't listen to our protests. Just as we were about to bunk down, we noticed an old man was already in bed and he started to rise. We certainly didn't want him to give up his bed so we barred his passage. Getting angry, he pushed towards us, and after a brief skirmish stubbornly forced his way outside. We quickly conferred and went out to bring him back, only to find he was relieving himself near a tree. Grumpily, he pushed back through us and into his bed.

After a sleep, some food and back out in the daylight and sunshine, the walk was stunning as we toured through villages and croplands, regularly meeting the smiling local people as they carried bundles of wood and supplies around the hillsides. It was fun to see the young children, running around in bare feet with humongous loads, and always thrilled with the novelty of the racing team of foreigners they had stumbled across. We were racing in fifth place and enjoying it.

On day five we returned to the Sun Kosi and loaded up canoes for what was to be two days of paddling. The first stage was 40 km downriver where we would then transfer to rafts for another long section. We loaded up the canoes with food and gear for an overnight camp. The river was larger now and contained some significant rapids. I was guiding the canoe with Jeff and Louise, and in one rapid we dropped into a hole which flipped us over, leaving us clinging on to the canoe as we were swept down in the turbulence. Through another river feature the canoe went one way and I went the other, and next thing my arm was dislocated again. Regrouping downstream, it took a while for the team to understand that I was stuck on some boulders in pain. Jeff ran back along the bank and asked what was wrong. I explained that my shoulder was out but we should be able to get it back in and gave him instructions on what to do.

With my dislocated arm dangling off a rock, Jeff swung most of his body weight on it, but I couldn't relax the muscles enough to allow it to be manipulated back in. It felt like if I relaxed my arm fully it would fall off. By now a group of villagers had gathered and one of them was keen to try. We didn't have anything to lose. After a few painful attempts I politely declined his offer. Coincidentally, a staff canoe came by and the river safety guys had a go too but time was running out. My shoulder was starting to seize up. They decided to call for assistance and moved me to the other side of the river where a helicopter could land.

About an hour later the helicopter started booming up the valley and touched down near us in typical dramatic fashion. A staff member came running over and asked if I could walk to the chopper okay. We explained I didn't want evacuation, that I wanted my shoulder fixed. After a few radio calls the helicopter took off again and returned an hour later with a doctor. After a few attempts to get my shoulder in without success he suggested we go to the hospital. Hours had passed by now and four different lots of people had tried to get my shoulder back in place. Exhausted and in pain, reluctantly I gave up, accepting that we'd done all we could on the riverbank. The decision to withdraw from the race was a tough and emotional one, both for me and the team, but we couldn't see an alternative. There was no way I could race on in that condition.

Once in the air, I thought I'd be in hospital promptly but that wasn't the case. I was taken to another transition area and told to wait there. I lay on the dirt floor of a hut for hours, covered in flies in 35-degree heat, waiting for an ambulance. It arrived sometime during the night. I was fairly delirious and can't recall much apart from inhaling a general anaesthetic once I was in hospital. My next memory is waking up the following day in a hospital bed, the shoulder fixed, sore, bruised and weak. I was later discharged and dropped off to the race hotel. The team finished unranked.

As disappointing as it was not to finish the race, there was nothing I could have done. There would be more racing to come and I knew I was going to have a successful career in the sport. I had a more pressing matter to attend to now anyway – Jodie and I were getting married the following month.

CHAPTER FIFTEEN

NOW FORMALISED

Returning to New Zealand, I ran another Outward Bound course and then got married. Jodie and I both wanted a small wedding, but I wanted the smallest wedding. We had seen a few friends and family get married who had ended up having weddings that were too big, too expensive and too much hard work, often a result of the proceedings being hijacked by their families. My ideal was the bare legal requirement – the two of us, a witness and a celebrant – I was sure you could get the marriage licence with four people maximum. Jodie wanted our families there, which I agreed to, and she wanted some of her friends there too, which I took some convincing on, but in the end we agreed on a three-friend limit each. On 20 May 2000 we got married on a beach in the Abel Tasman National Park using water taxis to transport us there, 20 people all up. May is a stunning time of year in the park and we had the beach we wanted to ourselves and it was a really enjoyable day. Jodie and I then popped off to the Cook Islands for our honeymoon – a week of paddling, swimming, biking, hiking, and adjusting to newly married life. The highlight was getting our wedding rings tattooed on for $20 each – it was a steal.

I was also keen for a small wedding because a high percentage of my mates, me included, are often caught saying, 'I wish I could but I have to go to a fucking wedding this weekend.' I didn't want to cause that sort of problem for my mates, or to put financial strain on people either, with the usual costs of attending (travel, accommodation, presents etc., which I reckon add up to about a thousand bucks a person on average). There was a massive snow dump the weekend of my brother's wedding – fresh powder skiing – but my masterful bro had arranged for me to put a hangi down so I had to go, although even he said later that they could have had a smaller gig. Each to their own, I guess. However, Jodie did manage to convince me to throw a party after our honeymoon. I was okay with that because most of our friends liked to party and people don't feel the same sense of duty to attend parties as they do weddings. I haven't been much of a party person since I was a teenager either, though, because avoiding alcohol and drugs removed me from an array of such environments after I decided to make some fundamental life changes.

Married life was going great, we were very much in love and excited about our future together. Our plan was to finish our Outward Bound contracts and then move back to our house in Nelson to start a family. I could see myself pursuing a career in adventure racing – the prize money was good and sponsorships were there – I just needed to get some results and prove my worth in a team. Back at work I ran courses and trained for the Southern Traverse later in the year. It was now sponsored by Discovery Channel and had some decent prize money on offer. Aaron wasn't available to race as he was engulfed in study so we invited Jeff Mitchell to race with us. He already knew Steve and Kathy well. Two of the top international teams were racing, from Finland and the US, plus some very strong New Zealand teams. While this would be only my third adventure race and the most competitive field I'd raced in with a top team, I was confident we could win it.

The race headquarters were in Methven where we were given the course briefing. This was my first race as lead navigator. It started at Mount Cheeseman ski field with a trekking stage through a series of ranges exiting out to Lake Coleridge. As we stood in the car park and surveyed the route exiting the ski field, we agreed we didn't want to be leading because the team in front would be plugging the steps in the snow for the others to follow. Guess what happened. On the gun, Kathy leapt to the front and starting plugging steps up through the snow, the following teams happy to sit behind while we broke the trail. It seemed pointless to me but that's how Kathy raced, from the front. About an hour into the race going up the Harper River I started to feel weak and noticed straight away my heart problem had returned. As far as I was aware, it was the first time it had happened since the race a year earlier.

I lay on the ground with my feet elevated trying to compose myself. Steve was a little stressed but Kathy and Jeff especially were really calm, assuring me we'd get back into the race, even if they didn't believe it. It was still a bleak time as we sat around in the forest with team after team zipping by, all asking if we were okay, but we knew they were all thinking the same thing: 'Great, one less team in the race!' After an hour or so I could feel my heart rate return to normal and I was keen to go – giving up was not an option for me but fighting to the bitter end was. It helped that the team were really relaxed, insisting numerous times that it was a long race and we'd be fine. They carried my gear for now and I just focused on navigation.

Opting to take a gamble on a very direct line through the forest to the alpine tops, when we got to the ridge we were very surprised to find that we'd nearly caught back all the lost time on the lead teams. An abseil created a bottleneck and next thing we knew we were chatting with the team in first place. By the end of the day we were back in first ourselves. There was a dark zone at Lake Coleridge where we were not allowed to start kayaking until daylight the following morning. This meant I could nestle into my sleeping bag in the tent and get a full night's sleep, the ultimate recovery. I hoped that would be the end of the heart problem, for this race anyway. From then on, the race couldn't have gone much better for us, as we paddled kayaks and rafts, mountain biked and hiked our way to Lake Tekapo to win the race by a comfy margin.

My navigation had been nearly perfect. I blew a line descending off the Two Thumb Range at night which cost us about an hour but that was the only error in the whole race. It was an amazing feeling winning the race and pocketing prize money, which was nearly as much as my annual Outward Bound salary. The course was incredible and still rates as one of my favourite race routes. Jodie had been part of the support crew and was tossed into the lake by the other crew members once we'd won the race – I think she had been a bit bossy, but she got the job done. I remember sitting with Jeff in our accommodation looking down Lake Tekapo as a nasty weather system engulfed the mountains where most of the teams were still racing while we were warm and cosy, enjoying a hot drink and some cookies. We'd just converted the US dollars prize money to New Zealand currency, and erupted into uncontrollable laughter – life was glorious.

Jodie and I returned to Outward Bound and completed the working year. After being diagnosed with atrial flutter, I was determined to sort out my heart condition, which was getting worse with repeat episodes. I was starting to get it at work and it was putting limitations on me I didn't like. The medication I tried didn't seem to help, but rather made it worse. It was hair-pulling frustrating at times. The school marathon was held at the end of each course and I tried to run it each month. Typically, I would be one of the first finished and posting competitive times. One day, I started running and my heart switched into an arrhythmia. Determined to finish, I struggled to the finish line with a few runners in front of me. One of the other instructors couldn't contain himself. He dined on it for weeks, saying things like, 'I had such a good run that day, I totally knew I could beat you.' Hard as it was for me to hear that kind of stuff, I was determined to suck it up and never told anyone when I was suffering from my heart condition. Words didn't need to be exchanged. I'd just log it and make sure I'd give that person the thrashing from hell when the time came. That scenario repeated itself countless times over my sporting career. I've lost dozens of races because of my heart but I'd rarely tell anyone what was happening, not even Jodie. I'd let people enjoy their victory, even if it tore me up. I wasn't swallowing my pride, I was swallowing my soul. Sport was my identity.

Early in 2001, I received an exciting email from the Natural History film unit in Dunedin. They had been contracted by National Geographic to make a documentary about mountain biking. The concept was to use a cross-country rider and a downhill rider to portray the sport and the technology. It was a fully funded four-week trip – not only were we getting paid but we'd be given a mountain bike to keep. The best part was that the filming location was Bolivia. So I trotted over to the school director's office and had a chat with the ever-obliging Gaike who granted me the time off.

Just a few days later I got another email from Louise, with whom I'd raced in Nepal, asking me to race in Canada with her and whether Jodie could be support crew. It was right after my month in Bolivia. Back to the school director's office – thanks, Gaike. Now I had May and June off. A little while later, our team secured a sponsorship deal to compete at the Adventure Racing World Champs in Switzerland and again Jodie was asked to be support crew. I had September off as well. The Eco Challenge, by now the grandest adventure race in the world, announced they were going to hold the 2001 event in New Zealand, so Gaike gave me October off too. Later I got November off for the Southern Traverse, but that's a whole other story.

While Gaike was incredibly supportive, it was the programme manager Nikki Wallace who was breaking her back to accommodate my demands. Nikki was a tough nut and shared my view that most people, including instructors, could do with a bit of hardening up. She once told me that out of all the instructors she had met, I was one that clearly lived and breathed the Outward Bound values, plus she was intrigued to see what I would do after Outward Bound. Outdoor education is generally a low-paid industry and has limitations as a career. It's a fun job through your twenties, but working for outdoor wages long-term is a hard grind. I was making a lot more money from sport and other initiatives at the same time as I was working as an instructor. Always entrepreneurial, I was always thinking about how one component could leverage another. So Nikki and I made a deal that if I ran eight Catalyst courses in 2001 I could take the four months off, and I had two months' leave owed anyway – suited me fine.

Meanwhile, on doctor's advice, I travelled to Christchurch for an ablation procedure to sort out the arrhythmia. The four- to five-hour operation involved making cuts into my femoral artery and carefully feeding catheters up into my heart to place some small electrodes and possibly inject me with adrenalin to see where the electrical problems were. If any were found, scar tissue would be burned onto my heart to stop those pathways. Obviously, there were risks, the worst being that I could die. I drove myself down and checked into hospital, had the procedure, stayed overnight and checked out the next day. Afterwards Jodie and I couldn't believe how relaxed we'd been about the whole thing. I simply took a few days off work to go and get a heart operation. I was back at work two days later, against medical advice, but I hadn't planned any extra days off and I didn't want to ask for any more time off. It was really dumb as I ended up doing some very challenging work in the following days. Unfortunately, the surgery didn't work and the condition advanced. I was diagnosed with atrial fibrillation.

In May I popped down to Queenstown to start the filming for the mountain-bike documentary. Tony Moore ('T-man') was the downhill rider selected, and we were both ex-New Zealand team riders. After one shoot high in the mountains the helicopter pilot was annoyed as the cloud had rapidly moved in and he wasn't prepared to fly in the whiteout. We had a 4×4 truck with us so he was preparing to leave the chopper on the mountain overnight. I had decided to bike back to Queenstown and got ready, putting on a bright-red jacket. Sensing an opportunity, the pilot came over to ask if I was willing to lead him down the ridge using my jacket as his point of reference. I couldn't go too fast, though, because if he lost sight of me through the whiteout it could be disastrous. He started the helicopter, rose a few metres off the ground and hovered above me. I was getting the full force of the downwash but was still able to ride. The noise and turbulence as we moved down the ridge was freaky. Visibility was almost zero so I worked hard to stay on the track, every so often looking over my shoulder to see the grinning pilot giving the thumbs up, just a few metres away. Once or twice the skid damn near tapped my shoulder. After about ten minutes we descended below the cloud and could see the valley below, so he zoomed off.

After a few days filming in the mountains we spent a day at Otago University getting a VO_2 max test. We did them on bicycles and the testers were impressed with my results – apparently one of the highest levels they had recorded. Next stop was Intense Cycles in California. They had agreed to sponsor bikes for us so we filmed a visit to the factory. For bike riders this was striking gold – Intense were and still are one of the finest bikes made. We had lunch with the company owner and then he took us to the factory and said, 'Tell me what frame you want, suspension, wheels, parts and components, then we'll assemble the bike for you.' As a cross-country rider the decision was easy, but T-man had a hard task building up the best bike for what he was expecting to ride in Bolivia.

We had a few days spare in Los Angeles before we flew to Bolivia. I was keen to visit my adventure-racing team-mate Louise, and T-man didn't have anywhere to go so he joined me for a few days at her place. The mountain biking close to her house was excellent so it gave us time to set our bikes up. By pure coincidence, while I was staying with Louise, Discovery Channel broadcast the documentary they'd made of the 2000 Southern Traverse, calling it the Discovery Channel World Championships. We got some popcorn and drinks and hunkered down to watch. My team featured regularly in the programme because we led for most of the race and went on to win. The other team that got attention was Team Seagate, a team of executives from the global technology company based in Silicon Valley, San Francisco. At times the doco jumped from my team to Team Seagate, highlighting by contrast how poorly the corporate executives were getting through the course. However, what impressed me was their attitude. Even though they were going slowly and were making mistakes, they were in high spirits and enjoying the adventure-racing challenge, a galaxy away from their corporate planet. In contrast, our team was blitzing the course and the field.

T-man, who had spent time at adventure races as a cameraman, felt that they were so far out of their depth they were just a liability and shouldn't have been allowed in the event. I had a different view. To my mind they had the most import- ant qualities needed in adventure racing – positive attitudes and an unfaltering commitment not to give up. They had team spirit. From what I could see, all they needed was a bit more fitness and better navigation skills. They were highly suc- cessful businesspeople so they weren't stupid. I said that if I spent a week training them before the next Southern Traverse I reckon they could finish it. T-man wasn't convinced. We carried on debating the issue until Louise suggested we test the theory and find out. She would try and contact them to ask if they wanted some training from the guy who navigated the team to first place in the race. We dis- cussed how much I should charge them but in the end I told Louise to tell them I'd do it free – I wasn't doing it for a job, I was just keen to get them to the finish line.

We flew into Lapaz and immediately got acute mountain sickness, T-man, the film crew and myself. Our hotel was at 4000 metres – from zero to 4000 in a day, mad. After a few days of feeling ill and sleeping with throbbing heads we started to come right. The plan was to film T-man and I training for our ultimate goals and weave the bike technology into the story. T-man was going to attempt to ride the Takesi Inca Trail, a very technical trail that took up to six hours. People had ridden it before but there were a few sections deemed unrideable, and T-man was aiming to be the first to complete it in its entirety. My challenge was an endurance climb from the sweltering Amazon Basin at 700 metres up to Chacaltaya, at 5345 metres, which at the time was the highest ski resort in the world. The road route was 90 km and ascended over 4500 vertical metres. It had been done before but took the rider two days – my challenge was to do it non-stop in one.

We had an absolutely amazing three weeks mountain biking all over Bolivia, both of us completed our missions, and it took me eight hours to complete the climb. I then flew back to Los Angeles to meet up with Jodie and the race team coming from New Zealand. After a few days with Louise we flew to Canada for the adventure race, being held on the island of Newfoundland. Much to my surprise, Louise had managed to talk with the Seagate executives and they were very keen to meet me in New Zealand before the Southern Traverse and get some training tips. Our team took fifth place in the race. It was stunning landscape and we saw all the wildlife we'd expected – whales, eagles, caribou, beavers, bear and moose. However, after a month in Bolivia not doing any running and a mistake in using Gore-Tex shoes for the first time ever, my feet became a mess of sores and redness, skin coming off everywhere. I could hardly stand on them at times because of the blistering but we had Vicodin in the first-aid kit so that stuff enabled me to carry on, although my feet suffered even more as a result. Valuable lesson learned. Afterwards Jodie and I rented a sea kayak and did a week-long trip from Corner Brook to the Bay of Islands and into the Gulf of St Lawrence – it was amazing. It was then time to return to New Zealand to work and I needed to keep training for the 2001 Adventure Racing World Championships in Switzerland.

CHAPTER SIXTEEN

NZ FAIL

The balance of travelling, training, competing and working in the outdoors at Outward Bound was enjoyable. I think it made me a better instructor too. It certainly helped to keep things in perspective. Because I was regularly pushing my own limits and challenging my own boundaries, living the challenge/reward model, I had empathy with my students who were doing the same thing. Some of the other instructors made their courses pointlessly hard while others made them ridiculously easy. Perhaps I was unfairly critical of the quality of courses they were delivering, but I felt they weren't getting out enough in their own time and being reminded what it's like to be challenged. Later I learned that it was unrealistic to expect all the instructors to operate at my level and ability. They had their own unique skill set that they applied to their programmes, even if I did think they were a bit soft.

In our build-up to Switzerland, Steve Gurney opted not to race with me in the team given my heart condition. I fully understood his concern but fortunately Jeff and Kathy still preferred to take the risk. We invited Neil Jones to join us, a kiwifruit grower and pig hunter – known fondly as the 'White Maori' to other adventure racers – with a young family. He was an exceptional racer and navigator and fitted in really well with the team. Neil had won major races before, plus he and Jeff had been team-mates a number of times, and I had raced with him in Tibet. He had a reputation at post-event parties of being highly committed to rehydrating. My heart had settled down, my training was on track, and the medication I was taking to manage the condition seemed to be working.

In August we travelled to St Moritz to spend a period there at altitude before the World Champs. Jodie came with us as support crew. We were having a great year and the fully funded travel was a huge bonus. We did a few sensational mountain-bike rides in the Swiss Alps, stopping at chalets for a coffee and congratulating ourselves, 'We're doing something right, cheers.' Each day the risk was doing too much as the quality of the hiking and biking trails was immense. It was one of those times in life where you pinch yourself to make sure it's not a dream. It was summer, we spent the days playing in the mountains, we relished the food selection, and the major race looming was the one thing stopping it from being the ultimate holiday. After a week of some of the most primo single-track mountain biking we'd ever had, we discovered that the signs which we'd interpreted as marking the biking trails were in fact 'no mountain biking' signs – whoops.

The race started up high so everyone rode a gondola to the top of the local ski resort. It was a crazy start with hundreds of athletes tearing down the ski field which was still holding snow up high. After that the race settled into a more predictable rhythm and the favourites established themselves in the lead pack. It was mainly a biking and hiking race with one small rafting section on the first day. There was a canyon swim which turned out to be a controversial stage when a young woman from England, Carolyn Jones, a former member of the British and Scottish rowing teams, was swept away by the flow of water before becoming wedged under a rock. Rescue teams took nearly an hour to free her. A doctor taking part in the event revived her before she was flown to a hospital. She did survive but was permanently injured, very tragic. We had been one of the first teams to go through, and it was freezing cold despite the fact we had very good gear on. We'd been forced to abseil into the canyon in darkness and wait for a few hours before daylight to swim down the river. Everyone had mild hypothermia before the stage even began. As we plunged downriver, Kathy called out to me to look after her, but I felt I could only look after myself. It was spectacular, but it felt very dangerous – you could see it in people's eyes, they were swimming for their lives.

Towards the end of the race a large storm passed through and slowed the speed of travel. With over a day to go, Kathy was getting sick but not slowing us down, she was seriously tough. We were leading by about four hours and were trudging over a glacier to a mountain hut. It was a checkpoint and there was a Kiwi mountain guide there. We lay down on the beds for a sleep. After about 30 minutes the guide woke me to say the course had been shortened and that perhaps we should keep going. Dazed and tired, I just fell back to sleep. A few hours later we woke to find that the second-placed team had arrived and were camped in the doorway blocking our exit. We had to wake them up to leave but they managed to get away before us and trotted off up the mountain. We plodded after them, still not fully focused on the race. Once off the walk we had a short mountain bike to the end. What was meant to be a further 12 hours of racing had been reduced to about four. We chased hard to take second place close behind the Finnish team. We were disappointed in ourselves for throwing the race after going so hard for the first three days but the Finns were justly rewarded for their fighting spirit.

Pre-race, Kathy had been trying to tell us that the fresh water in the Swiss Alps wasn't safe to drink, that it was nuclear reactive or something. She tended to get ideas in her head and argue them firmly, but Jeff, Neil and I didn't buy it – it was the Swiss Alps, surely the water would be safe to drink. 'What are you smirking at, you little cunt?' she snapped at Jeff who couldn't hide the sceptical look on his face. It was a classic Kathy moment if not quite the ideal level of communication between team-mates. One of my other trip highlights came from the tip-off that a New Zealand 50 cent piece was the exact size and weight of a 5 franc coin. To buy 5 francs at the time cost us about NZ$9. So we could buy a can of Coke for 50 cents from a Swiss vending machine and get about 4 francs change. It really helped our budget a lot.

Unbeknown to us, travelling home through the US, we were the last plane to depart from LAX. Just as our flight was taking off, the World Trade Center terrorist attacks were happening in New York. Not long before landing in New Zealand an announcement was made that there had been a major hijacking and air accident and we could be required to wait on the tarmac before we could leave the plane. They didn't give us any more information and once we landed we were cleared to disembark. I couldn't believe what I was seeing when I watched the TV news in the airport. I didn't understand politics then and still don't. However, I do remember thinking that there are some very pissed-off people out there but that this was only going to piss others off even more.

I managed to run an Outward Bound course and then headed to Queenstown for the Eco Challenge. This was a huge event for New Zealand to host and without a doubt the biggest race I had been in, for media exposure and hype. Our team was picked to win it as we were the strongest Kiwi team entered and in the 11 years that adventure racing had been going in New Zealand no international team had ever won on our turf. The race included horse riding, rafting, mountain biking, and hiking with glacier travel.

We boarded buses to the start at Lake Tekapo, which was quite fitting as that was where the Southern Traverse had finished a year earlier. I was apprehensive about the horse riding because I wasn't a rider and horses in races often resulted in injured athletes. My main concern was that I was again having trouble with my shoulder dislocating. It had come out four times that year and while I was getting good at putting it back in place, it always left my arm weak and bruised for a few days. Before the race I used three rolls of strapping tape to keep it firm. I could hardly move my arm at first but it felt a lot stronger. It turned out I didn't need to ride the horse in the end, as each team was allocated only two of the beasts, but the funniest part was that our team won the stage trophy for the fastest horse riding.

The Eco Challenge was an epic sporting event but it was also an epic television extravaganza, and when push came to shove, it was more a TV show than a race. I didn't mind that at all as it drew sponsors to the sport but it changed the way it could be raced. The experienced teams and athletes knew that the integrity of an authentic sporting event could be compromised and they used that knowledge to their advantage. The race started with two people riding horses and two running. After about 5 km Kathy and Neil rode the horses around to the Cass River while Jeff and I ran over Mount Joseph. We were the first team over the hill and started the trek up the Cass Valley. In the race rules it stated that teams must stay on the right of the river. Leading the race, we stuck to the rules, although somewhat puzzled about why we couldn't use the track on the other side. For 4 km it was extremely slow travel but we finally made it to the checkpoint at Memorial Hut where the race director Mark Burnett greeted us and pointed out that the chasing teams weren't far behind. We spun around to see a group of teams marching up the track that was out of bounds. Mark had no idea of the rules and didn't care – the tight racing was going to look great on TV.

It was like that all the way through the race. We were always in the lead but our efforts were regularly undermined by rule interpretations or teams that played the system. For a few days we traversed the eastern side of the Southern Alps to Wanaka. From there we had one more hike and one raft stage to the end. We'd been forced to race through a southerly storm over dividing mountains, in extremely cold rain and wind, and after a long and arduous night we emerged sore and weary for the final stages. We'd been racing for three days on only two hours' sleep.

The final hike stage started around the shores of Lake Wanaka and headed up Minaret Burn. It was searing hot and there was no shade, the welcoming lake begging to be swum in but just a little too far away to justify a detour. I'd been navigating until that point but started to feel really dizzy and tired so gave the maps to Neil. I was getting slower and slower, struggling to stay awake. We knew we had a few hours' lead and the team was keen to keep pushing on. I was in a dream state and kept falling behind. At one stage I decided my pack was too heavy so I stopped and took out all the food and threw it over a bank. I simply wasn't thinking logically. On a few occasions I dropped back and found a shady tree to lie under, falling straight asleep. We were making dismal progress so my team-mates decided to let me have a power nap for 15 minutes but I woke up in an even worse state.

For the next 12 hours I was completely out of it. I was in a different world. I was convinced that the event hadn't started, that it was the night before the race and we should be getting some good sleep. I believed that I was dreaming and that my team-mates should get some sleep too. Instead they were in my dream and trying to get me to race and I began to get annoyed with them. Apparently I was ranting about how unethical it was for them to enter my mind. Physically I was still strong and would travel forward fine whilst being coaxed along. Later that night the team decided to stop for an hour's sleep, and that's when the second-placed team, the Americans, passed us, unaware they'd taken over the lead. Morning came and we carried on. I even did an abseil down a cliff face in my sleep-befuddled state. Halfway down the mountain during mid-morning I remember fully waking up, the glaze I'd been viewing the world through like a dirty window cleared, and I was back.

It was difficult to grasp exactly what had happened and that we were now hours behind the new leaders. With only half a day of racing left we chased. Although we closed the gap to 17 minutes, in the end we ran out of race course. Second place was difficult to accept, but what really hurt was that the Kiwi legacy of being unbeaten on home soil was over, and to make matters worse there had been quite a few narrow rule breaches or marginal things that the other lead teams had done that made us feel the race hadn't been a fair fight. The next day Mark Burnett even came to our team and said we had reasonable grounds to lodge a protest but that he wanted to film the whole process, as it had potential to add to the drama, to build ratings. We weren't interested. Even though we felt a little hard done by, we also knew we'd still had plenty of opportunity to win the race. What was more important was focusing on the following year and I had never felt more motivated.

Kathy announced that she was done with adventure racing. While she was a truly elite-level athlete, she was often difficult to race with, as she only had one tactic, which was to go as fast as you could for as long as you could and hope you reached the finish line still going fast. It won races but we could have probably won a few more if we had been able to pace ourselves and be more strategic. We'd still made good prize money coming second though.

I needed to shoot back to Outward Bound to run a course before getting back to Queenstown for the Southern Traverse. During the Eco Challenge the guys from Seagate had contacted me. One of their team members was injured and couldn't race, and while they were aware I had just raced Eco Challenge they wanted to know if I could race with them after I had given them some training. It sounded appealing to do a race and not be trying to win it, so I agreed to meet them in

Queenstown. Bill, Pat and Marie and I spent a few days doing some training in the area. We had tons of fun and I was sure it was going to be a great week. I was very confident we would finish the race.

When the race got under way we were careful not to start too hard. Sensible pacing was vital and I was used to travelling at slower speeds from working at Outward Bound. We got through the first few stages, a bike, paddle and hike around the Wakatipu Basin, then onto bikes for the first longer stage. Nearing the end of the first day we were biking on a technical trail along the lakeshore. I was slightly ahead and heard someone yelling and then the sound of falling. Bill had hit a rock and fallen off the trail into the lake, some 4 metres below, hitting his head in the process. He was really dazed but determined to keep going, impressive after such a massive crash. We kept moving forward slowly but I was really concerned about him. Through the transition area we changed to a walking stage. I wanted to get a doctor to check him out but he insisted we just keep going, he'd come right. During that hike he just froze a few times. He'd simply stop still, vacant. We kept him moving and a few hours later when we finished the stage, Pat and I took him to the medics. They said he had concussion and they were taking him to hospital for monitoring. That was a major blow – only 12 hours into the race and we were unranked and down to three – but Pat, Marie and I were determined to finish so off we set.

We completed a difficult trekking section in Wye Creek and then a mountain-bike ride back to Lake Wakatipu where we narrowly missed a cut-off and were directed onto the short course. We were the first team on it so our goal became to win the short course. We paddled half the length of the lake, did another hiking stage to Cecil Peak, and then it was back into kayaks on the lake and to the final mountain-bike stage. We were racing well but knew there were teams close behind. We had come out in front of the teams on the full course and it became another goal to stay ahead of them too. In a strange way, it really felt like we were leading the entire race. I was super-impressed with the team, especially Pat who knew how to suffer. Quite a few times he threw up because he was pushing himself so hard, his body unable to digest the food he was eating. At one stage he was keeled over on his hands and knees vomiting, and I said to him, 'Do you reckon you could keep walking while you're throwing up – it would save us a bit more time.' Looking up at me with vomit dribbling down his chin, disbelief written on his face, he could see I was serious and got back on his feet. On the last hiking stage with the main race leader breathing down our necks, we raced on through the night. Pat's kids were flying in from the US that day and he said that if we stopped for an hour or two of sleep they'd be able to watch us finish the race. I told him they'd have to watch it on TV, we weren't stopping.

One of the things Pat and Marie really enjoyed was racing with a confident navigator. On the final night, in complete darkness, we reached a saddle where there was supposed to be a staffed checkpoint. I wandered around a bit and Pat asked me what I was doing. I explained that the checkpoint wasn't there so we should carry on. Pat and Marie felt we must be in the wrong place but I assured them we weren't. Normally they'd assume they were wrong and would keep searching, but I was 100 per cent certain we were in the right spot and I wasn't going to waste any time. About ten minutes later down the valley, we came across a tent and I woke the occupants up.

'Are you the checkpoint?'

'Yes, what team are you?'

'You're in the wrong place – you need to be up in the saddle.'

'We were, but there's no water up there – it's better camping down here by the stream.'

'You can't do that. You need to be where the checkpoint is marked on the maps – teams won't know you're here! I suggest you break camp and get up there pronto.'

Grumbling, they got up and started to move.

We were delayed for a period when we dropped off the final mountain we'd climbed. There were two obvious routes, one of which descended to a valley that showed a walking track, and we headed for that only to discover that the track was derelict and completely overgrown. We knew we were in the right place so we battled down the valley, fighting through dense vegetation. Pat and Marie hadn't experienced a classic Kiwi bush-bash before, and they weren't impressed. However, humour did prevail when we came across a bridge, in perfectly good condition, leading nowhere, which Pat found highly amusing. But we did it, we managed to travel fast enough over the last day to stay ahead of the team behind, we won the short course and broke the finishers' tape ahead of the real race winners. It felt great that we'd achieved something special.

A few nights later we were having dinner in a Queenstown restaurant and Bill joined us. Despite being taken off the course, he was really happy with the team result. We got talking about racing and Eco Challenge. He asked me if my Kiwi team could win Eco Challenge. I told him we could. He asked me how certain I was. I told him 100 per cent. He questioned how much it would cost to sponsor the team so I told him, he reached over the table offering his hand, and we shook on it – one Eco Challenge victory ordered. The waiter arrived at our table so we ordered meals as well.

CHAPTER SEVENTEEN

NI SA BULA FIJI

Our Outward Bound contract was coming to an end. Jodie and I had four more courses to deliver and then it was time to move on. We were offered extensions to our contracts but we were both keen to get back to Nelson. We wanted children and I had a career in sport to pursue. However, before I went full-time racing I wanted to get my shoulder fixed so I arranged an operation at Wakefield Hospital in Wellington. Afraid I wouldn't be able to kayak again for a while, Jodie and I decided to kayak from Anakiwa to Wellington in our double kayak. We'd paddled Cook Strait before but this was going to be just us on the water, one boat, a little more adventurous. We were getting into our kayak outside the school when another instructor jogged past.

'Where are you two off to?'

'Wellington.'

He laughed and kept jogging.

On the morning of the operation the surgeon was prodding my shoulder and commented that my muscles were really tight. I told him I'd just kayaked over from the South Island and he laughed too.

Leaving was harder than I had expected. Outward Bound had been an incredible experience and one of the best things I'd ever done. Without a doubt, what I learnt there set me up for being a team captain, a parent, and gave me even more confidence to chase my dreams. It had served me extremely well but I was ready to get back into the real world and put things into practice. Everyone should do an Outward Bound course at some stage in their life, ideally when they're under 30 but whenever you end up there is likely the best time. For anyone caught in a rut, feeling a bit flat, lost, or needing some change, inspiration or motivation, Outward Bound delivers. I felt the Catalyst students were going to suffer without me, as I had taken responsibility for the delivery of the courses even if I wasn't working directly on them. There was only one other instructor at the school who had the same passion for that specific programme and it would be a challenge for him on his own. But that's life and everyone is replaceable in time.

We moved back to our house in Nelson which by now we nearly owned freehold. We had used one wage to pay the mortgage plus my prize money had provided some large payments. If I won Eco Challenge later in the year we'd be able to redeem our mortgage. We did splash out on a vehicle, spending a small fortune on a Toyota 4×4 van and modifying it into a camper. It was our ultimate adventure touring vehicle and quite an investment at the time but well worth it, and later it served as the perfect family vehicle for road trips all over the country.

I turned 30 in April 2002 and was proud of my life and who I was. I certainly had nothing to complain about. I was a highly qualified outdoor instructor, I was married to the woman I fell in love with 10 years earlier, I'd travelled the world, owned a home, and had just signed a contract to be a professional athlete. My shoulder was fixed and my heart was still beating regularly, which is normal for most people but a treat for me. I was well aware that I measured the success of each day by how much outdoor activity I'd done. If a day went by where I didn't do any, it was usually because I was sick and wiped out. Of the 3650-odd days I lived in my twenties, I would have spent well over 3000 of them doing something sporting or adventurous. If I missed a day, I didn't function well. It was a blessing to have been able to spend so much of my time doing things I truly enjoyed, and untold exciting things more were going to happen in the decade ahead. I'd spent my twenties gathering skills and figuring things out, my thirties would be the time to reap the benefits of that work, and my forties? Life is kinda over by then, isn't it? Retirement?

The first race for the elite Team Seagate was being held in Colorado. Bill Watkins, whom I raced the Southern Traverse with, wanted to see an equivalent event in the US so he made it happen, investing a significant amount of his personal capital to inaugurate the Primal Quest event. Neil, Jeff and I were being joined by Kristina Strode-Penny who was an emerging talent in New Zealand multisport and adventure racing. She had done a handful of expedition-length races plus had a wide array of outdoor skills making her a highly worthy addition to the team. I had asked her at the end of 2001 if she'd be keen to join the team if it came together and she was 100 per cent committed. She'd risen to fame in our sport with a dominating performance in a multisport race that traversed the length of New Zealand, a three-week event called the Mizone. Typically it was the sort of event I would have started in myself but it clashed with Eco Challenge and the Southern Traverse.

Jodie was a few months pregnant when we travelled to the US for the Primal Quest. The team spent 10 days at Crested Butte, having a really productive training camp while getting adjusted to the altitude, although we nearly got in strife for kayaking down a river that was privately owned – a foreign concept to New Zealanders who are used to public access to waterways. Some aggressive local men chased us in their truck and intercepted us where the river and the road met, but when they realised we were from New Zealand they were very understanding. We then shifted across state to Telluride for the race. We had spent time mountain-bike racing there years earlier. Coincidentally, there was a World Cup mountain-bike event on as well so we met up with a few of the Kiwi riders, including an ex-team-mate of mine, Kashi Leuchs, who was by then a highly successful pro rider.

Primal Quest was launched with gusto and it was a huge buzz to be part of it. The sport of adventure racing was thriving with some major events and significant prize money to chase. Disappointingly, our team didn't race well and we ended up in fifth place. Despite the course being spectacular, the race was simply too high for too long and we battled altitude-related illnesses for nearly the entire race, it was pure slog. I suffered from vomiting and diarrhoea for much of the time, repeating the classic mistake of feeling that I was well adjusted to the altitude and foolishly going hard from the start, carrying more than my share of the team load, and paying the price.

The worst was a long paddle stage down the Animas River. We were expected to be paddling for about eight hours, and the water was cold so we had to wear wetsuits and splash wear. Although I was experiencing terrible diarrhoea, stopping was not an option so I was forced to go in my wetsuit, at least every hour, all day. Taking that wetsuit off was something I'll never forget and I shudder to think what the support crew had to do with it before they could pack it in the van. We were fit and strong but we were competing against teams that mostly lived at altitude. It was a pity not to win the prize money too, as it was US$100,000 for the winning team, which back then equated to nearly NZ$200,000. This was pale in comparison to other professional sport, but for me picking up NZ$50,000 for a five-day race was highly worthwhile.

We headed to Oregon next for the Gorge Games 24-hour race. This was a three-person team race with the winning time expected to be 12 to 13 hours. All the top teams from Primal Quest had gone too. The appeal was the US$50,000 first prize. Given all four of us were there, we needed to drop a male athlete for the race. Neil had been the strongest at Primal Quest so it was clear that he would race. Jeff was keen to race too so we sat around at a Mexican restaurant trying to decide which of us would race the next day. We were splitting the prize money equally between the four of us so that wasn't an issue. The discussion was going in circles until I said to the team with absolute conviction, 'If I race, I can guarantee we will win.' Jeff had no comment. I raced, we won.

It was now time to set our sights on Eco Challenge Fiji, the trophy race of the year. For all the pro teams, if you wanted to win one race, this was it, it was the media monster. We headed directly to Fiji for a 10-day training camp. After a sea-kayaking trip and some hiking, we gained a feel for the land and country. It was similar to Samoa in many ways. I had a good feeling. Back in New Zealand I trained harder and more specifically than I ever had before. I knew the importance of this race and the deal I had made with Seagate. It was my job. I was being paid to race. Before we knew it we were in Fiji again getting ready. After our narrow defeat in the previous year's event, we were favoured to win, but the best of the best were gathered and we knew that it was going to be an extremely brutal week.

Eco Challenge had come under criticism in 2001 for the course being too sterile and easy, an off-road Ironman event. The feedback had been taken on board and they were delivering a race that was big and raw – it was payback. At the race briefing Mark Burnett said repeatedly that the Fiji course was the hardest they had designed. It was remote, rugged, and we'd be in areas where our safety could not be guaranteed. Teams that wished to pull out would be offered a full refund of their entry fee ($20,000). North American and European teams are exceptionally fast on trail systems and easy travel, dressed in tights and clicking along with their walking poles, but when a course gets brutally rough, bush-bashing and no trails, Kiwi teams rise to the challenge, so this excited us. With 80 teams with a designated camera crew each, helicopters and hundreds of staff, Eco Fiji (as it is commonly called) was set to be ginormous.

While there was a long list of strong teams from Australia, Finland, France, Spain, South Africa and the US, the only team we felt we were racing was the US squad who won the previous two Eco Challenges. They were friends and well-respected athletes but we had a score to settle. After a long bus trip through the night we arrived on the east side of the main island, Viti Levu. The race route traversed the island to the western side, followed by several days of sea kayaking in the Yasawa island group.

It started with a jungle run and canyon swim. Race starts are always chaotic so we just took things easy, well aware it was going to be a very long race and we didn't need to be leading at the start, we only needed to be leading at the finish. The next stage was building a bilibili raft from bamboo poles and traveling 40 km downriver. This was a really fun stage and filled with some classic moments. We were comfortably positioned in the top ten. Once off the river it was dark and we headed back into the jungle for another trekking stage. Late that night we decided to take an hour's sleep so we pushed on to a village and found that the local church was open. We crept in and rolled ourselves up in the floor mats to stay warm, and after a good sleep were back on the course.

After a night of jungle trekking, mainly in a riverbed, we exited to our mountain bikes, sitting around fifth place and feeling in control. In the back of our minds was the knowledge that the race ended with a huge amount of sea kayaking and we knew for certain we could out-paddle the US team and that only the Australians and South Africans could match us on the water. Rain fell, turning much of the mountain-bike stage to mud, and we were surprised at how cold it got – anticipating tropical temperatures, we were not prepared for the wet chill making it quite miserable.

Late on the second night Kristina leapt off her bike and started vomiting violently. In a very short time she had deteriorated immensely. Typically strong and reliable, it was not good news to see her get sick. Over the next few hours we moved forward as best we could but she was getting noticeably worse and it felt cruel to continue. We needed to get her better and fast. Huddling in a roadside shed, Jeff took care of Kristina while Neil and I studied the maps and planned our routes. Unable to hold down any fluid or food, it was a hellish night for her but we finally made it to the end of the stage. We had another trekking stage to the Navua River where we would have a whole day of river paddling, and Kristina trusted the paddle would allow her some recovery time.

At the start of the paddle she had a violent fever and the race staff did all they could to help her while the rest of us readied the kayaks. We requested a doctor to come and check her but the organisation radioed back that if they sent one we would be disqualified. We weren't sure if that was a rule or if they wanted us out of the race, but Kristina told us to forget the doctor and get on the water. She paddled well down the river and recovered a little but still wasn't in good shape. Starting the next trekking stage we knew we needed to do something radical. Reaching a village we opted to give Kristina a long rest. We were barely halfway through the course and all teams were making mistakes or travelling with sick or injured teammates – the race was far from over.

A family invited us into their home, offering up their beds, and the village doctor examined Kristina and gave her some medication. We decided that we would maximise the opportunity and get a decent rest as it would benefit all of us. After a hearty meal and an eight-hour sleep Kristina had noticeably improved and was keen to get going. As we were preparing to leave we bumped into Pat O'Malley from the Seagate corporate team – the village was part of a loop on the trek so they were a day behind us. I explained to Pat what was going on. He was sympathetic and encouraged us to do our best, but he knew our race was probably over. Despite things looking bleak at that point – we were outside the top 10 and at least a day behind the leading team – we had not given up.

The next trek stage was a mammoth one that included scaling a 200-metre waterfall through a series of rope activities. After that we had to travel along the highlands for about 20 km, which we did at night. It was bone-chilling cold and we were forced to swim the small lakes scattered throughout the dense jungle. After an extremely taxing stage we collected our pack rafts and enjoyed paddling on the water rather than swimming in it. This wasn't the fastest option but we were warm and dry so figured it was best. These stages had been super-hard and Kristina was going downhill again. At one point in the early hours of the morning, as Kristina stumbled and suffered through the muddy jungle, Neil pulled me aside and suggested we seriously consider withdrawing from the race for her sake. I wouldn't have a bar of it and knew that Kristina wouldn't stop anyway. Despite what was happening, I still believed we would win. It was a welcome relief to exit that part of the course and reach the dry side of the island. The jungle turned to grass and the sun's warmth gave us desperately needed energy.

Nearly five days into the race, we arrived at the end of the stage. Much to our delight, we had made up some significant time on the leading teams, except the Spanish team Buff who had flown out to a big lead, but they were not strong paddlers so we weren't too concerned about that. Talking to teams after the race it transpired that some had hired local Fijians to guide them through parts of the stage, while some of them hired horses too. When the documentary was released we saw teams with guides carrying their packs and even teams riding the horses! Because we had come off a big sleep and didn't use a guide or spend time negotiating guiding rates we had clocked a fast time for the stage.

Ending that section was a major turning point in the race. Kristina was almost back to full strength and Jodie had flown up from New Zealand and got herself to the transition area. She had a strong relationship with the team and seeing her refocused us all. She briefed us about what was happening in front while we assembled our bikes. She was full of good news, the most positive thing being that we looked exceptionally good compared to all the teams she had seen, who appeared to have at least one member with foot problems who was struggling to walk. We were using a very strong anti-chafing cream from home on our feet that contained antibacterial properties and they were all healthy and ready to run.

It was an intensely hot day for the next mountain-bike stage so we stopped in every river we passed to swim and cool off. While it cost us time, we could feel the benefit in looking after ourselves. Team spirit was high and we were on the rampage. After a full day of riding and passing a few teams we arrived at the final trekking stage on the mainland. One of the teams we passed was the 2001 world champions. The Finns had completely run out of food and were moving agonisingly slowly as we caught them. I had an abundance of food so I gave them as much as I could. They were sincerely grateful. At the hiking stage, a large group of teams had not long departed in front of us. Feeling great, we jogged up the road and once into the mountain climb we soon caught and passed them. We were now in third place and gaining rapidly. We were travelling radically faster than the other teams so when we passed them it was like we were in a different race. By the end of the stage we caught the US team. This would have been very bad news for them as they knew they had little chance of paddling at our speed, plus the fact we'd just eaten up a 12-hour deficit with consummate ease.

Because Chevrolet was an Eco Challenge sponsor, they had shipped some big off-road beasts to Fiji which were being used to shuttle teams 20 km down to the coast. We could have run but they wanted to feature the vehicles in the show. We were told the vehicle transfer was not included in race time and it would be fair to all teams. It was a joke but we climbed into a truck next to the Americans' one and started the drive. I don't know if it was planned or not but their driver shot off at high speed and our driver, bless her, seemed like she'd just learnt to drive. We sat in bewilderment as she cautiously crept down the road, rapidly losing minutes which would likely add up to a considerable amount of time. I was in the passenger seat egging her on, and even offered to drive. She assured me that the drive time didn't count but I asked how that was going to work, as the US team were way ahead by now. She had a staff radio and was speechless when I picked it up and called ahead to the transition area. Startled that a competitor was on air, the transition area staff wanted to know what I wanted. I explained to them what was happening and they assured me that when the American team arrived they would make them wait in the vehicle until we got there. I was super pissed off when we arrived at the transition area and the others were not in their truck waiting at all, but were a significant way through their transition. My fury just fuelled my motivation. Fuck you lot, we're on the water now – the race is ours. We had 100 km of ocean paddling broken into four stages. In the middle stage there was a 25 km island trek, which was another bonus for us as we were clearly the fastest team at this end of the race on foot.

Victory was near. All we needed to do next was reel in the Spanish team who had a few hours' head start on the water. Sadly for them, one of their team-mates had developed a severe foot infection (trench foot) and couldn't walk, so they arrived at the island trek to discover they couldn't go anywhere. Now we were leading. The Fijian locals were so excited and supportive, they sang and screamed and danced when we went through their villages, making it really emotive for us. The final stages went as expected. We could smell the finish and accelerated away from the field. If you ever watch the documentary of the race, ignore the commentary – they manufacture drama by making it look like the race was close in the finishing stages. It wasn't. We cleared out unchallenged – but that's not much of a story, unless you're a Kiwi.

After about 50 km of ocean paddling to the outer islands, we spent the best part of a day doing a hiking section. It was about 25 km and ascended to some high rock spires where we could see quite a way below us. Spying no other teams gave us confidence that we were doing damage to the chasers. Climbing a series of waterfalls, we took time to soak in the cool pools to combat the heat. We passed some local farmers who gave us fresh ginger to chew, my taste buds ever so grateful for something zesty with a living enzyme. Going into the night, I did the final part of the stage along the coast in bare feet, and the sensation of wading through the warm salt water felt rejuvenating and therapeutic. Finally we rounded the end of the island and returned to our kayaks, which were at a small resort. It was pitch black and we had about eight hours of kayaking to the finish, but the sleep monster surely wouldn't allow us to escape that easy. We opted to take an hour's sleep, backing ourselves to out-paddle any team that arrived in the interim.

Jeff and Neil disappeared into the bushes for a lie-down while Kristina and I spent some extra time preparing the kayaks, readying them for a fast getaway should that be required. When it was our turn to sleep we couldn't find Jeff and Neil. We wandered into the resort but still couldn't find them. One of the race media was following us getting some photos and offered to let us sleep in their room – a bed, for sure! Unbeknown to us, Jeff and Neil had got their hour's sleep but couldn't find us. It was bad planning on everyone's part.

By the time we eventually regrouped and got into the kayaks we had no idea how far back the next team was. I was sure it would be hours but Kristina was really paranoid that because we'd overslept and wasted time, our race was unravelling and could be lost. In my view, we just needed to paddle well and stressing about the teams behind wasn't helpful. Charged by emotion and exhaustion, we got into a heated discussion, and somewhere in the mix she asked me why I'd even invited her to be in the team. In the heat of the moment, I told her she was essentially mandatory equipment – the rules said we needed a woman. It couldn't have been more hurtful and I spent the next few hours reassuring a very upset team-mate – and rightly so.

I was saved a little by the conditions. The wind and swells increased and the night navigation was quite tricky, so we became very task focused, making it to the final checkpoint on Beachcomber Island. Race staff informed us we had a big lead. The next team hadn't yet started the kayak. We were lined up to be Eco Challenge champions. The sun rose, we wandered around the resort, read about the race online, had some juice and returned to the boats.

The last paddle was incredibly special and we made sure we savoured the victory. Paddling into the finish line was electrifying and I couldn't have been more satisfied. It had been a truly epic race. We raced for nearly seven days and overcame numerous adversities to reach the finish first. It was the ultimate example in sport of an unrelenting desire to succeed and to never give up. Kristina had been the main contributor to the victory – she had suffered beyond all expectations for the sake of the team – and I owed her a sincere apology. I'd stuffed up big time and I had some major grovelling to do at some stage in the future.

A few days later, one of the best handshakes I have ever had was with Alfie Speight, a helicopter pilot from New Zealand who was flying a film crew in Fiji. The production team for the filming had been so impressed with the Kiwi pilots from Eco NZ they'd shipped their choppers to Fiji for the race. From the start the film crew asked Alfie who would win, and he loyally said the Kiwis of course. As the race unfolded and we slipped back it became a running joke. 'Who will win, Alfie?' 'How are the Kiwis going – in seventh, eighth, or is it tenth?' Despite how grim it looked mid-race, he stood by us the whole time. 'You guys wait and see,' he told them, 'the Kiwis will prevail.'

In the space of 24 hours we went from outside the top 10 to leading the race. Our stampede through the field was jaw-dropping and Alfie took great pleasure in pointing out that we were in the lead and even more pleasure when we won. Pat from the Seagate corporate team who'd seen us mid-race and didn't fancy our chances of finishing, let alone winning, had a similar experience. He was still racing when a media person told him the race was won and did he know by who. He guessed half a dozen teams before giving up. When he was told we had won he simply couldn't believe it.

Unfortunately that would be the final Eco Challenge. Mark Burnett decided to focus his energy on other shows he was developing, *Survivor* being the main one, and I heard that he was also concerned by the ever-increasing liability risks. The stark reality is that if you organise an adventure race long enough, someday someone will die. In a multiple-risk environment where it's impossible to guarantee anyone's safety, it's an odds equation, plain and simple.

After Fiji, Jodie and I said our goodbyes to the team and took the opportunity to shoot over to Samoa to visit my family there. The night flight with Air Pacific was scheduled to go to Tonga then on to Samoa. On the tarmac the pilot announced the flight details, the Tongans smugly pleased they were being dropped off first. It didn't worry us – it was only an hour or so between the islands. Coming in to land I was staring out the window at the flickering village lights and the outline of the coast, thinking how much it reminded me of Samoa the further we descended. After we touched down the pilot announced, 'Ladies and gentlemen, we seem to be in Samoa. If the Samoan passengers would like to disembark here we'll then fly down to Tonga.' The plane erupted with laughter and delight from the Samoans but the Tongan passengers were understandably a bit crestfallen.

Back in New Zealand we had one more race left for the season, the Southern Traverse staged in Marlborough. Kristina still wasn't back to full health and wanted to step aside so we persuaded a reluctant Kathy to come out of retirement to race with us. We had a comfortable race leading from early on to take the win, my third Southern Traverse victory. One fond memory I have of that race was on the last night, when we didn't have enough time to complete the stage in daylight so were forced to camp on the riverbank until sunrise the following morning. We'd been racing solidly for nearly four days and the final stage was a 60 km kayak down the Wairau River. A mate of mine and Kathy's, Brendan Neylon, who had been following the race, figured out where we'd be camped and that we'd be in need of a good feed and a decent night's rest. From the riverbank we heard him calling out to us from high up on the road above. He brought down fish and chips, some mattresses and bedding, we lit a fire and had a superb night. The next morning we paddled for a few hours to the finish line. My first season as a professional had been eminently successful – three wins in four major events and the Eco Challenge crown. Jodie and I said goodbye to our mortgage. I was chuffed. She was well and truly pregnant.

CHAPTER EIGHTEEN

NEW FAMILY

The start of the New Year revolved around the birth of our first child. Due in late December 2002, we moved into January and the days started to tick by. On 4 January 2003 we were at a friend's wedding and Jodie came over to me and said, 'Take me home, please, I'm going to have the baby.' Our daughter Jessie was born the next day. If Jodie was writing this book she'd probably devote a chapter just to the birth, but I don't have much to say, except that we had a home birth. It didn't look like much fun, but having Jessie in our lives was marvellous. I had always looked forward to having my own family, and because I had helped raise my sister, handling a baby was something I was comfortable with. We were determined to retain the essence of our lifestyle. We were having a grand adventure and we wanted our kids to be part of it, not change it.

Soon after Jessie was born I had to travel to Australia to speak at a Seagate conference. The company had adopted adventure racing as the vehicle for instilling their corporate values and they were having a race there, the Eco-Seagate. As captain of the pro team and Eco Challenge winners, I was asked to be the opening speaker. I had done quite a bit of speaking already and by all accounts had done alright, so when Bill Watkins came up to me afterwards I was expecting him to say, 'Great job, Nathan, excellent speech.' Instead he said, 'We need to get you some speaker training.' Bill was good like that, straight to the point.

One of my goals for the season was growing the team and getting a succession plan in place. Jeff and Neil were superb expedition racers but there were some lucrative stage-racing events developing that suited the younger, faster athletes. These were typically multi-day events where teams would race up to eight hours per day then stop overnight. The pace was much quicker and younger athletes were training more specifically for them. Balance Bar was the premier 24-hour racing series in the US and Seagate wanted us to compete in that too. We agreed to race the Primal Quest and the Raid Gauloises with the expedition team and then introduce Hadyn Key and Richard Ussher into the squad for the short-and-sharp-style events. Our first race was the Raid Gauloises in Kyrgyzstan. I didn't even know the place existed. Getting there was an expedition in itself, going through Singapore, Germany and Turkey, arriving in the capital Bishkek 55 hours after leaving home. It's the only airport I've landed at with an air-force fighter jet alongside for company. It didn't make me feel any safer.

The race itself was very fragmented. The early part went high, to nearly 4000 metres above sea level, and while we were only at that elevation for a brief moment on a mountain pass, I was at the limits of what I could handle while racing. We came off the peak in fourth place, not trailing the leaders by much. On the second day we entered a river section. Kristina and I were together in an inflatable canoe, both of us qualified instructors and very capable in white water, but it got more challenging and dangerous as we progressed. It was swift-flowing with trees on the sides and in the river itself. To make it even more testing, safety staff had gone through before the race cutting foliage back but leaving sharp branches exposed that would puncture the canoe if they came in contact. The hazards were coming at us so thick and fast that at one stage I said to her, 'Someone will drown on this river!'

When we reached the lake which we needed to paddle on for a few more hours to the end of the stage we were informed that there had been some accidents behind us. The race was paused but we needed to finish the stage and await instructions, although we could take our time. Under the circumstances, it was a strange feeling paddling quietly along the calm blue lake beneath lush green hills transforming into snow-covered alps. At the end of the leg we learned that a French woman had drowned. Graded 2 to 3, the river was normally relatively light-flowing and presented very few risks but for some reason it flooded that day. There hadn't been any rain in the region so the likeliest explanation was rupture of a natural dam somewhere upriver or on one of the tributaries. When we reached the midpoint of the next trekking stage there would be a meeting with the teams to decide what should happen.

Although close friends of the victim withdrew and some teams said they would complete the race but non-competitively, once we'd casually hiked our way to the meeting point we discovered the plan had changed again – the course was still open. We'd just wasted time thinking the race was going to be stopped. Meanwhile, a group of eight or so teams was long gone, charging ahead through the course. We opted to stop for a sleep while we had access to a warm and comfy yurt (round tent) and would get back into race mode afterwards. Our next setback came in the horse-riding section when my horse refused to move forward, collapsing to the ground twice with me on it, and we spent a freezing-cold night in the saddle, minus 12 degrees Celsius. I was wearing seven layers, including two down jackets, on my upper body and was still ice cold.

On the following mountain-bike stage we were again so frozen that we detoured to a small village to seek warmth. A family welcomed us in beside their fire and we purchased some woollen jerseys from them and they gave us a hot meal. Here was a bunch of foreigners, dressed in bike and race gear, and they probably had no idea why we were there, yet their impulse was to help us. It was a really special moment but when we went to leave we discovered that Neil's bike was gone. The family were furious and started yelling out to neighbours, and before long a crowd gathered, deeply unimpressed about the missing bike, and then the police turned up. This all happened in the space of 10 minutes, and while it was hugely entertaining we still had 100 km to traverse. What the thief hadn't accounted for was the fact the tyre tread was very distinct, showing up nicely in the clay road and leading directly to somebody's shed. We grabbed it and quickly departed. A further two stages remained – another hiking section and another canoe stage over a lake to the finish.

The last hiking stage was a mixture of desert-like terrain and dry, rocky landscape. The race had been tracking west and we were nearing all the 'Stans' – Kazakhstan, Tajikistan, Uzbekistan. We were getting very low on food, and it was dark and really cold again. Hiking towards a distant campfire we encountered a small group of herdsmen, huddled around a big pot over a flame. They motioned for us to sit by the fire and swiftly filled some bowls of soup for us, ripping bread off a loaf to accompany it. We gobbled it down hungrily, the hot liquid soothing our mouths. Fifteen minutes later when we got up to leave with full bellies, out of curiosity I lifted the lid and shone my light in the pot to find a goat's head staring up at me. It was still the best soup I've ever had.

When daylight greeted us so did the top British team who were strong runners. We had just crested a mountain pass and had about 25 km to go on a rough trail down to the lake. The Brits were renowned for their foot speed and it seemed inevitable that having caught us they would disappear down the track. We had been going slow, had sore feet and believed we couldn't go any faster, but the Brits provided a second wind. We started jogging too. I thought it wouldn't be long and we'd be back to walking but after a time I felt good and we stayed with them, much to their frustration. Both teams knew that our team was stronger on the water, so the race for fifth place was on.

The day started heating up and we were still in our bad-weather gear from the previous night but we didn't want to lose contact with the Brits. The pace slowly increased as they tried to shake us off but by now we were hanging on like pig dogs. As we descended closer to the lake we knew we'd finish the stage together or at least within minutes of each other but the pace never relented. We'd all run out of water but no one even dared to stop to fill a bottle, which was a shame as when we arrived at the lake it was filthy and stank of chemicals, most likely thanks to the huge factory on the shore. Although they fought honourably, it wasn't long into the paddle before we left the Brits behind. The day turned into a real scorcher so we enjoyed leaping off the boats to cool off from time to time on our way to finishing fifth.

The run down the hill that day taught me something I carried with me into future racing. Prior to the Brits showing up, had someone suggested we run hard down to the lake for a few hours, I wouldn't have thought it possible, having raced solidly for five days already. But given a purpose and some competitive juices, we went beyond what I believed was possible. It had been an extraordinary journey through an enchanted land. The scenery had been breathtaking – massive snow-capped peaks, arid deserts, tundra, grasslands, big lakes and rivers. My personal highlight was the white-water rafting stage about mid-race. I've never been through the Grand Canyon, but from all the images I've seen this was how I'd describe that section of white water amid rocky brown screes and ravines. Yet again I was amazed by marijuana growing wild and concluded that this must be the part of the world where the plant originates. The finish line and campsite were created by a tractor mowing down a field of the stuff, which they shoved into big piles and burned each night –very relaxing. The memorial service for Dominique Robert, aged 47, from Team Endurance-AGF, who died on the second day, was a sombre affair. Afterward I said goodbye to the team and travelled to the Seagate head offices in the Bay Area for my speech and media training.

I hadn't been back in New Zealand long before I had to return to the US for Primal Quest. The second version was being held in California and again we had altitude to contend with, but not as severe as at Telluride in 2002. Jodie and Jessie came with me as I intended to train in the Lake Tahoe mountains for a few weeks beforehand. Through Seagate we had the use of a luxury log home nestled in the woods, the most amazing training base one could wish for. The team was in great shape and keen to improve on fifth place from the year before.

As expected, we struggled at times with the higher elevations but made up for it in the lower reaches. We were lined up to take second place but received a four-hour penalty for walking on a forbidden road – it wasn't a short cut, we'd just failed to read the course notes closely enough. We got to the penalty box in second place but while we were serving the penalty a team went through leaving us with third. We'd made a few bad navigation route choices, but the penalty was severe considering there was no advantage to be gained by the route we had taken. That said, we'd had a fun trip and the race course did contain some magic sections, plus the prize money for third was still good. We decided then and there to win Primal Quest the following year, no two ways about it.

I spent some time with Bill Watkins after the race and we chatted quite a bit about racing, how I was finding being a full-time athlete and how life was going. I explained to him that Jodie and I owned our home but had decided we wanted to move to the coast. We wanted to raise our kids on the beach and we'd been trying to buy a piece of coastal land but we'd had a few failed attempts, each time missing out to foreign buyers and investors. Bill said he and Pat were interested in buying land in New Zealand and that I should keep an eye on any land that perhaps we could buy together. He also said I could mortgage from him if that helped, which was outrageously generous.

Following some more training in New Zealand we travelled to Malaysia for the Mild Seven Outdoor Quest, the premier stage race in the world. One of the reasons it had taken me this long to get to the race was because it included inline skating. I didn't know how to skate but the event was getting so popular the time had come to learn. It was to be four days of high-speed racing through a number of environments – mountains, jungle, rivers, ocean and urban. Richard Ussher and Hadyn Key joined me and Kristina, and although it was our first attempt at the race we were very confident of winning.

The first day ended with a white-water rafting section and we beat the next team off the water by 20 minutes. In a stage race 20 minutes is a seriously huge margin so we just had to protect that lead, but we extended it as each day went by. Richard and Hadyn were super-fast plus they were fresh – the team felt really good. The only negative was that during the first two days of the race I was having episodes of atrial fibrillation, and while the team towed me through these moments it was less than ideal. Being at the end of the year the event was somewhat of an end-of-season party for the pro teams. The hotel we were based at was five-star and the banquet dining was tastefully decadent. Everyone still has stories of how awesome those trips were, and the Australian athlete John Jacoby's astonishing Magnum ice-cream-eating record – something like 50 Magnums in five days.

The final hit-out for the year was the Los Angeles Balance Bar race, only a three-person team so Kristina, Rich and I shot over and won it fairly easily, beating our main rivals, Team Nike, who had won the first two rounds and the overall series. We'd had a good year with winning our final two races. It did raise the issue that Rich and Hadyn were great athletes plus closer to Kristina and I in age which socially made a difference. The problem we had was that we now had six people in the team and only needed four. The hard decision fell on me – who was going to be in the squad for 2004?

That summer I had regular problems with my heart – the episodes of atrial fibrillation were becoming more frequent and starting to affect my everyday life. Some days I would struggle to walk around the property and training was getting severely compromised because I was missing about 20 per cent of my scheduled sessions.

Meanwhile, I was looking out for pieces of land and one day spotted a very small advert in the local paper. It was a discreet ad that simply read, 'Coastal property at Kina Beach, serious buyers only' with a phone number to call. I phoned and spoke to the agent who was not very forthcoming. Offers over $1.9 million would be considered, but they had been trying to sell it for $2.1 million. I said I'd talk to my colleagues and get back to him. I don't think he thought he'd hear from me again. When I called Bill in the US and told him about the property, he suggested I go and look at it and if I thought it was a good buy, offer $2 million cash, first and final offer. He said he'd call Pat and tell him what was happening, suggesting that the three of us form a company and buy the property together. We arranged to view it the next day.

I cycled over from Nelson, about 40 km, while Jodie drove over with Jessie. It would be fair to say the agent wasn't used to buyers turning up on a bicycle. Back then there weren't many young couples with a baby looking at $2 million-dollar properties. Understandably, he felt his time was being wasted, and while he was polite, he stayed in his car doing other work while we looked around. We walked along the beach and discussed our options. There was a big shed with a small flat attached to it, and we agreed that we could sell our house and live happily in the shed. We decided to go for it so went back to the agent and offered $2 million cash. 'But don't you want to see the house?' he spluttered. We didn't even know there was a house on the property. It was a two-bedroom mud-brick house on an elevated platform above the beach with stunning views out over Tasman Bay and as soon as we saw it we knew we'd found our new home. We went straight to a friend's house and emailed Bill and Pat that we'd put an offer in. The offer was accepted next day and not long afterward we sold our place in Nelson and moved to Kina Beach.

The property was divided into six titles with Pat, Bill and ourselves taking two each. An earth house was of little value to the guys so Jodie and I eagerly took that. There's no way we could have bought our new home without their help, so not a day goes by that we don't appreciate how lucky we were for that to have happened.

We live in our dream home, which has doubled in size and grown astronomically in value since we moved in. Now we part-own one of the few blocks of bare coastal land in Tasman Bay, quite possibly the best site along the entire coast for vast ocean views and privacy, and when I'm paddling home after a surf ski and look at our cliff-top mansion nestled in the forest overlooking the bay, I think to myself, 'That's pretty choice.'

TOP Braden (left) and me, c.1974. With only 13 months between us we've always been close, spending significant time together growing up and sharing many of the same interests.
ABOVE Tahuna Soccer Team U10 with our coach Mr Grey, c.1982. I enjoyed his freedom coaching style and remember that our team won the league most years. PHOTOS: FA'AVAE COLLECTION

TOP Bogan boys! Braden (right) and I were teenagers when Zariana was born in 1987.
PHOTO: FA'AVAE COLLECTION

ABOVE My family on my wedding day, Awaroa Beach, 2000. In fear of a massive Samoan wedding, Jodie and I opted for something small and private. PHOTO: NICOLA DOVE

TOP The day's catch at Roaring Lion Hut, a few days after I'd nearly drowned in the Karamea River, 1989. PHOTO: NICK KING

ABOVE Climbing Takaka Hill on my first mountain bike – the pink Avanti – during my first real endurance triathlon, 1989. PHOTO: FA'AVAE COLLECTION

ABOVE Sub 3! – what I thought was going to be relatively easy turned out to be the biggest physical and mental challenge I'd faced, but I was extremely stubborn to make sure I broke 3 hours in 1990. After the race a doctor told my mum that I was too young for marathons – such sustained efforts weren't good for a developing heart. PHOTO: CHRISTCHURCH MARATHON

OPPOSITE TOP As a teenager, the excitement and thrills of mountain biking, mixed with the wilderness environments I could access, smoked my tyres. PHOTO: MIKE GANE

OPPOSITE BOTTOM Finish of Day 1 at the Coast to Coast, 1991. I was race leader and had just set a new record for the individual mountain run stage, but where are my support crew? PHOTO: BOB MCKERROW

ABOVE 1999 Coast to Coast Longest Day was also a lonely day. I raced at the front for about
9 hours and saw only Steve Gurney the whole day. I was in excellent physical condition but I still
had a lot to learn regarding how hard I could push myself. PHOTO: PAUL'S CAMERA SHOP

TOP Travelling home from Otago University in 1992, checking out O'Sullivans Rapid on the Buller River to see if it was worth getting the kayaks off the roof. Our little Subaru was an adventure sports store on wheels. PHOTO: FA'AVAE COLLECTION

BOTTOM My time as an instructor at Outward Bound in 2000 is probably the single best thing I have done in my working life. It was immensely satisfying and also a place of valuable learning about myself. PHOTO: OUTWARD BOUND

ABOVE 2001 Southern Traverse, Kingston, Lake Wakatipu. I enjoyed racing with the Seagate Executives at a social level after the rigours of the Eco Challenge the month prior. Getting to know the Seagate guys was another massive life-changing period for me. PHOTO: DEREK PATERSON
OPPOSITE TOP 2004 Nelson Rollo's 24-hour race. Hadyn Key, Richard Ussher, Kristina Strode-Penny and myself were the core Team Seagate. We used local events for training for the international competitions. PHOTO: IAN TRAFFORD
OPPOSITE BOTTOM 2004 Primal Quest, USA, drawing first place with Team Nike, the greatest team of that era of the sport. It was a hugely emotional and challenging week, but finishing the race together felt like the right thing to do. PHOTO: DAN CAMPBELL

TOP Kristina and I finishing Stage 1 of the 2005 World Championships, landing at Waimangaroa Beach. We'd just negotiated a huge surf landing and, unknown to us at the time, the rear of the kayak had all but snapped off – we had to get a replacement for the next kayak stage.
ABOVE Tyrolean Zip-line at Charleston, 2005 World Championships. Ropes stages in events can sometimes be a nuisance but can also be a pleasant break from the relentless intensity of the race.

TOP 2005 World Championships, rafting the Buller River earthquake section. It was a bonus that I had done my rafting guide training many years earlier on this section of water and had kayaked it regularly. Obscured behind us is the safety kayaker, my good mate Don Allardice.

ABOVE Adventure Racing World Championships 2005 with my son Zephyr (Zefa) and the team, Marcel Hagener, Kristina and Rich. It was an extremely satisfying time, winning the race and bowing out – time to enjoy retirement. PHOTOS: CHRIS MCLENNAN

TOP Racing in the 'empty quarter', the desert of UAE, 2009. The heat at its hottest is indescribable, something like racing in an oven.

ABOVE Rich and Elina Ussher were great to race with in Abu Dhabi. They won all four of the events staged there and I raced with them for two of those. I was always at the back in the desert – because I was heavier than all of them, having footprints to step in made a big difference to my work rate. PHOTOS: CHRIS RADCLIFFE

TOP Wulong, China, 2012. I've raced a dozen or so events in China and they're always interesting because you can be guaranteed something random will happen. PHOTO: RONNIE HAMMER
ABOVE Hiking with Trevor Voyce in Patagonia, 2012. We loved the race there, the changing landscapes and scenery. It's somewhere high on my list for further travel and exploring.
PHOTO: DIEGO COSTANTINI

TOP Sophie Hart and I crossing a river in France on Day 2 of the 2012 World Championships. After the debacle in Tasmania during the same event in 2011, we were extremely focused for this race. PHOTO: AYA KUBOTA

ABOVE Winning the 2012 World Championships is possibly the most satisfying victory I can recall, for many reasons. We didn't have it easy, we had to work super hard as a team and, for me, I could finally lay the demons of 2011 to rest. PHOTO: ANDREAS STRAND

TOP Pre-2014 World Championships in Ecuador we made a big effort to adjust to the altitude, spending a few weeks training in the mountains, with the highlight summiting the volcano Cotopaxi. PHOTO: EDISON OÑA

ABOVE Sophie and I nearing the end of an excellent downriver paddle in Ecuador, 2014 World Championships. As both of us are passionate paddlers we've always been very strong in the boats, which has been a big advantage to our team – every team in the world expects to concede time to us on the water. PHOTO: AYA KUBOTA

TOP For Stuart Lynch, Chris Forne and myself, winning in Ecuador was our third World Championships title (second for Sophie). We were happy to be finished and win but it felt more like relief than jubilation. For me, the novelty of winning is not what it used to be. PHOTO: AYA KUBOTA
ABOVE One of the spoils of being a World Champion – Toyota sponsorship! We're about to do a family overnight rafting trip on the Buller River for my 43rd birthday, with Zefa and Jessie.
PHOTO: FA'AVAE COLLECTION

TOP Rafting the Jatunyacu River in Ecuador during a memorable multiday family trip in the headwaters of the Amazon, 2014. PHOTO: VICTOR AGUIRRE

ABOVE Bagging another high point – Beebys Knob, Mt Richmond Forest Park, 2014. As a family, along with our dog Sunny, we've had some excellent adventures wandering around the mountains and valleys in the South Island. PHOTO: FA'AVAE COLLECTION

TOP Hiking the infamous 'Queens Mile' that starts at Remarkables ski field and returns through Wye Creek, 2013. Jodie and I create regular time for our children to be in nature, where some powerful learning often takes place. As a result, they are strongly connected to the outdoors. PHOTO: FA'AVAE COLLECTION

ABOVE Jodie and our children canoeing in the Amazon, 2014 – they spent a week in the jungle while I was training in the mountains of Ecuador. PHOTO: SANI LODGE

TOP A summer cruise down the Upper Grey River in one of our many watercrafts, 2014. The kids have named this boat 'Big Chili'. PHOTO: NATHAN TOPP

ABOVE Zefa with his Ma'ma and Pa'pa, 2010. Mum always supported my sport because I enjoyed it, not because she was interested. Dad always supported me because he was a sportsman himself. PHOTO: FA'AVAE COLLECTION

TOP Start of GODZone 2015 Adventure Race, Makarora River near Haast Pass.
ABOVE Beginning the final stage of GODZone 2015, Lake Wanaka. We'd just found out the size of our lead, so the pressure was off and it was time to enjoy the last day racing.

TOP GODZone 2015, heading into the Garvie Mountains at the end of Day 3. A southerly storm was about to hit us making for a testing night out. Chris is applying his trade – map and compass. ABOVE GODZone 2015, making it four wins from the four GODZone chapters. After the race, I said to the team, 'that's my last GODZone', at least in a team that's trying to win. Maybe I'll be back one day with one (or more) of my children. PHOTOS: ALEXANDRE SOCCI/GREEN PIXEL

GODZone 2015. PHOTO: ALEXANDRE SOCCI/GREEN PIXEL

CHAPTER NINETEEN
NUMBING FRUSTRATIONS

Towards the end of 2003 I was invited by a group of Canadian adventure racers to attend an event in Toronto. They were inviting Ian Adamson, one of the most successful adventure racers at the time, and I to run some clinics and speak about the sport. Added to that, teams who wished could enter a competition and the winning teams would have either Ian or I join them for a one-day adventure race combining city parks and some urban areas. It would be a two-day event including the race and clinics. Because it was being held as a fundraiser our travel and accommodation expenses were covered but we'd need to volunteer our time. I was happy to help out, I had the time and it sounded fun.

Very soon I was boarding my flight to Canada via Los Angeles. Twelve hours later I landed at LAX and proceeded to immigration. For a number of reasons LAX is my least favourite airport in the world, especially when in transit because you have to clear immigration even if you're about to board another flight. This was about the tenth time I'd been through LAX in the past 10 years. Tired and grumpy, I finally got to the immigration counter and handed over my passport. When the officer asked me if I'd been arrested in the United States before, I answered, 'No, are you mad?' He asked me again. 'No,' I repeated firmly, thinking this guy is stupid. He then asked me to follow him. I was led to secondary immigration and asked to wait. I was really confused – what the hell was going on?

After about an hour of sitting in the waiting room observing the immigration staff I had drawn a few conclusions. The first was that collectively these people seemed totally lacking in intelligence. They were mostly obese and despite being armed I wondered how many actually had the sense and skills to handle such weapons. Extremely rude and condescending to the travellers they were processing, it seemed to me that here was a group of people who had wanted a job with a uniform

141

but that Burger King considered them unemployable. I have little tolerance for stupid people in power so I braced myself to deal with them.

Finally it was my turn and I was taken to a room with one of these idiots with a gun. Without any explanation he asked me why I had lied to the immigration officer. By now I was completely confused. 'I didn't lie,' I told him. He asked me again if I had been arrested in the United States and again I told him no. After we played this game a few times he asked me what happened at Mammoth Mountain in 1994. Then the penny dropped – I finally knew what they were talking about. I actually laughed out loud. 'Oh that! The flag incident.' He got me to explain what had happened and was satisfied that my story matched what was on their records. But the issue was that I had lied to an immigration officer and they were not letting that go.

Despite my assurances, he would and could not believe that I had forgotten about the incident. In his mind, I was arrested in the United States about nine years ago for petty theft, surely that's not something you forget. He informed me that lying to an immigration officer was an offence and that I could expect a penalty of some sort – either a fine or maybe just refused entry into the US. I didn't even want to go to the US – I had just missed my flight to Canada. After about an hour of getting nowhere with this monkey I asked to speak to his superior. He refused, saying his boss would only agree with him. Clearly I was no threat to national security but it would require someone with a functioning brain to deduce that, and no one at US Immigration I could talk with seemed to have one. Watching these people waddle about I felt trapped in a world of idiocy.

Hours went by as they tried to decide what to do. At one point I lashed out, asking if anyone in the office had any common sense, but they threatened to put me in a jail cell so I quietened down. Eventually monkey man had finished his donut stack and was back at work, informing me that lying to an immigration officer was a serious crime and that as I did not have a visa I would be on the next flight back to New Zealand. Although, following 9/11 anyone with a criminal record in the US needed a visa to enter, so I simply wouldn't have got one even if I knew it was a requirement, because I had completely forgotten I'd been arrested there in the first place – it wasn't a major life moment never to forget. Despite my explanations of the truth of what happened and the fact I was wanting to get to Canada for a charity event, after 12 hours flying to LAX, 12 hours stuck in LAX trying to communicate with Neanderthals, I was back on a flight to New Zealand for another 12 hours.

Before departing immigration I was allowed to make one phone call to a US number. I called a friend in Los Angeles and asked her to call Jodie in New Zealand, saying as loudly as I could, 'The fucking clowns at US Immigration are sending me home because all they have between their ears is soda and burgers!' I asked her to tell Jodie that once I landed in New Zealand I needed to get to Canada as fast as possible but couldn't go via the US. I still had time to make it to my Canadian commitments if the flights worked out.

I was handcuffed and led onto a plane. Because of my frequent flyer miles, I was on a business-class upgrade, but the dicks from US Immigration weren't happy about that and ignoring the protests of the Air New Zealand flight attendants, they found me a seat in economy. This seemed clearly personal and nothing to do with policy. Perhaps they saw themselves as heroes, stopping a known criminal at the border and saving the country from certain doom, but once I was seated and they were heading off to Starbucks, I couldn't help myself. I looked them in the eye and said, 'One day I'm going to write a book and dedicate a whole chapter in it to you arseholes!' As soon as they were gone I was whisked back to business class and had a very comfortable return flight.

Back in Auckland I called Jodie to discover I had a 10-hour flight departing to Osaka in a few hours, followed by a 12-hour flight to Vancouver and a six-hour flight to Toronto. I emailed the event organiser and told them I was running late – that I was getting some sushi on the way. After 75 hours of travelling and transit time, I finally arrived in Canada with about eight hours to spare before the race started. The weekend was successful and I was really pleased I made it after all. It felt like a victory over the muppets at US Immigration. Back to Japan then back to New Zealand.

I did have a problem, though. I wanted to return to the US later that year to race Primal Quest. Making some calls to both the US Embassy and Consulate in New Zealand, I wasn't too surprised to discover that the embassy staff were equally as IQ challenged as their countryfolk at border control, but at the consulate it was refreshing to find people who could listen and understand the situation. It also helped that they believed my story – after all, I didn't have any motive to lie. They agreed to help me as much as they could but a few weeks afterwards I received an apologetic letter saying they couldn't do anything as the matter was managed by Homeland Security in the US.

Basically I was still seen as a threat to US security and not allowed entry. So I launched a campaign. I was going to be annoying. I wasn't going to go away. I rallied my friends to write to the consulate and embassy endorsing my character and assuring them that I was indeed no security risk. I reckon they must have received about 200 letters that week and as a result I got a letter from the US Ambassador to New Zealand assuring me he'd look into it. At the same time I spoke to Seagate – as captain of their professional adventure-racing team it was a problem that I wasn't able to take part in the major race of the season – and they had their lawyers investigate.

What transpired ended up being quite funny. Between the US Ambassador and the Seagate lawyers, it was discovered that what happened to me at LAX was a major mistake by US Immigration. They were correct that I needed a visa waiver to travel through the US after 9/11, but my situation was not an inadmissible one, I should have never been refused entry and they admitted the error. Seagate wanted to sue but in the end we settled for a 10-year visa – one with a big 'NOT GUILTY' stamped on it that the orang-utans at immigration couldn't possibly miss. While I still have to go through secondary immigration when I travel to the US, which is a hassle, each time it's easier, as they look up my file on the computer, say, 'Please enjoy your visit, sir', and I throw them a few peanuts.

CHAPTER TWENTY
NIGEL FATALITY

We celebrated the start of 2004 with a whole bunch of friends for a New Year's Eve party at Kina Beach. Jodie and I were adapting well to life as parents but it seemed to take a while for Jessie to settle at our new home. We were keen for another child but for the moment had a fun summer of kite boarding, taking turns at going out on the water while the other looked after Jessie on the beach. Racing professionally enabled me to spend quality time with the family and do the training I needed to, which was typically about 25 hours per week. I'd spend another half day a week on team management, booking flights, travel, entering events and dealing with sponsors. I'd made official changes to the race team by retiring Neil Jones and Jeff Mitchell who were both very understanding. It was a really tough decision but that was the reality of being the team manager as well as a team member. I had a responsibility to Seagate to field the best four I could and Rich and Hadyn would add another gear to the team. Summer turned to autumn, I was fit and ready to get into the racing season, and we discovered that Jodie was pregnant again.

The first race of the season was in Sweden, an event called the Airborne Expedition. We wanted to improve our inline skating, and containing 125 km of skating spread over two stages, this race provided good motivation to get better. Jodie and Jessie made the trip with me so that we could take some time after the race and travel around Norway and then Thailand on the way back to New Zealand and miss some of the winter. We arrived at our accommodation around 11 p.m. yet it was still light enough to see, because of the short nights, so Rich and I strapped on our skates and went out training. It was a novelty to be out skating in the middle of the night, on smooth roads and with zero traffic.

The race was divided into three sections, each of which ended at an airport where we boarded a flight to another part of Sweden. We raced well but lost time to the Swedish and Finnish teams who were all very accomplished skaters. Some of the skating was down rather large hills at high speeds, which I found terrifying, in an out-of-control way. Scenically, the coastal archipelago, mountains and rivers were amazing. After a few days of racing we reached the airport for the first flight. Tired, dirty and smelling, as you'd expect, the teams who made it boarded the flight, most falling asleep instantly. Landing at Kiruna, the northernmost town in Sweden, situated in the province of Lapland, close to the Arctic Circle, the next stage was to climb the highest peak, the Kebnekaise massif. We took buses to the edge of the national park and spent the night there before the race restarted. The local Sami people reminded me of Native Americans, living in tepees and with similar totem poles. It was a long trek into the climb and another out, close to 100 km.

Descending off the mountain, one of the points on my crampons caught my pants and I tripped up, tumbling down the ice at high speed, flipping a number of times before I could manage a successful self-arrest into the snow to stop my fall. I was fine, a bit shaken, but my heart was now in arrhythmia due to the spike of adrenalin. That made the last few hours extra hard. Once back in the village we laced up for a 90 km skate back to the airport. We'd been racing for about four days at this stage and we only just made it in time, much to the surprise of the local teams who didn't rate our chances of pulling it off, especially as most of it was at night. I nearly had a spectacular wipe-out close to the end after we spotted a fuel station and zoomed into the forecourt to buy some supplies and hit oil patches, sliding wildly but recovering in time (wearing inline skates whilst shopping was also quite unique). By making the cut-off time, we'd secured a place in the top three as only three teams made it. After some white-water rafting, a 200 km mountain ride and some challenging orienteering, we couldn't move any higher than third place but we were happy and we had raced well as a team.

The rest of the team headed back to New Zealand via New York for a (three-person) Balance Bar race, and Jodie, Jessie and I rented a car and went touring in Norway for a few weeks, camping and doing some easy hiking trips. The scenery really made the trip and we had a great time exploring. After a race I'm happy just to relax and take it easy so it was a perfect break. We stopped off in Thailand for a week on the way home and then I needed to get back into regular training.

In the spring I was contacted regarding a support role to Phil Keoghan, producer and host of *The Amazing Race*, on another show called *No Opportunity Wasted* (*NOW*). The essence of the episode was that Phil would select three 'ordinary people', fly them to Queenstown and give them an intense, non-stop, action-crammed, life-changing 72-hour experience. Part of the concept was to remind people of what can be achieved in life with a bit of effort, much like Outward Bound. My job was site safety as many of the activities were adventure based and also to support Phil, if he needed it, dealing with the contestants facing some massive challenges in the outdoors.

It was a fun few days and the contestants were nice people. One thing I didn't count on though was being part of a world record bungy jump. I'd jumped a few years earlier and dislocated my shoulder so I wasn't that thrilled, plus I'd always viewed low-risk, low-skill activities as somewhat lame, naturally preferring the high-risk, high-skill pursuits. As nine of us stood on the platform preparing to jump, the only reassuring thing for me was that AJ Hackett Bungy co-founder Henry van Asch was roped in too. I knew Henry from mountain-bike racing days and I asked him quietly seconds before the jump if this was all legit as he looked mildly concerned. Huddled on the jump platform designed for two, wriggling nine people to the edge was an undertaking in itself. As the countdown began, Henry assured me he thought we'd be okay. A terrifying few seconds later, I believed him.

Our big goal for the year was to try and win Primal Quest. Apart from wanting to improve on our fifth and then third placings, it was the most prestigious race since Eco Challenge and had the biggest prize pool. Adding to the situation, it was funded by Bill Watkins, CEO of our sponsor Seagate. We wanted to win for Bill. Before we departed for the US, the team met in Nelson and did a five-day training camp, hiking in the mountains, mountain biking and sea kayaking. It was a fun time and we had a really strong team spirit. The itinerary included a trip into Harwood Hole, New Zealand's deepest vertical shaft, the highlight being a 180-metre abseil down, then taking the Starlight Cave passage out.

Local caving friends Mike and Terry managed the trip for us. The weather wasn't ideal and they were concerned that the water levels in the passage might be unsafe. We decided to abseil in and assess. It's a mind-blowing abseil, massive exposure. Once we were all at the bottom Mike felt the passage was not an option, it was raining outside the cave, and he suggested we reascend, but to speed things up we should go two to a rope. I'd spent years working with ropes but I'd never heard of two people ascending together, although Mike assured us it was fine. Hadyn and I went together. With so much rope above us, there was metres of stretch in the system, so we were bouncing around like mad and feeling very vulnerable. But we worked together to reach the top – it was the ultimate in teamwork.

During this training camp I noticed that my relationship with Kristina had changed. When she first joined the team I found her hard work at times, mainly because she was so proactive and confident. For someone joining an existing team she wasn't afraid to express her views, which I found mildly disrespectful, feeling that she had to serve some time as a new team member first. I was inexperienced in my leadership role. I think we both used to get on each other's nerves quite a bit but we matured and adjusted our behaviours to ensure we raced professionally. But as time went on, we developed a special friendship and became close. Within the team, Neil and Jeff were good friends so Kristina and I tended to spend more time together, plus we paddled together in the kayak so that naturally bonded us further. During the training camp I felt that my attraction to her had grown. I guess we'd shared intense experiences, rich ones, along with many highs and lows, so we knew and understood each other very well. As I started to process what was happening, I realised I had developed strong feelings for her – not intentionally, it just happened. I knew Kristina valued me as a friend and I didn't want to do anything stupid that could put that at risk. I was happily married and had no intention of having any other form of relationship, so I let it be.

The Primal Quest event was based in the Orca Islands, in Washington state, so we were excited about the course potential. My brother Braden and Kristina's brother Karl (an adventure racer as well) were happy to come along as support crew. Hadyn's wife Katie joined in, as did Rich's partner at the time, Anna. Mike Gane, a friend and sponsor of mine who owned the local bike shop, was invited along as team mechanic. All up we had an entourage of nine. I found it difficult leaving home with Jodie due to have another baby in about three weeks plus looking after a one-year-old, but it was my job and this race was a big pay cheque if we managed to win. However, as we prepared for the race on location, I couldn't deny my feelings towards Kristina, making it a very confusing time. I looked to her for support in the race environment and close to the big races I depended on her as we had a strong connection and were firm friends.

Race day rolled around and soon we were kayaking in the San Juan Islands. The race started with a long kayak stage, about 80 km back to the mainland. Because it was a very long course, possibly taking five to six days for the winner, our race strategy was to start conservatively. We wanted to invest in looking after ourselves, with the hope we'd be able to finish strong. The first day went by uneventfully, kayaking, hiking and biking. We were sharing third and fourth place mostly with the US team Nike, the two-time undefeated Primal Quest champions. It appeared they had a similar strategy – it was a long race, start slow. In first and second were the Australian team AROC and the US/Australia combined team Montrail, both highly experienced and talented units. They had opted to go faster from the start and take less rest than us and Nike so had built up a lead of a few hours.

Another day went by with more hiking and biking as teams progressed through the race. Due to weather, a stage over Mount Baker was shortened which cut time out of the full course. Our team was not racing particularly well. We'd made some navigation route errors and generally weren't moving as fast as we would have liked. We were still with and around Team Nike but the teams ahead had pushed the lead out to a margin that was looking close to impossible to pull back. We had heard that one of the Team Montrail members was injured and starting to slow but Team AROC was still racing strongly.

After a particularly long night of carrying bikes though a hellish stage, we finally managed to get going well and felt like the lead teams were within reach given the amount of time and distance we still had to race. We felt rested as we had had daily sleeps. We weren't far behind Team Nike, climbing a hill toward the end of the bike stage which led on to a hiking orienteering loop, when an event vehicle caught up and stopped us. We were informed that we needed to return to the valley and meet at a camping area by the river. The race had been stopped but they couldn't give us any more details. Team Nike had reached the end of the stage and had been told the same thing and had already started back down the hill. Discussing what was going on as we rode with them, we all concluded that there had been a major accident – someone was either seriously hurt or dead. When we arrived at the camping area our support crews were waiting. We were told there would be a briefing that evening and that we should rest. However, rumours started to circulate around the camp to the effect that an accident had occurred and some-one from one of the leading teams was most likely dead. This sent us into shock as we knew all the members of those teams well – who was hurt or, worse, dead?

Later that evening I attended a captains' briefing where we were told what had happened. Teams AROC and Montrail were descending off a peak when a large rock was dislodged and went tumbling down the mountain. Nigel Aylott of Team AROC was a fair way down already and never heard the warning cries as it hurtled down, killing him instantly. Nigel was dead. This was really heavy news and we grieved for him, devastated that he had died from an accident that could have happened to any of us. The race directors needed time to formulate what to do next – I suspect they needed to seek legal advice before making any decisions – but one thing was for sure, the race was stopped until further notice, at least another 24 hours. Back in our RV we sat around in a state of disbelief. It was a surreal situation. A few hours earlier we were in the thick of an adventure race, and now we were sitting around a table drinking tea, eating food we had no appetite for, and coming to the acceptance that Nigel was gone. We'd raced against him regularly, and while he was annoying and cheeky at times (exercising healthy trans-Tasman rivalry), he was an exceptional athlete and we had huge respect for him. Wearily we went to bed.

The following day was occupied with getting ready for restarting the race, obviously without AROC as well as Montrail, who had a team member badly injured from the accident. The race directors had contacted Nigel's family and they wanted the race to continue, in remembrance of him. The plan was to send teams off at evenly spaced intervals in the order in which they were at the time of the accident. We couldn't deny that we had benefited from the stoppage caused by Nigel's death. We were in second place, just minutes behind Team Nike.

In the dark of night in heavy rain we got under way on a biking stage. Midway through the stage we missed a turn over a bridge. We realised the mistake quite quickly but decided that rather than going back to the bridge we'd hardly lose time if we continued to the end of the road we were on and crossed the river by foot. When we got there we carried our bikes down to the river which was much more flooded than we anticipated. But under the light of our torches, we thought we could see a place to cross. It was swifter and deeper than expected but luckily we managed to stay on our feet, despite our bikes catching water and almost pulling us off our footing. After a few high-fives when we made it across we started to move towards where we expected to find the road.

Bad news. We were on an island and still had another channel to cross, except this one was bigger than the first. After closer examination we decided it was suicidal to attempt it. We had to retreat. Frustrated, we returned to the first crossing. More bad news. The angle returning was more difficult and dangerous, it was not looking good, but the river was clearly rising so we couldn't delay. I went first and managed to cross, partly swimming. It was cold and still dark and raining. Then we helped each other over, the risk of someone getting swept off their feet very high and most likely disastrous, it was so fast moving, contained rapids and was littered with trees.

Once all back on the road with our bikes, I called a team talk. We'd lost close to two hours and everyone was feeling down. I pointed out that we could have lost someone, but because of our fast action, decisions and teamwork, we were all alive and safe. The race was insignificant in comparison. After a quick hug we started riding and singing songs to warm us back up. Not long after that we started passing other teams. We were really happy, singing, joking and riding along surprisingly fast, and by the end of the stage had made our way back into fourth place. It was an incredible recovery and another valuable lesson in the power of team spirit. Dropping our bikes, we set out on a hiking section followed by another bike stage. We travelled really well and entered the transition area in second place, a few hours behind Team Nike. Luckily for us, the final stage was a long kayak with a portage in the middle. The first 50 km or so was downriver so it was a dark zone, meaning that no teams could start paddling until 6 a.m. the next morning. We could get a full night's sleep.

Due to the logistics of making sure everybody got on the river quickly to maximise daylight, teams would set off just two minutes apart the next morning. When we heard this it sent us into fits of laughter. We were the strongest paddling team left in the event and ahead of us lay a kayak race from which we stood to earn US$100,000 if we won, which seemed highly likely. We were due to start just a few minutes behind Team Nike and there was no way they could match us in the kayaks. We even discussed the fact it was likely the highest-paid kayak race ever.

It was a beautiful morning as we loaded the kayaks with food and drink for the day ahead. Nike departed on time and then a few minutes later we set off, a South African team behind us who were fairly strong paddlers too, but we were confident no one could rival our pace. Soon after starting we caught and passed Team Nike who were good friends so we exchanged some jovial banter and soon afterward left them in our wake. As we paddled downriver we extended our lead. It was going to be a long day in the boat but we were fresh and leading the race, certain victory ahead. In my mind, though, I was wrestling with a dilemma. We were on the verge of winning Primal Quest and making a decent amount of money – it was all but signed and sealed. But we weren't in this situation solely because we'd raced well, but largely because we had benefited the most from the circumstances of Nigel's death. In fact, it was unlikely we would have won had the tragedy not occurred. Team Nike was probably still the team that would have gone on to win – you never know what's going to happen in sport, but that was my pick. It didn't feel right to take the victory so I asked Kristina what she thought, and it turned out that we were thinking the same thing. We paddled over and spoke to Hadyn and Rich. We all agreed that the only good reason to win the race was for the money, but for all of us that wasn't a good enough reason. We threw options around and agreed that perhaps the best option would be to see if Team Nike would like to draw the race, so we decided to ask them.

The problem was that they were back upriver somewhere so we got out some food and sat just drifting down the current. It must have been 20 minutes before they caught up, very confused as to what we were doing. We explained our situation, and although they were somewhat surprised at our offer, agreed immediately, so we started to paddle downriver together. It soon became apparent, though, that we were much stronger and we kept needing to ease up. After having to wait a few times I said to Mike, the Team Nike captain, that while we were happy to draw with them, if they didn't go faster it was likely the South Africans would catch us both. We agreed to paddle a little slower so that they could stay in our draft and that helped, even though we had to reduce our speed. It was rather comical that sitting on our boat wash was the greatest adventure-racing team of the period calling out to us 'slow down please'.

We reached the portage section and they got slightly ahead as they had carried inline skates in their kayaks. Back on the water but the ocean this time, we quickly caught them again, although now our speed differences were even more noticeable – to paddle at their speed we felt like we were hardly moving. So I checked in with my team and we agreed to offer Team Nike the chance to mix the paddlers up. We suggested that we all pull over at a beach to swap paddlers around so each kayak had one from each team, and that way we would stay together. After a short discussion as to whether that was within the rules and figuring it was, plus in light of what had happened during the race with the accident, we all agreed it felt like a better way to finish the race. Early evening we climbed out of the kayaks and staggered up to the finish line to be crowned Primal Quest champions – two teams. It had been a big week and it felt great for the two emotionally charged teams finishing together to have that support and camaraderie.

The next morning a float plane took me to Seattle and I boarded a flight to New Zealand. I'd found it difficult saying goodbye to Kristina, and flying home I still felt very confused. I knew I had a lot of love for her but I didn't know what that meant. I had to get home as soon as possible, though, as Jodie could be having our second child any day. My mind was spinning.

A few days after getting back, I received a call from one of the Nike executives in Oregon to congratulate me on the race but more importantly on our sportsmanship by drawing it with their team. Apparently the story had made mainstream news in the US, so they were very happy. They understood that we took a $25,000 reduction in prize money by drawing with the Nike team so wanted to offer us that value in product and clothing for the race team. It was an amazing gesture and we cheekily got some Nike golf clubs each thrown in as well (I still play with those clubs today).

I started into some light training which allowed me time to process the battle that was taking place in my mind in regard to how I felt about Kristina. I decided the best person to discuss it with was Jodie. We went for a walk along the beach one afternoon and I told her what was happening for me, but it didn't turn out to be the discussion I'd hoped for and I regretted bringing it up. Jodie was angry and not very open to discussing it. I didn't appreciate how bad the timing was – she had been home alone with a one-year-old for a month and was heavily pregnant. I loved Jodie as much as I ever did, there was no question there, I just had strong feelings for another woman as well and I didn't know how to deal with it. When the initial shock passed we talked things over in more detail and agreed that I needed to set and keep some clear boundaries for myself. Kristina was a special friend and an excellent team-mate. I didn't want to jeopardise that. Because I felt like I could control my mind but not my heart it was a challenging time for me and new learning.

Life went on, and I started training again for our next race. On 5 October Jodie went into labour and by early morning, 6 October 2004, our son Zephyr was born. It was amazing to have another child and we were both so happy we had a healthy baby boy. Although it took us some time to adjust to having two children, we coped fine. A few weeks afterwards I departed for the next race, the Mild Seven Outdoor Quest in Malaysia.

We had won the race the previous year and were keen to win it again – the prize money was high and the style of racing suited us. Unfortunately, my heart condition was starting to flare up more regularly and my training was getting compromised. I talked to the team about it and about me not going to the race, but they decided they would rather take the risk of racing with me and maybe having some heart issues, than taking someone different.

Being back with Kristina was both good and bad for me. I didn't want an affair or anything like that but my attraction to her was engulfing. I drew a line and knew I wouldn't step over it but it wasn't easy. It was a situation I'd never been in before so I didn't have any skills or experience to draw upon. I didn't want to do or say something stupid to Kristina and lose a friend as a result. Fundamentally, although I never have and don't intend to, I don't see anything wrong with having intimate contact with another woman. I'm not governed by religious dictates and I tend to resist social expectations, preferring to make up my own mind about things. Because Jodie and I were speaking very openly about what was happening, I knew that whatever I did I would discuss with her, so that naturally controlled my actions. I had this conundrum going on inside of me and I needed to get control of it.

The race didn't go well for us. We were racing superbly as a team but I had heart problems throughout the race and Hadyn had a bad day when we ran up Mount Kinabalu, possibly getting a mild dose of altitude sickness. We did manage to finish third, which was still a very respectable result, considering the level of competition. Back to New Zealand for a few weeks and then to Los Angeles for the final of the Balance Bar 24-hour series, Kristina, Rich and I going as the three-person team this time. We won the race but paid the price afterwards.

In the first stage we had to climb a small mountain to an abseil, and then run down to our bikes. Soon after it started I was surprised that the main field and local teams started running around the mountain, when the first checkpoint was directly uphill. I wasn't sure why everyone was going that way but I suggested we should just go direct. We pushed through the forest and reached the checkpoint about an hour later, pleased to learn that we were the first team when we headed off. We went on to win the race and the series but on the flight back to New Zealand we started to break out in a rash. Little did we know that we had bush-bashed through poison oak for nearly an hour – we were covered from head to toe in it, the reaction I had was so severe that I needed steroid injections to make it manageable. I still clearly remember how terrible it was. The first week, I was thinking to myself, it was worth it, we won. The second week, I decided it wasn't worth it, despite the prize money. Now I knew why the local teams had gone around the mountain. Still, it was summertime in New Zealand and it felt like we were having our first 'real' family Christmas – mum, dad and two kids.

CHAPTER TWENTY-ONE

NAMIBIAN FISH

The New Year ushered in some significant changes. The first was that Seagate wouldn't be able to continue sponsoring the team. We'd been very successful and they were extremely satisfied with our performances but they needed to pull back on costs. It wasn't a complete surprise as they had said from the beginning they could only commit to three years. The good news was that former Seagate CEO Steve Luczo had set up a personal project called Balance Vector and would pick up the sponsorship. Balance Vector was essentially a philanthropic organisation Steve set up to help his friends do cool stuff, a common theme being people chasing their dreams through business, art, film, music and sport, often with an environmental benefit. The second change related to team personnel. Kristina announced that she wanted to reduce the amount of adventure racing she was doing to concentrate on qualifying to represent New Zealand in sprint kayaking at the 2008 Beijing Olympics (Steve, through Balance Vector, was keen to help her achieve that goal too). Hadyn was also stepping down to put his energies into his young family as well as a new business he was starting. He was a significant loss, although thankfully there was no major shortage of strong male athletes to replace him, but it could take a few more years for another New Zealand female to reach Kristina's level. For these reasons combined I decided that 2005 would be my final year adventure racing.

By the end of the year I would have done seven years of adventure racing and I felt it was time to move on. Discomfort and hardship are all part of the job description for an adventurer racer, but I wanted an easier life, to enjoy the outdoors in a more sedate way. Jodie and I were also keen to have three children, so that was on the horizon too. A further reason I wanted to retire was that despite trying countless medications, together with lifestyle and diet changes, my atrial fibrillation (AF) was occurring more frequently and hindering my ability to train properly. Too many sessions were being missed or cut short and it frustrated me immensely. I clearly remember one day when I was scheduled to do a long road ride and several kilometres into it my heart went into AF. I tried to push through it, but after a few more kilometres I was so tired and weak I couldn't stay on my bike. Pulling over to the side of the road, I collapsed onto the grass, my heart in a major spasm. I was so angry and upset that I starting punching my chest as hard as I could, cursing my heart for failing me. Crying tears of frustration, I slowly made my way home, my training over for the day. When this happened, I would be depressed and negative for the rest of the day, which was a strain on Jodie and the kids. The World Champs were announced in New Zealand so Kristina and I agreed to make that our adventure-racing farewell.

I needed to get my heart sorted so for the first few months of the year I was in and out of hospital for regular blood tests and injecting myself with Warfarin daily. After one particularly long blood-testing session the nurse wouldn't let me leave for a while, as I was almost passed out. But I'd reached a point where I was tired of underperforming due to my heart condition. Another ablation procedure was scheduled for March. After being virtually unbeatable in long-distance mountain-bike races, I'd done an event at Lake Taupo where I was in AF for the entire 12 hours. It was like riding through mud with the brakes on the whole time, but I was determined not to give up – the race wasn't against the other riders, it was between me and my heart. Amazingly, I managed to take second place. In a similar event, this time a 24-hour team mountain bike, I had such a bad episode of AF I had to stop and lie down at the side of the track, the clock ticking and my team-mates waiting for me to complete my lap. I wasn't even sure if I was going to survive, but after a few minutes I was able to sit up, then stand, then slowly ride to the end of the lap and tag the next rider. We had lost significant time and I needed to return to the hotel to rest. After a shower and a few hours' sleep I woke up and felt great. I called the team, who were doing it hard with one rider down, and told them I was on my way back. They weren't that keen but I insisted I was fine. I went out on course and started producing some of the fastest lap times of the event, but we never managed to claw back the lead, again taking second place.

The other big project I had on for the first half of the year was building an extension to our house. We treasured our little adobe brick and wooden joinery home that had been built toxin free, but it had become too small for our growing family. What started off as a project to add two rooms to the south of the existing building ended up being four bedrooms and two bathrooms to the north (funny how these things happen). Our challenge was to merge the extension with the existing structure so that it matched. Partly to control costs but mainly for personal reasons, Jodie and I wanted to do as much of the work as we could, to feel like we had contributed a large part to enhancing our home. We enlisted the help of a few close friends and family who would add some heart and soul to the project and for a few months worked non-stop to create our cliff-top palace at Kina Beach, looking out over the waters we had grown up with. I would go to bed each night hardly able to sleep with the excitement of completing more of the building the following day. We laid over 5000 mud bricks, put a roof on, fitted doors and windows and did all the finishing work. It was a richly rewarding experience and has inspired me to build again given the chance.

March came round and I headed to Christchurch for the heart ablation. It's a weird feeling walking into a hospital seemingly healthy to subject yourself to a procedure which carries an element of risk. There was a chance I could die during the operation, albeit an extremely small one. Was I prepared to risk my life just so I could do a few more races with a normal heart? That was the big question that I had deliberated over for some time, but in the end the condition started to occur so regularly that it began to impact on everyday life. Some days I struggled to finish a round of golf, and once I couldn't keep up with Jessie, then about two years old, on a walk back from the beach. Something needed to change.

It was an emotional experience saying goodbye to Jodie and Zephyr at the hospital (Jessie was in Nelson with family), as it could be the last time I would ever see them, but I had decided that the rewards outweighed the risks. I was in theatre for about four hours, sedated most of the time, but occasionally aware of what was taking place, including the burning and popping of the laser as it carried out its task – it was heartburn at a whole new level. Afterwards I was advised to take life very easy for six weeks, to allow plenty of time for recovery. Eager for this procedure to work, I stuck to the instructions. Counting the time spent working on the house, the ablation and then six weeks of rest, I had gone four months without training. It was the most unfit I had been in about twenty years.

My plan was to build up to the World Champs in November, using three international races as stepping stones. The first was in Mexico, thankfully a stage race, not a non-stop expedition. It was only a three-person team so Rich and I invited emerging athlete Sally Fahey to join us. The race contained three stages, a short, medium and long, spread over four days. It was held in the middle of summer, in the middle of a very hot region called Nuevo Léon, with most of the racing being in the middle of the day. It was a competitive field but we had a chance of winning despite the fact I was far from my full race pace.

The first day involved mountain biking, running, navigation and a huge zip-line which only one team-mate had to do, so Rich volunteered for that, and we finished in a respectable second place. The second day began with a mountain-trekking stage which we nailed, navigating precisely to move to the front. It was burning hot and getting hotter, well over 30 degrees Celsius and still rising. We had carried enough fluid but some of the teams didn't and ran into serious trouble. A US team who had dropped off the wrong side of the mountain into a baking canyon with no shade had run out of water and luckily were spotted by a passing helicopter and given a box of water and told how to get back on track. The transition area was in a small town and we had to do an abseil off a cliff to end the stage. I guess nothing much ever happened in that town because thousands of people gathered to watch us abseil and change over to the bike stage. Adventure-racing rock stars! Opening our gear box amid the cheering and screaming of the crowd we were hit by a wave of toxic fumes. The heat inside the box had got so high it had started to liquefy the glue on the soles of Rich's bike shoes and they were peeling off.

Speeding along the barren trails past the mud buildings and desert plants it was swelteringly hot and there wasn't a drop of moisture anywhere. Water stations where we could refill had been marked on the race map and we desperately wanted to reach one. Although we had carried plenty of water from the start, it was so hot as soon as you opened your mouth (a helpful thing to do when riding hard) that your tongue would instantly be desert dry. A few hours into the ride we reached the water station only to find that it hadn't been set up – such was racing in Mexico. With about 40 km to go on a flat gravel road, we had no option but to ride on into the wind and heat dreaming of a cold drink at the end of the stage.

Rich and I were having turns up front riding into the wind but Sally was struggling to keep the pace. She was keen to keep pushing on but was having trouble controlling her bike, continually hitting the build-up of roadside gravel and eventually losing control and crashing. She got up, dusted herself off and got back on but the same thing happened again soon after. This time she didn't get back up. Rich and I stopped and I went back to help. Temporarily stunned, when Sally regained consciousness her eyes were wide open but staring through me, terrified. As I got closer she started to panic and scurry away, screaming at me to leave her alone. I tried to explain to her what was happening, that we were in a race and she had just crashed off her bike, but she was completely confused. Then she got up and started sprinting through the needle-laden cactus plants into the desert for about a hundred metres before collapsing somewhere out of sight. What the fuck?

By now Rich had joined me and we decided that since he knew Sally best he should go and get her. Tenderly picking his way through the cactus field Sally had just dashed across without flinching, yelling every time he got spiked, he finally got to where she lay and started talking to her. I watched intently, wondering what on earth we were going to do. Just then Sally reared up with a piece of wood the size of a baseball bat and started chasing Rich through the cactus. I had one of those 'Jesus Christ' moments – here I am in the middle of the desert, in the middle of the day, and one of my team-mates is chasing the other through the middle of a cactus field – someone pour me a tequila, please! Sally collapsed again but this time thankfully closer to the road.

Before either Rich or I could say much, a large pick-up truck came barrelling down the road sending up a billowing cloud of dust. We waved it down and it came to a rumbling halt beside us. A large leather-skinned Mexican with a handlebar moustache slowly looked out from under his hat. It was like being in a Tarantino movie. Using sign language we explained to him that our team-mate had been badly affected by the sun and crashed off her bike and we needed to get her to the end of the day's racing at the next town. He slowly got out of his truck and surveyed the scene, taking a long hard look into the sun. Sally was watching from a distance with a crazed look. Sizing us up and down (Rich and I wondering if our lives were going to be ended there and then), eventually he nodded and signalled us to load our bikes into the back of his truck. Then the three of us went to get Sally who by now seemed to be sleeping.

When she woke up she struggled to break free as we carried her to the truck. We got her inside and Rich climbed in next to her. She was terrified of the driver and sat as far from him as she could, jamming Rich against the door and window. I jumped on the back for a frightening high-speed trip to the hospital, sliding all over the road a number of times as the driver fought to stay in control on the loose gravel. In a matter of minutes Sally was safely in the care of the doctors and there wasn't much for Rich and me to do other than go to the hotel at the finish line, drink some fluid and wait. We had some drinks and then dived into the swimming pool and I immediately cramped up. Unable to swim, I started sinking, just managing to cry out to Rich before my head went under. He dragged me to the side of the pool, nearly another hospital case.

Sally had been put into an ice bath as her core body temperature was at a very critical level and she remained in hospital care for a few days. Our team was out of the race but Rich and I carried on through the final day for fun. I'm glad we did as the canyoneering section remains one of the best adventure activities I've done whilst competing. We spent a hot afternoon leaping off cliffs into pools, abseiling down waterfalls, and even down a waterfall inside a cave that the river went through. Sadly for Sally, it would be years before she would fully recover from that degree of heat exhaustion. She was a great athlete and I really enjoyed racing with her so it was a shame the event ended the way it did. At the airport I bought her a souvenir fridge magnet that pictured a cactus tree under the sun but I don't think she appreciated the gift. Sadly for me and Rich but on a far lesser scale, we had both managed to get another good dose of poison oak rash.

Back home in New Zealand I didn't have long before we departed for our next race in South Africa and Namibia. Rich and I were teamed up with two other Kiwi athletes, George Christison and Lisa Savage. The plan was for George to take Hadyn's place in the team for the remainder of the season. Lisa was brought on board as she would also be the reserve female for our bigger races should anything happen to Kristina. Jodie was keen to visit South Africa so we decided to make a family trip out of it, see some wildlife and stop over in Singapore and Indonesia on our return, a winter escape. I was still very focused on using the races as training, so while we were keen to win, I was equally focused on getting stronger with the World Champs being the ultimate goal. The race was to be held in the Richtersveld Transfrontier Park close to the border of Namibia, so we enjoyed a few days of pre-race training in the area, spotting giraffe and zebra as we biked and hiked around.

The race started with a hiking stage which meant we started running. George and Rich are both exceptional runners so the pace was fast – too fast for Lisa whose strength was mountain biking. Eventually things settled down as we went into the first night. We were travelling well but in the early hours of the morning we lost a few hours when I was looking for a checkpoint up the wrong valley – I was in the neighbouring valley but it took some time to realise the mistake. It always took me a while to adjust to the scales, magnetic declinations and symbols of a different country's map. As a team we had plenty of speed so the next day we easily pulled back ground and were soon in second place and moving well. A strong memory of the race is the massive date plantations we went through, a few of which sold fresh dates at the roadside. We loaded our pockets and packs with them, making them a staple fuel source as we raced towards Namibia.

On a long mountain-bike stage the roads were soft and sandy – it was like riding on a beach, slow and heavily taxing, the wind at times throwing up large plumes of fine dust (some swimming goggles would have come in handy). Struggling into the sandstorm, George started to cough uncontrollably and pulled over to the side of the road. I came alongside and asked if he was okay and he told me that his chest was hurting and he was having trouble breathing and he was going to have to pull out of the race. I was gobsmacked. George was regarded as a very tough guy within our sport, and rightly so, he had a long list of achievements plus he was a hunter, and Kiwi hunters are typically hard men. We still needed to finish the stage so we carried on, although George showed no sign of changing his mind. We got to the end of the stage and he quit the race. Rich, Lisa and I were all a bit stunned but we loaded up our packs, said goodbye to George and carried on racing, except we were now unranked. From a training perspective it was good for me as we settled into a more relaxed pace and enjoyed the course, taking more sleep and spending extra time to appreciate the surroundings. After doing one of the most terrifying abseils of my life descending about 80 metres down a cliff with rocks the size of footballs hurtling past me, we then completed an incredible canoe stage down Fish River Canyon, a gigantic ravine.

The Fish River is the longest interior river in Namibia. It cuts deep into the plateau which is dry, stony and sparsely covered with hardy, drought-resistant plants. We were lucky it wasn't a hot day – a few months before the race it hit 48 degrees Celsius in the canyon, but it was only 30 degrees when we were in there. The white water was exciting with some large rapids to negotiate. After a full day on the river we headed into the hills on a long trekking stage. During the night we opted to stop for some sleep and decided we might as well sleep until sunrise, such is the life of an unranked team. Camped high on a mountainside, we checked our shoes for scorpions at daybreak and then descended to the open plains where once again Rich and I found ourselves in a desert without water.

The hiking section ended with about 40 km of flat gravel road, which we were due to be doing through the hottest part of the day. A well where we could resupply had been marked on the map so we rationed ourselves to make it to that point. The well was about a kilometre off the route but we needed water as we still had a few hours remaining to reach the village. The well was dry. Back on the road we swore and cursed and wondered how on earth the teams behind us were going to cope – the day was still relatively cool but was only going to intensify. Rich still had a few mouthfuls in his bottle that he was rationing carefully and when Lisa asked for a drink he somewhat reluctantly handed over his bottle and before he could say anything she had drained it completely – now we definitely had no water. It wasn't a major issue, though, more just a miserable way to finish the stage.

Lisa was walking ahead of us when an approaching police car stopped beside her. As we drew closer we caught the tail end of one of her signature tirades of expletives. She started walking again and the car slowly drove past us and onwards. We caught up to Lisa to see what had happened, and it turned out that they had driven out into the desert to check if the teams were okay but hadn't brought any water with them. Lisa let them have it. Half an hour later they passed us again heading back to the village ahead. We walked on, sweltering in the sun and generally suffering, still cursing their stupidity. Then, with an hour still to go, we saw them returning, this time slowing up and holding giant 500 ml cans of cold Coke out the window. They had gone back to the village, filled their car with cold drinks and were now taking them to the teams – thanks, Lisa! By the time we reached the village we were totally parched again and straight-lined past the transition area to the local store and the chilled drinks. I drank three cans before even moving from the fridge, and paying for our big pile of empties up at the counter must have been quite a sight.

Finishing the race unranked wasn't very satisfying, but we'd had fun and seen more of the countryside. It taught me a valuable lesson in making sure beforehand that all team members are committed to the same goal. It had always been our team's rule that the only way someone could withdraw from a race was if they sustained an injury that made it impossible for them to continue or the race doctor stopped them. Because we had had a few team changes I hadn't gone through these expectations and conditions beforehand, so I vowed to always make that clear in future. After the race we spent a few days doing a safari and then returned to New Zealand via Asia. It was a superb family adventure and the kids proved they could travel really well.

The next race, the Raid, based in Annecy, was our last shake-out before the World Champs. We enlisted the help of friends Mike and Benjamin (a French guy living in New Zealand) as our support crew. Kristina was back on board and we invited another friend, Marcel Hagener, to make up the fourth spot. It turned out that George did indeed have a serious lung infection and was expected to be out of racing for the rest of the season. We raced okay to finish fifth, and given it was the first time we had teamed up together it was okay. I struggled through the higher-altitude sections and made a few navigation errors that set us back. While not usual, the race allowed GPS use and that actually put us at a disadvantage because we didn't know how to use one and poorer navigating teams were not making mistakes. I was still building up my strength, fitness and endurance from my heart operation, but I was really pleased with where I was at. We asked Marcel to join us for the World Champs too – he was super-strong and despite not being overly impressed with our ability in France, I assured him we would be a completely different unit at the World Champs.

I had found a way to be around Kristina without it being complicated. On a spiritual level, I believed our lives were destined to intersect and that there was a life lesson there for me. I was excited to be racing with her in the World Champs, and because it was her last race before she switched to kayaking and I only had one more race in me, it was going to be a legendary one. I was looking forward to life after racing and Jodie was pregnant with our third child. It was time for a change.

The 2005 Adventure Racing World Champs were held in Westport, about four hours' drive from home. Even so, I knew very little of the country in that area and we had only done one training trip there – three days of hiking and biking. Because we would be racing with our own maps and food, in our own time zone, I felt we had a competitive advantage. The event had been the main goal of our year and the one race we had peaked for – this was the race we wanted to win. Actually, this was the race we *had* to win – we couldn't allow a foreign team to triumph on our turf again.

We built a strong support crew to help in our bid to win the title. Two days before the race we went to Drifters Café for coffee and a team talk, the aim of which was to get us all centred and focused for the race ahead. Together, we built a clear picture of what a champion team would look like and agreed that it would race by the following values:

- 100 per cent commitment to put the team first; not afraid to look bad as an individual if it meant putting the team first; doing it for the team
- great honest communicators; not holding back in asking for help or sharing ideas or concerns; constantly checking in with each other and supporting each other
- highly efficient and dedicated to doing everything as quickly and efficiently as possible
- never giving up, no matter what was happening.

While we all wanted to win the race, we placed more importance on striving to perform like the champion team of that vision. If we achieved the goal of racing like a champion team we would be satisfied, because the chances were high that if we met that goal, we would win the race too. It helped us to think of the team as a separate entity. The team was not just the four of us, it was a fifth being that we had created, and it was up to us to race hard and do our best for that new fifth party – the team. 'For the team' was the catch phrase. We talked about what the checkpoint staff, other teams and spectators would say when they saw this champion team. Things like, 'It's no wonder they won – every time we saw them they were a well-oiled machine, racing hard, supporting each other, having fun.'

Unusually for me, I was really nervous the morning of the start. I'd had a very sleepless night sweating over the navigation challenges that lay ahead. As the team's lead navigator, I felt I held many of the cards that would determine the race's outcome. I was confident, though, that I had the support of the team and that we were all in this together. The race started with a short 3 km run to the beach where we entered the kayaks and set out through 2- to 3-metre breaking waves. Our team quickly got clear of the break line and headed up the coast into fog, paddling on a compass bearing. After more than an hour of kayaking and a few dolphin encounters, it was time to start our approach into transition area one (TA1). By this stage the waves had increased significantly in size. Kristina and I ended up surfing in a wave that we actually tried to avoid, and while we made it to the beach unscathed, sadly our kayak didn't – the force of the wave had cracked the rear of our boat. Although Rich and Marcel sustained some rudder damage, they landed safely and we headed out on the first mountain-bike stage.

This ride took us through old coal-mining settlements and into the wilderness. The ultimate fantasy in an adventure race is to choose a navigation route that gains you considerable time over your opponents. The first trekking section turned into just that. We headed up into the mountains for what was going to be a 16-hour hike with tricky navigation and chose a route that was different to most teams. We took a risk and rather than using an old trail opted instead to drop into a river valley for a few hours and then bush-bash up a spur to the checkpoint. I was fairly certain it would be the quicker route, but never guessed it would be hours faster. Later that night, we met the field on a high ridge – en route to the checkpoint while we were on our way out – and figured we had a lead of about four hours. Although the race had been going for just 18 hours, we agreed that it felt better to be four hours in front than four hours behind. The highlight of the night was going through a section of bush full of calling kiwi – a comforting omen.

A quick raft section saw us back into another mammoth hike. This hike turned into an epic in all senses of the word. Once darkness set in, so did the rain and fog. Navigation went from challenging to bordering on impossible, but I managed to keep the team moving along the ridge. It was windy and cold, and the light of our torches was reflecting into the fog making it difficult to see, so we had to walk holding the torches beside our knees, which happened to be aching from all the steep ascending and descending. Finally, unable to make efficient forward progress, we holed up in our tent for two freezing-cold hours until daylight. While the night had gone, the rain and mist had not, making navigation still difficult. However, we finally found the route to the transition area at the end of the section. Thinking we would have lost our four-hour lead, we were astonished to hear instead that it had opened out to six hours. Even though we were having problems, it seemed other teams were having more.

The next bike stage was supposed to be 90 km and take us about 13 hours. It was 130 km and took us 20 hours. Arriving at a checkpoint at a hut during the night the staff invited us in for a hot drink. We thanked them but said we needed to stay focused on racing. They reckoned we had such a big lead – over 10 hours and maybe even 12 – that we needn't worry too much. Inside we went. Mid-race it was strange to be sitting in a warm hut, sipping a cup of tea and dunking gingernuts, reading the newspaper about the race we were currently in. 'Team captain said he was expecting the bike ride to be extremely demanding . . .' I had another cup of tea before we departed.

The next morning dawned fine and we were informed of a course change. Doing some quick math and calculating that if we wanted to get past the dark zone on the river-kayak stage we needed to race like cut cats, we set the tone for the day by running from the transition area up into the hills. We pulled out our team drug on this stage – an MP3 player – and gave everyone an equal dose. Once over Mount Kirwan the navigation got tricky again and our speed was slowed but we never gave up pushing hard, knowing that if we could get off the river that night the race was all but over. Once into Larry Creek we found some old bits of trail that enabled us to run most of the valley and reach our bikes for a quick sprint to the river. We got on the river about 5 p.m. which meant we had four hours to get to the end of the kayak stage, about 50 km downriver. Race director Geoff Hunt had predicted it would take most teams five to six hours to do this stage but believed our team could do it in around four.

All was going smoothly for the first quarter of the paddle until Rich and Marcel broke the rudder from their kayak which had been damaged in the surf from day one. They struggled to steer it so we decided to swap boats. While it required a little more effort, we made the dark zone with 15 minutes to spare and were rewarded with the knowledge that the other teams couldn't start on the river until 6 a.m., if they even got there by then. All we had to do now was close out the race with no injuries or silly mistakes. Ahead of us was a 14-hour hike, a cave, a bike ride and a beach run to the finish line.

This was a very special time for our team for a number of reasons. It was the final stage of what had been an epic week of suffering and discomfort. The next team was over 12 hours behind. We were about to win the World Champs. For Kristina and I, it marked the end of what had been an incredible journey in the world of adventure racing. In the final metres of the race, arm in arm, we all agreed that we had achieved our goal of racing to our values. We had striven to race like a champion team and we had done it. As expected, we won the race as well.

While the race had many hard times, it did not feel to us that we had raced very hard, but rather that we had timed our peak to perfection. You know when you peak perfectly because the ultimate performance will seem easy, and it did. Whenever I look back at some of the major events I have won, I can normally find a turning point in the race, and put some of our victory down to luck. We may have been lucky with the weather, a route choice, another team's error, or whatever it may be. This World Championships victory felt different. Sure we had some luck go our way, but we set the fastest times for all but one of the race legs. This proved that it was more than luck that won us the race. It was quite simply an unbeatable performance. Midway through the race when we had about a 12-hour lead, we knew that not only did the chasing teams have the mammoth job of catching us, they still had to get past us, and there wasn't a single moment in the race when we felt we couldn't have gone faster if we'd needed to. We were on fire for that race and no one could have put the fire out.

The finish line was right beside a popular restaurant at Tauranga Bay, a picturesque location with fine dining. When the waitress took my order, I requested five steaks and five lattes, one for each day I was on the course. Less than half an hour after finishing the race we lavishly indulged. That was me – I retired world champion. Thank you.

CHAPTER TWENTY-TWO

NEW FRONTIERS

The New Year kicked off in 2006 at a party with mates, hosted by a friend Lawrence who had established an accommodation business, the Golden Bay Hideaway, with a strong point of difference. Inspired by the level of construction he'd seen in Germany, he crafted a lodge that utilised modern energy-saving and environmental technology and materials which won an award for being New Zealand's most 'eco' building. He has since built another that has surpassed the original. I first met Lawrence at Outward Bound where he worked as an instructor. He has had a number of careers and professions, giving him a wealth of knowledge in a variety of fields, and I always find his take on things thought-provoking and insightful.

Parenting was one of his passions for a while and we had some lively discussions about the upbringing of children. Lawrence was quite appalled by how he saw people raising their kids these days, in terms of spoiling them, lack of discipline, and the general lack of respect many had for their parents. I don't like telling my kids that they can't do something, but I do teach them appropriate behaviour for different environments. For example, if they're playing with the campfire, I won't say, 'Be careful' or 'Don't touch that', but something more like, 'I wouldn't do that if I was you – I've been burnt doing the same thing.' It empowers them to weigh up the risk and make their own decision. Lawrence and I were in agreement that kids need to learn from an early age that life has consequences. One of the beauties of the outdoors is that there are very few limitations, but very real consequences.

As a parent I place high value on adventure and I encourage other parents to consider the importance of it. I know many parents whose children are involved in great activities – music, dance, sport, art, drama, the list is endless. While I think academics are important I don't consider them to be as critical as many parents do – they develop the mind whereas the outdoors develops the person, and both are equally important. As parents you naturally make the most of your skill sets and what you have access to, but I think adventure into nature is something that is an 'add-on' to whatever else you do. Once Maslow's hierarchy of needs is met in your household – food, shelter, love – the benefits of being immersed in nature are infinite. It doesn't have to be hard-core extreme sport, it's more about being removed from 'life as you know it' – TV, the internet, mobile phones and the daily comforts.

It's been important for me to teach my children a wide range of outdoor skills and introduce them to the seasonal environments, so that as they live their lives they are aware of the possibilities and ways to escape from the 'real world' and are able to understand what that means. Many of the lessons of the wilderness are transferable to everyday living – goal setting, perseverance, time management, hardship, adversity, making sacrifices, earning rewards, failure and success – to name a few. Expanding comfort zones is almost a given. Team sports teach many valuable lessons too – as well as the obvious, teamwork, there are tightly regulated rules, clear boundaries, uniforms, referees and officials, a scoreboard with losers and winners. In contrast, the outdoor sport environment offers up some other qualities – no boundaries, no limits, complete freedom, real risks, where the rules of engagement and consequences are set by Mother Nature. To my mind, there is no substitute for climbing a mountain.

Whilst in Golden Bay I woke one morning to go for a run in the national park – an exhilarating start to the day. Flying up a ridgeline that afforded wide views of the ocean, I noticed another runner climbing up from one of the bays about to intersect the trail I was on. As we drew closer I noted it was a female runner of slight build, and mindful that I'm a big dark man running in the forest and based on previous experiences could easily scare her, I sped up to get in front. But she was too quick and popped out onto the trail in front of me. I then had the dilemma of trying to get past her, except that as we ran on, I wasn't actually making any ground. Now, I'm not a runner of any particular acclaim, but it is rare for me to be outrun by a female in the hills, not that I minded.

Eventually I did catch up with her on a rocky descent and called out a friendly 'Hello there'. Turning to greet me, not at all alarmed, we started the next ascent together and I told her that I thought she was running really well. She thanked me and proceeded to tell me that she was from the UK and her friends were trying to convince her to race the Coast to Coast in a few weeks, so was out for a run to see how she felt. I remembered her name, Chrissie Wellington, and was impressed to see that she finished second in the two-day event. I was even more impressed when she went on to become one of the greatest female iron-distance athletes of all time, and to discover that she'd mentioned running with me in the Abel Tasman in the book she wrote a decade later. So now it's my turn to return the compliment.

After the summer holiday I was working full-time on the Eco Seagate event, an annual team-building conference using adventure racing as the mode to teach their corporate values and develop their employees. Seagate would fly several hundred staff from over a dozen different countries into New Zealand for a five-day adventure-based event with a price tag of about $2 million, and after working on the event for a number of years, I was asked to be the event director, manage the skills training and deliver the one-day race that concluded the week. It was a great chance to give something back to my long-time sponsor and perfectly aligned with my skills.

Although I gathered together a 30-strong team of some of the highest-skilled outdoor professionals in New Zealand, and from our end we delivered what was required, it wasn't a true reflection of our capabilities and that was largely due to me. I'd never worked at that level of corporate events before and I got incredibly frustrated by the inefficiencies and egos involved. In my view, the management was overstaffed and all it was doing was creating unnecessary layers and delays. I wanted the freedom and independence to get my side of the bargain seen to, but I was caught up in politics – the reality of a multi-million-dollar event, I guess. I didn't have the maturity to deal with it, and after doing it for a year I stepped away. Understandably, Jodie was livid that I'd walked away from an income stream because my ego couldn't tolerate taking orders from people significantly less qualified than me purely because they felt compelled to justify their roles, yet I saw it as a stand for what I believed in – something that Seagate stood for too.

Having quit what could have been a full-time occupation and now retired from adventure racing, I wasn't entirely sure what to do. I'd spent the best part of seven years travelling the world and the previous 20 years training for sporting events. I wasn't training for a race and I wasn't working, but thankfully the adventure-racing years had been financially kind so I had time to decide what I wanted to do next and didn't need to rush into anything. With Jodie pregnant we decided to spend the year adjusting to family life, a life without sport, and to make a plan for the next stage, the future. I had barrow-loads of work to do around our property and made a concerted effort to improve my golf. I couldn't complain. Life was amazing – living the dream, you could say.

In the autumn I was contacted by a television production company asking if they could feature me in a show entitled *True Grit*. The pitch was that each week they'd screen a half-hour episode on an interesting Kiwi, in sport, arts, business, music, a wide cross-section. It sounded interesting and I thought it would be good to have something like that to my credit in future. The highlight of making the show was visiting the Sir Edmund Hillary Outdoor Pursuits Centre (now known as Hillary Outdoors) near Tongariro National Park. I was there to support a youth adventure race and do a presentation, but unbeknown to me, Sir Ed was there too and he attended my talk. It was extremely humbling to be addressing an audience that included the conqueror of Everest and I was delighted when he asked a few questions about adventure racing. (I'll be honest though – he did seem to doze off a few times during my talk.)

Jodie wanted to do an adventure before she got too heavily pregnant and we were keen to take Jessie and Zephyr to Samoa so we headed over there for three weeks. Jodie's good friend Cindy had biked around the main islands Upulo and Savai'i while on a kite-boarding trip a few years earlier and recommended it as a fun way to explore. Loaded with two bikes and a trailer that had seats for Jessie and Zephyr plus gear, and much to the disbelief of my family over there, we headed out of our village Afega with the goal of riding around both the main islands. Cycle touring in Samoa was not common back then – in fact, I'd even say we were the second ever cycle tourers to pedal around after Cindy. The locals rode bikes occasionally but certainly not in a recreational sense. They couldn't believe what we were doing, biking around the islands with a one- and a three-year-old, especially as Jodie was clearly pregnant too.

The total distance around both islands is only about 400 km, so spread out over two weeks was easily manageable. There are regular villages with some sort of accommodation on offer, typically a beach fale (hut), and most places could provide meals if needed. We had a glorious trip, living on the beaches, biking along the quiet roads (only busy around Apia) and enjoying the warm tropical climate. After the trip I put together a few notes about cycle touring in Samoa and passed them on to friends who we felt would enjoy the trip, which they subsequently have. Always happy to promote Samoa as an adventure destination, I also supplied a travel agent with the information. Since then, bicycle touring there has grown into a significant business with hundreds of visitors cycling around each year – thanks at least in part (I like to think) to the half-caste Samoan dude, his Palangi wife and their two kids.

Spending time in Samoa gave me some more time to ponder what I wanted to do career-wise. My qualifications and skills were in outdoor education, and while I was still passionate about that industry, the earning potential was relatively low. I needed a career that provided an opportunity to make more money. I did pick up a part-time job working for SPARC (Sport and Recreation, later rebranded Sport New Zealand) as part of a team of athletes on an ambassador programme. Our job was to visit secondary schools around the country and deliver a workshop to their elite sporting youth, the next Kiwi champions. I met many incredible young people, some of whom have gone on to represent New Zealand at their chosen sport, and it was privileged to work on the programme for eight years before the funding dried up. For my career, though, I needed a project and continued to search for what that could be. I bounced ideas around with various people, and a friend who had recently been through a similar life stage gave me some useful advice that he'd gleaned from a book. It basically went along the lines of ticking three boxes. Whatever I thought I might do, it had to answer the following three questions:

1. Are you good at it?
2. Do you enjoy it?
3. Does it make money?

I had untold ideas, but as I asked myself these questions, nothing was answering yes to all three. Eventually, after some serious reflection, I decided that a commercial events management company had the potential to make money. The trick was either to grow a major event or to get contracts to deliver events on behalf of clients. I had been involved in sport my entire life and had run a business and a professional racing team, plus my career in outdoor education and adventure tourism meant I had a wide skill set in managing people safely in the outdoors. I wasn't out to make a fortune – I just wanted a lifestyle and to be able to feed my children.

My plan was to launch a company with ten new sporting events in the South Island – trail running, kayaking, road cycling, mountain biking, navigation and adventure racing. I wanted to do original things, to create new markets. The events industry was competitive and I knew many of the other directors personally, so rather than start events that would lure people away from other events, I wanted to offer experiences that were not currently being provided. Originality was the key. There were some magnificent areas of the country that were not being utilised, so my other aim was to create opportunities for people to visit places that they wouldn't normally get to see.

The decision to start an events company finally being made, I knew that I could speed up the process and its chances of success if I had capital investment. Travelling home from France in 2005 I'd stopped off in California and hung out with Steve Luczo for a few days. We did some mountain biking, went to a major league baseball game, and chatted about life in general. Through Balance Vector,

Steve was keen to help me transition to life after racing. So I went to him with a proposal – rather than sponsor an adventure-racing team (which back then typically cost around US$100,000 for a season), how would he feel about investing in an events company, a provider rather than a user? Thanks to the incredible generosity of Steve and Balance Vector, I was able to launch Mission Events Ltd at a very professional level, without the stress of carrying huge debt. I spoke with Steve about repayment options a number of times, especially should the company succeed, but all he said to me was, 'Help others and help the environment – that's all the repayment required.'

Balance Vector was also enabling Cindy to run her women's kite-boarding event which was being held in Fiji that year so I helped on that too, as safety staff. My second daughter, Tide, was born in July, and Jodie and I were thrilled to have another healthy child. I'd been hoping for a girl because having two boys could change the energy in the house to a full-on destruction mentality which I didn't think I'd handle very well. Two girls should be a bit more mellow, with maybe fewer parenting demands on my part, and more responsibility swinging to Jodie's department. However, with three children in the nest we decided that was enough and took precautions to ensure a fourth didn't turn up in the family photos.

During the year I got a letter from a lawyer representing Mission Winery from Hawke's Bay threatening to sue me if we didn't stop using the word Mission in our company name. It was hard to take them seriously – the chances of someone going online to buy a bottle of chardonnay and accidentally ending up on our website and entering a 100 km trail run instead weren't high – but our lawyer suggested we just change the company name and move on because it wasn't worth wasting time and money over. So to avoid upsetting any more worriers, we renamed the company Ten Events Ltd, because we were running ten events at the time, and it seemed unlikely we'd be stopped for using the word 'ten'.

Meantime I was keeping fit, running and paddling most days, mainly for local orienteering and ocean surf-ski races. My plan was to participate in events for pleasure, so I did the local 24-hour race at home and the Southern Traverse, which in 2006 was a 24-hour race, winning both of them. Even with a young family we continued to live an adventurous lifestyle and were determined not to let having small children change things drastically. It didn't mean we needed to be kayaking off waterfalls and tearing down rocky trails on bikes every day, but we did intend to spend a lot of time in nature and having a dynamic existence. The vehicle for this lifestyle was our Toyota 4WD van, which we converted into the ultimate road-tripping machine. It enabled us to travel easily, explore and live a simple life – we discovered that it was much easier looking after three young children when we were on the road versus being at home. For that reason, we've hardly been at home since the kids were born. We're constantly on the move, either planning, in the midst of, or cleaning up from an adventure trip. Our kids, like most kids, get bored easily but when we're out on adventures in the outdoors they never complain of boredom. They may complain about the weather, the temperature, the sandflies, the level of difficulty of the challenge at hand, but never of being bored.

CHAPTER TWENTY-THREE

NOTORIOUS FAIL

What really motivates me is to create freedom and flexibility, so it makes no sense to bury myself so deep in work that it becomes my entire existence. Lots of people will work like beavers to enjoy just a few weeks' holiday a year. I prefer to work like a bear – go hard for a season and then hibernate. It's the same in sport – long arduous hours of constant training deliver little benefit, but planning your season, when to peak, when to recover, when to improve your weaknesses and when to play to your strengths, is what creates a more dynamic and motivating environment. That's the theory anyway. Although the goal was to keep life simple and focus on the events company while adjusting to family life with three children, the year couldn't have turned out any busier.

In January and February I was organising biking events in Southland and the Queenstown area. One of them was a 100 km mountain-bike event called Bike Wakatipu and the other was a five-day road cycle from Arrowtown to Lake Tekapo called the Alps Tour. Running the events inspired me to ride regularly and enter a few myself where I wasn't organising. The highlight of the season was winning the 2007 Magnum Grape Ride, a hugely successful 100 km road-cycling event that attracted several thousand riders, more because of the way I won it rather than the win itself. That year they introduced two new categories – the Magnum and the Speed Bunnies (a bit of a silly name as it was targeted at New Zealand's elite riders). The Magnum riders were to do 200 km, two laps of the circuit, starting and finishing near Blenheim, while the Speed Bunnies would start in Picton and do one full lap and a partial lap to total 160 km. There was reasonable prize money for the Speed Bunnies but I opted to race the longer-distance Magnum, plus I knew the pace in the Speed Bunnies would be a little too hot for my endurance legs.

The start time of the Magnum was 6 a.m., and as we waited a discussion began amongst my friends, all strong riders, about the fact that the Speed Bunnies were starting in Picton, just 40 km away, at 7 a.m. We joked about arriving in Picton at 7 a.m. and hooking onto the back of them. The more we joked about it, the less of a joke it became, so we decided to try. Right off the start, Chris Burr and I gunned it. Before the rest of the field knew anything about it, a small group of us were up the road and riding hard to keep our average speed above 40 km/h. Our speed dropped as we hit the hills, but we fought on, watching the clock. As we crested the last rise into Picton the clock ticked 7 a.m. The Speed Bunnies were under way, about 2 km ahead. All of us bike racers knew they could be rolling for a few kilometres warming up, so we kept chasing and after 10 km we caught sight of them and they hadn't started racing properly yet. Digging deeper, after 60 km of riding a team time trial we caught the Speed Bunnies, oblivious to our presence, and sat on the back of the bunch high-fiving each other, the other Magnum riders' chances of a podium result effectively ended. Soon afterwards the Speed Bunnies started to race and we were getting sucked along with them. No longer needing to be passengers, we began to mingle in with the bunch until a race official in a following vehicle announced over the loudspeaker: 'Magnum riders, you cannot ride with the Speed Bunnies!'

I rolled back to the official car and asked them what they expected us to do. I explained that we'd broken away from our race, caught the Speed Bunnies and now we were stuck with them. We couldn't ride away from them and he couldn't expect us to slow down – we were in a race too. He understood but didn't know what to do. Chatting at 45 km/h, eventually he said to me that we could ride with the Speed Bunnies but we couldn't do any work. I said that was fine with me but it wouldn't be fine with them, especially if we got in a breakaway. The race official understood, so pulling up alongside the peloton he announced: 'The Magnum Riders who have caught you are allowed to ride with you but they have been instructed they are not allowed to do any work.' A loud laugh erupted from the riders, many of whom were our mates – they thought it was priceless.

So, for the next two and a half hours, we sat on the back, saving copious amounts of energy while being slipstreamed along. As the ride went on, the bunch grew smaller as riders got dropped, and while I managed to hang on, Chris lost contact when he got a flat tyre. I ended up riding with the breakaway group and winning the Magnum race, riding the 200 km in under five hours, a time unlikely to be beaten for quite some time as the following year they changed the start times so Magnum riders couldn't possibly catch the Speed Bunnies.

The last race I organised that summer season was a three-day multisport event in the Marlborough Sounds. My friend and former team-mate Richard Ussher was doing the race and we discussed the possibility of entering the 2007 Adventure Racing World Championships in Scotland, mainly because it was a place I was keen to visit. Rich had won the World Champs in 2005 with me and again in 2006 with an American team. He was keen to race again in a Kiwi team but also with his partner, Elina, who was an experienced adventure racer from Finland, now living in New Zealand. Aaron Prince, another Kiwi athlete and ace navigator who was doing the multisport race, was keen to join us, so Rich had a team but not a sponsor. I decided to ask Steve Luczo if there was a chance Balance Vector would sponsor us, and Steve came back with 'Sure, why not?' Now building up to the 2007 World Champs, Rich and I entered the New Zealand Rogaine Championships, which is a form of orienteering whose aim is to score as many points as you can in 24 hours by navigating between control flags. I'd managed to get running fit because a few weeks earlier I had organised an ultra-trail run through the St James Walkway and had run it myself a few times while planning the event. Our map and compass skills, combined with our fitness and ability to run for 24 hours, rewarded us with the win.

It seemed that now I had stopped racing full-time and created more space in my life, opportunities were coming at me from all directions. Another one of these came through a friend, Tony Davies, who worked in the film and television industry, to design and manage outdoor challenges for a TV show in China. It involved approximately four one-month trips to visit the filming areas, plan the challenges for the participants, and then finally shoot and produce the content. It was in essence an outdoor adventure television game show where 16 international athletes took part in an elimination contest to produce the final six contestants. Once we had the final six, we did a road trip to seven different challenge sites throughout China. I had a staff of five working directly for me plus the support of the other Chinese staff. Overall it was an incredibly interesting job but the post-production side of it was a complete shambles and the shows ended up being rather pathetic. It was a pity as the basic concept was quite good. However, I got to live and breathe China and learn more about the culture, and although I'd had enough after four months, it was still a rewarding experience.

With some effort and creativity, I'd managed to do some good training in China while juggling the workload, and I felt fit and ready for the Adventure Racing World Championships. After two years away from adventure racing at that level I was excited to be there and we had a great team. The race, however, didn't go well for us. Part of the problem was that Aaron and I were both former team captains but Rich was the captain for this race, and it also became apparent early on that Elina only felt comfortable communicating with Rich and going to him for support, leaving Aaron and I somewhat in the dark as to what was happening and placing more workload on Rich. The other issue was that because I had sourced the sponsor, I felt an additional obligation. On top of that, although the course was engaging, the event management didn't suit our style. Kiwi events tend to rely heavily on the spirit of competition and fair play, whereas the UK race director had imposed so many rules and regulations you could hardly move without breaking some obscure rule or other. After the prologue there were so many teams with penalties that there was a call to wipe it and restart the race the next day, which was rejected. Some teams ended up being cut out of the race after the first day because they had to serve these farcical penalties. Because our team never really fired we were only mildly competitive and spent much of the race chasing second and third place.

After some particularly nasty and sustained cold weather, Rich got hypothermia during a kayak stage down a lake, despite wearing all the right gear and doing all he could to warm up. It was early afternoon, daylight hours were diminishing and we weren't sure how serious Rich's condition was, so we diverted across the lake to a series of buildings as a safety precaution. Aaron and I felt it was important to have access to a phone and roads should it be necessary. We landed on the opposite shore to discover it was a massive castle-type mansion with many sections, and spotting someone in the kitchen of one of the buildings, Aaron and I walked over the lawn and knocked on the window. Looking quite alarmed, a guy swiftly came out and proceeded to tell us that we couldn't be there and had to leave. As he escorted us back to the kayaks we explained about the race and Rich's condition so he told us to wait. Minutes later another guy came out, the security manager of the estate (who we found out later was an ex-British SAS soldier), and he took us to his residence where Elina helped Rich shower, put on dry clothes and get into a bed. We were given food and hot drinks but told we would need to leave in a few hours. About 10 km down the lakeshore was a hut, and we could load our kayaks with dry firewood, extra blankets and food and relocate to it once Rich's core temperature came up. It was an extremely generous gesture and we were even allowed to use the internet to find out where the other teams were. A few hours later Rich started to improve and we paddled to the hut, got the fire roaring, had some more food and slept for the night, hoping a podium placing was still possible.

The next morning we were all feeling re-energised. There was still about six hours of the stage remaining, kayaking and portaging, but because we'd lost the best part of 12 hours helping Rich get back to full speed, we needed to start the next hiking stage by 6 p.m. to stay on the full course. As the day went on, however, it became increasingly apparent that we wouldn't make the cut-off, even though we were going as fast as we could. By 5.30 p.m. we could see the end of the stage and it looked more than 30 minutes away, but we gave it everything and arrived at the transition area a few minutes before 6 p.m. It would take us at least 10 minutes to pack our hiking gear and sort our kayak gear though. Because the race had started nearly an hour late despite the fact half the teams including us were ready and waiting on the start line at the stated time, we hoped the race director would cut us some slack and allow us to continue. We were in sixth place and all set for a very strong finish. Staff at the site spoke to him via radio but he refused to budge – we were short coursed. It was utterly absurd that in a World Championships event only five teams finished the full course.

Despite the disappointing result, I'd got to see Scotland for the first time so I was happy. We had done an amazing sea-kayak paddle from the Isles of Eigg and Rum back to the Scottish mainland, swum across Loch Ness, descended a deep chasm leaping off waterfalls, mountain biked and hiked in the Highlands, and climbed Ben Nevis. But after a month in China and three weeks in Scotland, I was eager to get home. Unaware until I checked in at Heathrow that my return flight went through the United States, I didn't have a visa to pass through, so when I transited at LAX it was straight back to the zoo of secondary immigration. While they chewed on donuts the Air New Zealand flight I was meant to be on was loaded and waiting. When a staff member, an older Maori woman, stormed into the immigration room announcing she was looking for one of her passengers, the officers said I was not ready to be released. But she took my hand and started to lead me away, telling them very sternly that if I didn't get on the plane, it would be delayed for hours while my bags were taken off and she wasn't going to allow that to happen. They sat there gobsmacked as she led me away. Impressive.

One of the events I had always been keen to organise was a women's adventure race. For most of my adventure-racing years it had been a fairly common gripe from male racers that they couldn't find a female – or at least a decent female – to race with, meaning someone fast enough and strong enough. At that stage I'd done most of my racing with Kathy and Kristina who were considered two of the world's top female adventure racers, and I knew quite a few other outdoor women who could complete an adventure race without any problems whatsoever, except they weren't that interested in joining a team with three males – especially the type of males who view the female as nothing more than a condition of entry. So the question I asked myself was how could adventure racing be made more appealing to women? The answer was the inaugural 2007 Spring Challenge.

In my view, the two main barriers to women doing adventure racing were team composition and kayaking. Whilst it is my favourite sport, kayaking requires equipment and specific skills that need to be trained. The plan for the Spring Challenge was to make two big changes. The first was to replace the kayaking with white-water rafting and the second was to make the teams all female. Friends in the rafting industry told me that the only time we could rent rafts more cheaply was when all the guides were back in New Zealand after rafting the northern hemisphere summer, which would be at the start or end of the New Zealand summer, but for obvious reasons the start of summer had the best river flows. After juggling dates it was decided that we'd run the event in the spring, hence the name. We also decided to change the typical adventure-racing team size from four down to three, as we could then fit two teams into each raft comfortably. Besides, getting a team of three together had to be easier than a team of four. I selected Hanmer Springs in Canterbury as the location as it was a popular weekend destination, easily accessible and a good place to take families, figuring that most of the participants would likely have kids too.

This was the one event in our line-up that was not targeting an existing market and I had modest hopes for it. All our other events were providing options in established sports but there were no women's adventure races and equally very few women adventure racers. With minimal marketing and not overinvesting in the first event, I told the rafting provider that we could expect, at best, maybe 20 teams. But by the time race day came around we had 109 teams – 327 women. This really stretched me as I'd never expected that many entries and I was already having an incredibly busy year, spending nearly five months overseas. To add to the tension, Jodie was racing so she wasn't helping with the event in any way. When I set up the company I asked Mark Rayward, a friend and colleague from Outward Bound days who had also done some adventure racing including a few Southern Traverses, to work with me on the events. Mark was working with me in China for two months that year so we barely had time to plan a major event in New Zealand while delivering another one in China. However, with help from friends and by calling in some favours we pulled it off – just. I wasn't sure if the event was a one-hit wonder or if we had tapped into a large market, but the feedback was all positive and most teams spoke of returning the following year.

I learned a valuable lesson in event directing that year too. Probably my most creative event idea was a 12-hour race called the Control 90. It was divided into three four-hour stages – kayaking, hiking and mountain biking. It started at 6 a.m. and there was a two-hour break between each stage. During each four-hour stage, teams of two had to score as many of the 30 controls (checkpoints) as they could. As health and safety plus risk management was starting to strangle the life out of adventure sport, I was keen to protect the integrity of authentic adventure (I still am). So many events are dumbed down to such a simple level that they end up being boring. The Control 90 started with a four-hour ocean kayak from Okiwi Bay to the outer islands of Croisilles Harbour. A north-west storm system was hitting and it was big seas and high winds with an outgoing tide – epic paddling conditions for an experienced ocean kayaker but potential highly dangerous for the less skilled and timid. Despite the bad weather, I approved the stage to run because teams could stay in the tranquil waters of Okiwi Bay and only venture out into the exposed ocean as much as they felt comfortable with, and I briefed that clearly. I put trust in the teams that they would stay within their limitations, which in hindsight was a mistake. There is a false sense of security that because you're in an event you're safe, so people will stretch themselves further, and that was the mentality I was trying to break from.

After four hours almost all the teams had returned, some with wide eyes and tales of extreme conditions. I had two safety vessels on the water so I knew what the conditions were like. They rescued a few capsized kayaks and had to tell a couple of teams, clearly out of their depth, to turn around and head to calmer waters. The worrying started when our timekeeper informed me that one team was not back. I sent the support boats back out to search for it and I drove to a high view point where I could scan the ocean below with binoculars. The conditions far out were serious. The waves were metres high and the wind was sending white blasts of water screaming over the surface. If a team was out there, fallen out of their kayak or, worse, separated from their kayak, it was a fatality waiting to happen.

I'm blessed with Samoan genes and nothing worries me too much, but I was deeply worried at that moment. It was nearing midday and we needed to get the other teams under way on the next stage, mountain biking. I called the coastguard and let them know we were missing a team and they said they'd despatch the rescue helicopter. We were just minutes away from launching an emergency search-and-rescue operation when the two guys we were looking for rolled up on their bikes for the next stage. It turned out that they had finished the kayak but the timekeeper missed them and they had gone into the village to a friend's house to warm up. They hadn't done anything wrong – it was our error. Relief would be an understatement. But it taught me what it felt like to be faced with an incident of potentially disastrous proportions in an event I was running, and it has shaped my decision-making ever since. Typically I'm an audacious character and my personality goes into the events I manage, but I've come to accept that if people want extreme adventure and risk-taking, they need to do that in their own time.

CHAPTER TWENTY-FOUR
NARROW FOCUS

In 2008, the second year of the business, I was largely focused on running events and building the company. My plan was to run each event three times and then decide which should be dropped, keeping the ones that enough people supported to make them economically viable. The year had started with a fun summer road trip to Te Anau and Queenstown for the mountain-bike and cycling events before heading back home for the start of the school year as Jessie was now five. On her first day she wanted to bike to school with me, so off we went. Like all parents, five years old seems young to be fending for yourself, but Jessie was excited and happy to start at Tasman School, a small local primary with about 80 children.

I ran two more events that summer, the St James Ultramarathon and the Multi-Marlborough three-day race in the Marlborough Sounds. I was learning about the industry fast, running so many events it was a crash course on what worked and what didn't. Multi-Marlborough was one that I was positive would succeed. I had been racing multisport myself for 15 years and I believed I had designed the best circuit ever. We expected it to grow into a monster event but after running it twice we didn't even have enough people to host the third event, despite the fact we had poured vast resources into it. The Spring Challenge, by contrast, had hardly any investment made in it but was looking to be a huge success. It highlighted to me that if the product and timing are right, it'll work. So to test the waters in the North Island, we launched the Autumn Challenge at Lake Taupo, and were pleased to have 80 teams take part in the six-hour event at the end of April. Afterward, we spent May touring the upper North Island with the kids. These family road trips around the events we were organising became unforgettable times in raising our children. We'd camp in our van in idyllic locations, normally on the coast, and the kids would enjoy endless hours of play and exploration at the beaches. When possible we would cook on open fires and stargaze the evenings away. The trips were relaxing but intense holidays at the same time. With our outdoor instructor hats on, we were facilitating powerful team-building experiences for our three kids.

Browsing Air New Zealand's grabaseat site one winter morning I spotted flights from Nelson to Nouméa for $100 return and purchased five tickets on the spur of the moment. 'What are we going to do in New Caledonia for two weeks?' Jodie asked when she got home. I didn't know. We certainly didn't want to sit around a resort for a fortnight. The road network didn't seem to offer any viable cycle-touring routes, and the more we looked at maps, a water-based trip seemed our best option. In particular, a 100 km section of coastline between Thio and Yate where there appeared to be no roads and very few settlements, but an abundance of beaches, islands and rivers flowing into the ocean. Unable to find kayaks in New Caledonia, I researched options to travel with boats from New Zealand. Incept Marine in Taihape make a vast range of inflatable boats, canoes, kayaks and rafts, and perusing their range we decided on a four-person inflatable canoe weighing only 20 kg, which inflated would provide ample room for the five of us plus gear, keeping in mind that Tide was now one (nearly two), Zefa was three (nearly four) and Jessie was five. We also managed to source some basic information about campsites, places of interest and where to find fresh water from a local kayak company that had run a couple of trips there before.

We were dropped at our starting point by a taxi and asked the driver to collect us in 10 days' time 100 km along the coast. The boat was fully laden with all our supplies, food and water when we set off. In a bid to limit gear and save weight, I'd decided that we would only take personal floatation devices (PFDs) for Tide and Zephyr, based on the logic that Jessie was a big girl and a good swimmer and that the boat itself was a giant floatation device. It felt incredibly liberating to be finally on the water, soaking up the sun, a pleasant tailwind aiding us along the coastline, outward bound on an adventure. Given we only needed to average 10 km per day, our plan was to paddle for the mornings and then set up camp and spend the afternoons relaxing in the shade, swimming and exploring on land. Fortuitously, this schedule happened to coincide perfectly with the tides as low tide was in the afternoons when most of the beaches couldn't be easily reached from the water, guarded by exposed coral reefs.

It was very quiet and secluded as we paddled north along the uninhabited shores. Campsites were easy to find – it was just a matter of moving a few coconuts and leaves to erect the tent. The snorkelling was incredible, possibly the best we've done, the marine life abundant, including turtles, reef sharks and a huge spectrum of tropical fish. The canoe proved to be an excellent viewing platform for the kids. We could simply drift over the coral and they would be entertained for hours, observing life beneath the surface. On the second morning after a superb night camping, we were paddling over coral reefs as the day heated up, and as we rounded one headland Jessie was keen to snorkel to look at the fish. I jumped in first and then she followed. Adjusting my mask, I looked down and immediately grabbed Jessie and threw her back into the canoe. 'There's a shark under here!' I murmured to Jodie as I climbed back in. It was a reef shark, and I'm now aware that they're harmless, but there were bull sharks along that coast so it was best to be cautious.

By the end of the second day we couldn't imagine how this trip could get any better. We really felt like we'd stumbled onto the trip of a lifetime. We were having a grand adventure, it was hot, the sea was perfect for swimming, the beaches were pristine, the camping was peaceful and, to top it all off, the kids were loving it. Time, days and beaches drifted by as we paddled forward. However, after nine days of either no wind or tailwind in favourable conditions, on the final day the weather changed. A storm was brewing. The wind was lashing the idyllic little island we had camped on and whitecaps were forming on the waves as we readied the boat for a quick getaway. We had a kite on board and the conditions were picking up, so we thought it'd be a fun activity to show the kids how a kite could power the canoe. With the boat at the water's edge, we needed to launch the kite on land, keep it in the sky and powered up, then get into the canoe. Combined with the weather, the kids could sense the urgency and perhaps also the danger, although it wasn't much.

We managed to get it all working and in no time were speeding away downwind towards our destination some 20 km away. As we flew into the channel the waves started to grow in size and I decided it would be good if Tide and Zefa put their PFDs on. Jodie was busy flying the kite and I was occupied steering the boat through the waves so I asked Jessie to help fit the PFDs. She sensed that we were close to a line as we hadn't needed to wear them so far and she started to get upset, partly because she didn't have a PFD herself but mainly because she was feeling scared. I told her to grow up and help her little brother and sister. That didn't help. By now the wind was gusting over 20 knots, nearly pulling Jodie out of the boat when the gusts hit, the occasional wave was 2 metres and we were racing downwind at about 13 km/h – really fast for the type of boat we were in. But Jessie was really upset, crying, needing support, and the other two were starting to worry. Reluctantly we had to drop the kite and sort out the crew. Once the kite was down there was no easy way to relaunch it so it was paddling from there on out.

Looking back, I can't believe we (I) expected Jessie to stay calm and composed in that environment. It was unfair to expect that of a five-year-old, but she, like all our kids, had proven very sturdy in the outdoors from a young age. But it's easy to think of your eldest child as old, regardless of their age, simply by comparison to their younger siblings. I would never expect the same from Tide at the same age, simply because she's the youngest. While the finish to the trip was a little epic, it is still to this day one of the best family adventures we've had.

Not long back in the country, we had a distressing experience to cope with. Jackie, one of Jodie's best friends since they were children, who had suffered with depression, took her life, leaving behind her two boys who were of similar ages to our older kids. We couldn't believe it had happened, that she was gone. It made me appreciate how serious depression is. I'd always felt that the majority of people on antidepressants simply needed to sort their shit out – life's tough, harden up. But I could see with Jackie that she was way beyond just sorting things out, she was tormented by mental illness and was obviously backed into a corner where she felt she had no alternative. I developed a new respect for the illness and empathy for the people who struggle with it. While nothing in comparison, the time was made even more trying because both Tide and I had pneumonia. That period really sucked.

During the winter I was approached by a community group who were setting up a new multisport event in the North Island called the Lake to Lighthouse. The group had some funding support from Genesis Energy and skills in event management but not specific to multisport, so I was employed as an advisor. The race began at Lake Waikaremoana, in the midst of Te Urewera National Park, on the first day, with the second day spent travelling to the historic lighthouse at the small coastal town of Wairoa. Mark and I spent a few days going through the course with the race director Chris Joblin and made some recommendations. We then travelled back a few months later to help deliver the event. It was delivered in an exceptional manner but unfortunately it was at a period where multisport participation was declining and it was also a remote location for people to get to. Of significance to me, however, was that it was where I first met Sophie Hart and, although we didn't know it at the time, we would become influential in each other's lives in the near future.

Back in the South Island the Spring Challenge was held in the coastal town of Kaikoura and it had exploded. We had a full field of 200 teams – 600 women – our maximum field size. Mark and I had spent a good deal of time exploring the back country and had designed two intrepid courses for the six- and 12-hour categories. We hoped to use a couple of major valley systems for the race routes and had concerns about how rain would impact on these valleys, so we consulted some knowledgeable locals about the weather. The common answer was: 'That river only floods once in a hundred years.' Accordingly, we pressed on with our planning. Just six weeks before the event the Kaikoura coast was hit with major flooding – what the weather forecasters called a 'one in a hundred year weather event' – so we were comforted by the fact that it would be another 100 years before a similar flood. We couldn't have been more wrong.

Arriving in Kaikoura the week before the event to get organised, the forecast showed some heavy weather approaching. As the system advanced it became apparent that severe weather was going to hit and heavy rain warnings were in place. With the event starting on Saturday, on Wednesday night the rivers were in torrential flood with more rain approaching, and snow, and we accepted that we didn't have a race course. We had two days to design a new event. It was incredibly stressful and we worked almost non-stop for 80 hours to deliver the race. The courses we ended up with weren't great, but in light of what we had a few days earlier, they worked. Thankfully, the weather was fine for the race weekend except for a rapidly moving southerly sweeping over the area on the Saturday night. It was a huge lesson on weatherproofing courses, and making sure a course could handle bad weather became the primary focus in our course design from that point on. Jodie had raced, with her team placing second, and afterward I told her that she couldn't compete in the event any more as I needed her help in organising. We left Kaikoura knowing that the Spring Challenge was going to be our flagship event.

Perhaps the highlight of my sport that year was the Rollos 24-hour adventure race. Jodie asked me if I could race it with her and two friends, both females, Fleur Lattimore and Nic Kelly. They wanted to go hard and be challenged, but not have the responsibility of having to navigate, as the race director Chris James had said the event would include some tricky navigation. The team goal was to finish the race respectably – the girls wanted to cross the line knowing they'd given it everything they had, and placings and positions didn't enter the equation. Between them they had eight children under five years old, so training time was limited, but I did a few training sessions with them and was impressed with the speed they could maintain. We were going to be competing against some very good teams of three men and one woman, and I couldn't see how our speed was going to differ all that much from theirs, except in the kayaking stage, although with my navigation skills and local knowledge combined with sensible pacing, we could go well. Close to the race, Jodie wanted my honest opinion on how I thought the team would go. I told her I thought we had a good chance of winning. She thought I was out of my mind but I did manage to convince her to at least be open to the possibility of winning, because if you rule it out as an option before the race, then you'll never stand a chance.

The race started and finished at Kaiteriteri Beach with the course briefing on the Friday night. Much of the race was in the Abel Tasman National Park and surrounding area and the first stage was a 20 km paddle into the park. The girls were all capable paddlers but we were up against very strong male paddlers so we expected to lose time on that stage. However, as I was going through the maps and rules, I saw a potential short cut that could save us a good chunk of time. There was a checkpoint at Anchorage Bay which was around a headland known locally as the Mad Mile. I had guided around this stretch of water hundreds of times and knew that it was much faster if you wanted to get to Anchorage Bay to land at a small beach called Watering Cove and do a short walk over a saddle. The concern was that this meant leaving the kayaks on the beach but they were not listed as compulsory equipment. The only compulsory equipment for the stage, other than the gear we needed for the entire race, was our PFDs, spray decks, pumps and safety flags so, by adventure-racing standards, provided you carried what was listed as compulsory, you weren't breaking any rules. I pitched it to the girls and we decided to do it.

Once the race was under way we were paddling well, sitting mid-pack, but watching the leading teams pull away. At the rate the front teams were paddling I estimated we'd lose at least 30 minutes to them on the stage, which is quite a bit for a race expected to take the winners 12 hours. As we paddled through the park our team diverted to Watering Cove, trotted over the hill with our gear and were the first to reach the checkpoint at Anchorage. We could see the lead teams coming into the bay so we'd saved at least 15 minutes, probably more. Happy with the outcome, we ran back to our kayaks and returned to Kaiteriteri Beach for the next stage. Because we were now in front and had a good chance of finishing the stage in the lead, everyone was motivated and we paddled better on the return trip, exiting the kayaks with a handy lead. On bikes we had a short ride to Marahau to start the first trek. We rode well but I knew we would be getting pulled in by the chase teams and that some of them wouldn't be too happy with our short cut on the kayak stage.

We started the walk in first position and moved quickly on the coastal track, although once at Tinline Bay we could hear the voices of the team behind us. But I knew another short cut through the forest that saved us a further 10 to 15 minutes, so we were soon out of sight again. The girls were strong hikers and held a very good pace climbing to the Canaan Downs area, and eventually a team did catch us but they were only moving fractionally faster so we ended the stage not far behind them in second place. Next up was a mountain-bike ride that was mainly downhill. Jodie and Nic were both fast descenders so we didn't lose any significant time on that stage either. A couple of teams caught and passed us but we all started the final hiking stage close together. It was getting dark now as we climbed back to the Canaan area. Walking was a discipline in which our team could match or better most of the others and I was particularly motivated as the next stage was night orienteering on one of the most challenging maps in the region. I was confident I could navigate that stage faster than any of the other navigators in the race and that it was our chance to win. After that stage, there was a reasonably easy mountain-bike ride to the finish that was primarily downhill.

By the time we reached Canaan Downs for the second time it was below zero degrees and pitch black. We had managed to move into second place not far in front of the third and fourth teams. The leading team had started the orienteering about 20 minutes ahead of us. When I saw the orienteering map I estimated it would take us about two hours so I knew we'd catch them at some point. Getting past them would be the challenge as it would be easy for them to follow us to the end of the stage if they chose to. As expected, the navigation was challenging but we moved smoothly through the controls. Nearing the midway point we could see the lights of the team in front. We had to be really smart as we needed to lose them as fast as we could, so we hung back a little so we could catch them at the next control. Luckily, it was in an area with a series of small ravines under a beech forest canopy. Our plan was to get into the ravines and spread out so the other team wouldn't know who the person was who would punch our control card at the control flag. If they were going to try and follow us (which maybe they weren't) they would likely assume I would have the card, so provided they stayed close to me I would lead them to the control.

To counter this assumption Jodie had the control card and the plan was for me to go close to the control and whisper to her where it was while I pretended to still be looking for it and move away. It unfolded exactly that way. The other team started moving towards us searching for the control, and while I can't say they were deliberately following us, to be safe I pointed Jodie to the control and kept going, saying out loud that the control must be a little further on. Everyone followed including Jodie who had swiftly punched the control. We kept going and soon after-wards the other team knew we had gone past it, although they may not have known we had got the control already. Now we pushed even faster and made it to the end of the stage. Knowing the next team wouldn't be far back we transitioned rapidly to bikes and sped off on the final stage, the race win tantalisingly within grasp.

It was freezing cold but we had rugged up for the big descent. With less than 15 km to go, we had one final climb over the Marahau Hill. As we started to climb, Jodie said she would quickly stop to take some gear off. 'No way,' I replied. 'There isn't time.' I think the others were surprised as we couldn't see the team behind us, but I knew there was another navigation route they could have taken that could have them appear in front of us – unlikely, but not worth the risk if you're trying to win. We won the race, the girls raised over $3,000 for the Open Home Foundation, and the celebrations lasted for some weeks. It was an incredible feeling to walk away victorious and one of those times when you truly feel like you have overcome great odds to achieve the goal. In the words of one of my favourite sayings: 'They who suffer most win.'

CHAPTER TWENTY-FIVE

NAVIGATION FINDS

After winning the Rollos 24-hour race, it seemed like a fun challenge to defend our title in 2009. Jodie and I teamed with Fleur and Ralph Lattimore, a team of two females and two males this time. To be fair, none of us did much training as we didn't really expect to be contenders, but the race was in a great location and we wanted to enjoy sharing the experience. To our surprise, we won again. I think I also surprised Ralph when I hit the wall mid-race, managed to drink 1.5 litres of Coke on a short hiking stage, and then made a full recovery to race strong to the end.

At the end of autumn I got a call from an adventure-racing friend, Emily Miazga, of Em's Power Cookies fame. She was in a team for the Dream Raid Adventure Race in New Caledonia with two others and they were looking for a navigator. They had raced the event the previous year but due to some navigation issues they didn't place as highly as they would have liked. I explained that I wasn't fit for multi-day racing but Emily sold it to me more as a fun trip to Nouméa so I agreed to race. I would have time to train and prepare, and once I had committed to it, the idea of doing an expedition race again was exciting, especially because it wasn't a major event.

As winter approached and the temperature started to drop, we promptly decided that we needed to get back to the Pacific Islands to escape some of the cold and bleak weather. Once again inspired by Cindy's experiences, we headed for Vava'u, Tonga. It's not like we had surplus money lying around, it's more that both Jodie and I place a high value on providing the kids with unique experiences. This fitted with our belief in the Outward Bound philosophy that outdoor challenges impel young people into value-forming experiences, that adventure, risk, challenge and having to adapt to new environments, out of one's comfort zones, develops character and expands perceptions. The mission was to rent a 12-foot dinghy with a 25 hp outboard, load it up with supplies, camping gear, kites and boards, snorkelling gear and tour the Vava'u Island group for two weeks, with no plan other than the map, a desire to swim with whales and to fly kites. These trips may sound quite romantic but with three young children they are far from it. Most of the time they are idyllic but there is enough hardship and risk involved to make them challenging. We cook on fires, sleep on the ground, there is no power or toilets, very few comforts, and we are subject to the weather, sea conditions, insects and wildlife often unknown to us.

On this trip the weather was not particularly good with constant wind that was awesome for kite boarding but not ideal for family camping. Monsoon-level rain hit us for the first few days but we discovered that our inflated kites offered excellent roofing over the tent. Most days we moved to new campsites and kiting spots. We frequently saw humpback whales and had the opportunity to swim with a mother and calf one day but were too scared to get in the water – the whales were much bigger than we had anticipated, so viewing them from the boat was just fine, thanks. We had one particularly rough crossing but our kayaking experience in running down big swells paid off, essentially using the engine to surf the dinghy across the channel (fun but at the same time a serious situation with dire consequences had the dinghy flipped or got swamped by a large wave). The weather cleared, though, and we lazed by the fire at night watching bats fly around the coconut trees. The snorkelling was unique, with reef and ledge diving on offer, amid an abundance of marine life. Overall, it was a magical time.

On returning from Tonga I discovered that as a consequence of being a well-known local personality I had been elected onto the Network Tasman Trust by the electricity consumers of the region who are the owners of the distribution company. I stood for the trust in the first place for environmental reasons. Network Tasman had seriously looked at the Matakitaki – a wilderness river that flows from Nelson Lakes National Park through the small town of Murchison – as a source of power generation. The Matakitaki is exceptionally good for kayaking and somewhat of a lifestream for the community, so a hydro dam would be tragic for those who enjoyed the river and lived in the area. Many groups lobbied against the dam prospect and as part of the kayak community I was asked if I would stand. No one was really sure what it would mean having a kayaker (who was against the dam) on the trust, but it was decided that it was better than not having a kayaker on it. It's not that I'm anti hydro-electricity in any way, but what I didn't want to happen was for the river to be dammed and not have done anything about it. I've been on the trust ever since and it has been very interesting learning more about the industry and I feel good about being involved in something that directly impacts on the community. The fact that it's a position with remuneration (which I didn't know beforehand) is a bonus.

A few weeks before we were due to depart for New Caledonia I got a call from one of my team-mates, Eric Billioud, to inform me that Emily had contracted malaria while travelling in Africa and wasn't going to be able to race. He suggested we ask another Kiwi female racer, Sarah Fairmaid, to take her place. Although I was more than happy to race with Sarah as I knew she would be great, I told Eric that I was keen to race with Sophie Hart, an up-and-coming multisport and adventure racer who was living nearby. There were a few other New Zealand females who were racing exceptionally well at the time but they were already committed to teams. I liked the fact, too, that Sophie hadn't been out on the international circuit. If I was to return to racing, part of my motivation was developmental, helping some new athletes to race at the top level and exposing them to the global scene.

The New Zealand adventure-racing community is small and news travels fast. By 2006, while I was no longer racing competitively, I was still involved in the scene as I was organising events. I began to hear about a young woman at Otago University who was an emerging athlete with potential, some even saying she could be the calibre of Kristina, whom I considered the best female adventure racer there had been to date. Years went by and occasionally I'd notice Sophie's name turning up in the race results. In 2008 she competed in the Rollos 24-hour adventure race in a team with a few guys I knew. I vividly recall seeing her on course while I was racing with Jodie and her friends, and what struck me was how thoroughly she was enjoying herself even though she was racing hard. 'So that's Sophie Hart,' I thought, beginning to see why she was tagged for greater things. A few months later, she competed in the Lake to Lighthouse multisport event I was employed to help organise and I was curious to see how she would go against Elina Ussher. It turned out she went very well, making Elina work hard for her win, with Sophie taking second. What impressed me most was that Elina was a full-time professional and Sophie was a medical student who was doing multisport for fun. I congratulated her after the race and she told me she was heading overseas cycle touring but would be based in Motueka, my local town, for a while the following year. We agreed to catch up sometime.

The next time I saw her was in 2009 at the local adventure race again. This time we were both racing in teams with two females and two males. I expected her team to beat us and we raced closely most of the day, but my team managed to get a gap when a checkpoint wasn't clearly set and we went on to win the race. Once again

I was impressed with what I saw of Sophie. By this point I was starting to think about getting back into international racing but I'd also discovered another female with ample talent, Fleur Lattimore. I'd been training with Fleur and done a few races with her, and she too had the qualities needed to win major races, including a world adventure-racing title, but my intuition told me Sophie was the woman to race with if the opportunity arose. That opportunity presented itself not long afterwards when Emily had to pull out of the New Caledonia race. Worried that she hadn't done an expedition race before, Eric took some convincing, but Sophie jumped at the chance. We did a few training sessions and soon after we were racing in New Caledonia.

Our team was never a race-winning squad but we raced competitively for a podium placing and it was a legitimate challenging event to see how Sophie would cope with that style of racing. There were some hard sections of the course and there are naturally times in a multi-day race when people are tired, sore, sleepy and generally not having any fun. In one particularly arduous stage where we were all suffering on some level, her head hung low, so I decided to check in on her, expecting to have one unhappy camper on my hands. She looked up at me from under her wide-brimmed hat with eyes shining and said with a broad grin, 'This is awesome, I love it!' I knew then and there that she had what it took to be a champion.

We raced well enough, finishing fifth. The highlight was a kayaking stage that started down a river for a few hours and then went out to the open ocean. The race staff had told us we needed to take safety glasses as needle fish could fly towards us at night, aiming for our headlights. At first I thought it must be a crazy joke, but after a few strikes to my face I quickly put the glasses on. We had a strong tailwind and decided to erect our sails. We got them up and sat under the moonlight with the water rushing by, the sails shaped nicely. At first I thought the GPS was malfunctioning as it showed our speed at 1 km/h. Then I realised we were in a fast-flowing channel going against the tide. We were basically stationary. Sails dropped, we paddled on an angle to get out of the flood channel and started making progress again. In the distance, we could make out lights and a beach fire, our destination. Soon afterwards, still far from shore, we started surfing some glassy waves, a result of the water getting shallow, and had to portage the kayaks over a large sand island off the coast. I savoured being back in an expedition race again, and although I wasn't sure if I'd do any more, I wasn't opposed to the idea.

On the flight home I asked Sophie if she was planning to race the Coast to Coast. She said she'd done it a few times but wasn't interested in doing it again. This surprised me as from what I knew of her by then, I had no doubts whatsoever she could win it. She went on to explain that she'd trained really hard for it the previous year and had a disastrous race, vowing never to go back. Explaining that she wouldn't need to do a huge amount of training to do the next Coast to Coast given where she was currently at, I got my laptop out and together we designed a training programme. She could win the Coast to Coast if that's what she wanted but she needed to go back and have a strong race to benchmark where she was compared to the other athletes. Winning the race would be a two- to three-year project. By the time we landed she was happy to give it a go on the condition I helped her with her river kayaking. Even though she warned me that her river skills were non-existent, I couldn't see how they could be that bad – after all, she'd done the Coast to Coast several times already and I knew from paddling in a double kayak with her that she was strong. Time would tell.

November 18. Caller ID displayed a call from Richard Ussher. Rich traditionally does not ring for idle chit-chat so when he started asking me about how Jodie was, how the kids were and how my golf was going, I started to sense a hidden agenda.

'So, anyway, why I called . . . would you be interested in racing in Abu Dhabi?' Rich tentatively enquired.

The Abu Dhabi Adventure Challenge was a new race on the international circuit that had been going for two years and had built up a reputation as a demanding competition with an arduous desert run, and desert running was something I wasn't particularly into. Rich explained the situation – he needed a team-mate desperately as two athletes had been taken out with injury. Eight days later I was on the start line.

The race included some classy ocean kayaking on the Arabian Gulf but the crux of the five-day event was a 120 km desert trek. Over sand dunes and across salt pans, past nomadic Bedouin camel herders and the occasional desert flower, we climbed and jogged and sweated in temperatures hovering in the forties through the aptly named Empty Quarter. One enduring memory of the race was running out of water on a 100 km mountain-bike stage with 10 km remaining. We were all as dry as an Arab's sandal when I spotted a discarded 7UP bottle with some liquid inside it on the roadside. I looped back and collected it and then carried on riding. Logic told me it was fuel, water, or 7UP. The first smell suggested it wasn't fuel so I tasted it to determine it wasn't 7UP either. Great, it's water. Everyone opened their bottles and we divided up the 1.5 litres some sheik had chucked out the window of their Hummer, probably when they learnt it wasn't 7UP. The water gave us a boost to finish the stage, we won the race by a very comfortable margin (although it was far from comfortable for me achieving it), and it confirmed for me that I could still race at elite level.

It was enjoyable being back in the racing circuit and seeing the new era of athletes, many of whom knew very little or nothing at all about me. I knew some of them thought Rich must have been extremely desperate to get me, because at first glance I don't look like an athlete for a stage race which is largely a speed race, plus it's the desert, and big mammoth men like me weighing nearly 90 kg sink into sand. What they didn't account for was that when Rich and I team up, we're the dynamic duo, we have an incredibly strategic approach to winning races and we dissected this one into small components as to how it would be won. To the surprise of many, especially the elite triathletes who backed themselves to win, big guys have big motors when they're in a kayak, I could ride a bike, and I could suffer. It turned out that by the time we reached the desert-running stage, we'd built up such a good lead we just needed to trot through with the other teams and not concede any time.

But as crazy as racing in the desert is, perhaps the craziest thing to happen that year was representing Motueka at *Top Town*. It was a television game show I grew up with where teams from different New Zealand towns competed in various obstacle challenges against each other between 1976 and 1990. When it made a return, I was asked to captain the local team, the Motueka Marvels, and we had a blast filming the show in Christchurch. Our team had some exceptional athletes, including my training buddy Danial Bremner (who dressed up as a superhero, 'Mot Man'), and had the potential to win the competition, but there was an array of random happenings that made it impossible to take the show seriously. The rolling road was my specialist activity, a huge conveyer belt where three contestants climbed on and kept running until only one remained. I was unbeaten on the rolling road.

Although I'm always considered big for most of the sports I do, there are some situations where my size and endurance pay dividends, and I had a classic moment when I went outrigger canoe training with my mate Andy in Porirua. The club I paddle for at home is mainly made up of skinny white guys, who excel in long-distance events. They always have an issue when I'm racing as to where to put me in the six-seater canoe, to balance it, so I'm mostly in a centre seat. However, as I stood around with a bunch of Maori and Polynesian blokes in Porirua deciding who would sit where, the captain said, 'Let's put the little guy in the front seat.' Everyone nodded as I looked around thinking, there's no little guys here, everyone's friggin massive, easily over 100 kg per unit. But because everyone was staring at me it suddenly dawned who the little guy was – far out, I don't get that often. It was a fun session that ended in the hot pools for a soak. When the guys learned that I had been a professional athlete they wanted some feedback on their training session. To be honest, I told them, if you didn't spend 10 minutes at the start doing handshakes and hongis, saying a karakia once on the water, and then another 10 minutes at the end doing high-fives and bro shakes, you'd have nearly 30 minutes' extra paddling time. They thought I was a crack-up.

CHAPTER TWENTY-SIX

NEAR FOVEAUX

The Coast to Coast was the focus at the start of 2010. Jodie had set a goal of completing the Longest Day and had made a consolidated commitment to training with what limited time she had outside managing our home and children. Unfortunately she was a victim in a road-cycling crash in an event she was using for training, and recovery from the accident restricted her training further. But she was a good kayaker, could run in the mountains, and having been a competitive racer she also possesses the ability to push hard when in competition (she actually holds the record for the final cycle stage for the Coast to Coast two-day event). For that reason, we both agreed a top five finish would be a fair goal should she have a good day.

I was coaching Sophie, too, so the three of us did a few river trips leading up to the race. On our first I got to see how bad Sophie's river skills really were – 13 capsizes on the Waimakariri River. 'This is going to take some work,' I said to myself. I'd mentioned to Jodie that Sophie showed the most promise of an emerging athlete I'd seen but Jodie just thought she was a muppet – lovely person, but shit paddler. I wasn't going to give up on Sophie though, she just needed more river time, plus I'd told her I'd teach her to kayak. Sophie was a fast learner and prepared to work hard so it didn't take long for her to become the strongest female paddler in the sport.

That Coast to Coast the weather hit hard forcing many course changes. It was unfortunate for Jodie especially as her real strength was the paddle stage which was relocated to the Avon River that meanders through Christchurch City – no comparison to the rugged Waimakariri Gorge – and the run leg was over Arthur's Pass on sealed road, a nightmare compared to the original route. She did well, eventually finishing sixth, and probably could have finished fifth without too much more effort but she lost a bit of motivation after the weather turned the event into an urban challenge. Sophie finished third after a tough day's racing, and she didn't get any real support on the long cycle from Klondyke Corner to Christchurch, riding much of it alone. She did well, and from a coaching perspective I now had a benchmark as to her weaknesses and strengths. If the original course had been raced she would have most likely won. I encouraged her to buy a white-water kayak and said that next time she would win the race on the river.

I got back into white-water kayaking myself, a passion of mine throughout my twenties, when I worked as a kayaking instructor and spent as much spare time as possible on the rivers. Back then I was paddling mainly Grade 4 rivers and occasionally Grade 5 rapids by accident, missing the crucial eddy. Many of New Zealand's gem river runs are helicopter or hiking access only, so I enjoyed some very challenging trips on the West Coast and logged a first descent of a technical Grade 4 river, the right branch of the Waingaro in Golden Bay. When kids came along it was harder to get away paddling as it was so time-consuming. My measure for going boating was that I had to spend more time in my kayak than in the car, which meant I'd miss out on some trips. Then I decided one day, on the Arahura River, after a mate dropped over a waterfall and smashed his face into the deck of his kayak and rolled up with blood everywhere, that I'd make kite boarding my water sport. Teaching Sophie to kayak got me back onto the rivers and I loved it. My kids were of an age, too, where they could enjoy the rivers more so it was good timing. I've managed to do some great paddling since.

Sea kayaking has been another passion of mine, and the holy grail of ocean paddling in New Zealand is Stewart Island, if you ask me. I had always wanted to attempt the circumnavigation trip since we had paddled there in the early 1990s. So paddling friend Tony Bateup and I decided to head down in March, typically a settled season for the Foveaux area. We had done our share of paddling in high seas and believed we had the skills and experience for the trip, according the island the respect it deserved, over a period of about two weeks if we needed it.

Arriving on the island mid-morning, we opted to paddle anti-clockwise, meaning we had a following sea along the north-eastern and northern aspects with about three days of settled weather to paddle the west coast, typically the most exposed and difficult section of the trip. There was a storm system approaching but we felt we should be able to round South Cape before it hit. The first day was incredible, and with fully loaded kayaks we surfed the entire northern coast in an afternoon, getting sensational views of Mount Anglem and into Foveaux Strait. We had about 20 knots pushing us and some swells in the 2- to 3-metre region, huge grins on our faces. It was an excellent start and it meant on day two we would be able to tackle the west coast, fresh and with a whole day of light. Perhaps foolishly, the calm seas lulled us into believing the storm system was still days away.

The notorious wild west coast was calm and pleasant, it was a sunny day and the sea was as clear as drinking water. We even consciously slowed down to ensure we enjoyed the paddle. As we neared the Titi (aka Muttonbird) Islands we took our time exploring around them as they proved fascinating, especially the relics of the muttonbird trade. We could see South Cape, the gateway to completing the trip – get through the gate and you're done – so we decided to camp close and early the following morning we would round it. We were not complacent in any way, it was a sensible plan at the time, but what we didn't allow for was how fast the storm would hit. In the space of an hour it got nasty fast and we went from effortless paddling to battling gale-force winds and rising seas. Unable to paddle close to each other, we yelled over the noise of the droning wind to beeline for Easy Harbour, the nearest shelter we could see on the chart. I was more paddling fit than Tony and we'd been in the kayaks for over eight hours that day, so I found myself creeping away from him and then having to wait. Deciding that there wasn't much point in staying together and it would be better if one person was in a position to activate a rescue if necessary, I managed to get close enough to Tony to scream, 'I'm going ahead – see you there!' Had Tony been blown over and missed his roll, he would go past the entrance of Easy Harbour so I would wait there. It was all action getting into the harbour but I made it and Tony rounded in to safety soon after. 'Whoa!' Little did we know when we set up camp that Easy Harbour would be home for the next week.

The storm lashed with a vengeance, the seas grew humongous and the wind ripped. According to the live wind readings we were getting via VHF radio from the weather station on South Cape it was gusting to 75 knots. Thankfully there were two campsites in Easy Harbour so we were able to move between them daily, as it gave us something to do. There was a cave which we could live in at one camp, plus a lifetime supply of firewood. Each day we'd listen and watch the weather, the likes of which neither of us had seen before. It wasn't so much the swell and wave size that stopped us paddling outside the harbour, but the wind, which was hurricane force at times. After the trip, friends couldn't understand why we were stuck there for so long. You had to be there, I guess, looking out to sea, huge waves rolling past the entrance to Easy Harbour like buses, the sea a mess of blue and white, the air filled with driving spray and hardly any visibility. In the forest behind us there was widespread damage to vegetation, debris hurled about left, right and centre. At night in the tent the gusts sounded like freight trains careering through the forest, colliding with the tent, sometimes forcing the roof down so it pressed on your face, making sleep near impossible. Each day we'd venture out to the edge of the harbour in an attempt to gauge the weather – a mildly terrifying experience in itself. About the only bonus of staying there for so long was seeing kiwi in the wild.

Finally the day came when the weather abated, the clouds slowed and we quickly packed and started paddling. The seas were still massive but the wind had dropped away, so we gunned for South Cape, knowing that once around it we were home, sort of. What we hadn't anticipated was the tidal flow around South Cape and the effect that would produce – the highest, steepest seas I have kayaked in, which felt like you were kayaking down the side of a two-storey building. It was difficult to understand at times how the kayak was keeping contact with the sea – it really felt like you could free-fall from the top of a swell to the bottom, some 4 to 5 metres.

Before the trip, Tony and I agreed that should one of us wish to land because they didn't feel safe, the other person would respect that decision. As we approached South Cape it became obvious that the risks of attempting to round it were very high. Wind and swell were lashing into the cape sending powerful waves smashing into the rocks. Trying to stay in the middle of the channel between the Titi Islands and the cape was challenging enough. Tony paddled over to me and politely suggested we try the cape in the morning, as we didn't have much daylight left. I was happy with that but the next problem to solve was where to go. We could see a settlement on Big South Cape Island but the waves wrapping in there over rocks awash meant we couldn't see a safe passage in. We retreated to another small island, Solomon, and in the last light of day found a small jetty in a sheltered bay, with a rope leading up into the forest. It was our only option. Hoisting the kayaks into the trees, we followed a small trail up to high ground which led to an open shed that we could camp in for the night. However, we walked further up the trail to see what else was around and arrived at a small house. The door was unlocked so we went inside to find that it was a classic Kiwi bach – a few rooms and kitchen. After being in harsh camping conditions for the previous week it felt amazing to be inside a building, protected from the weather, so we decided to stay there instead. It had some food stocks so we enjoyed a few treats, some canned fruit and endless cups of tea, read old boating magazines, and slept on the beds that night.

The next morning we were enjoying breakfast and getting ready to tackle South Cape again when we heard a helicopter fly overhead – the first sign of anyone else we had had all week. Tony was looking at a calendar on the wall at the time, from 2009, trying to figure out some numbers that were scribbled on it for each day of May. Then we clicked – it was the daily catch of muttonbirds, or sooty shearwaters, known to Maori as titi. According to some, these seabirds taste remarkably like sheep meat, and are harvested by Stewart Island Maori once a year as part of their cultural legacy. There were a number of calendars all on the same hook so we started to compare seasons by looking at the daily catches. We could see that the season ended in May and I casually asked Tony when it actually opened. He flicked back, paused for a bit, checked his watch and said, 'Today!' Right on cue, we heard the sound of a boat. With lightning speed we tidied the hut and got our gear out. We had always intended to leave a message, our contact details and some cash for the owner (which we did), but we didn't want them to arrive while we were spread out in their place.

Loading our kayaks, we started to paddle back to the South Cape. It wasn't looking very inviting. The problem was that should we encounter any issues, we'd end up getting pounded to death on the rocky coastline. As we approached, we agreed it was better to wait a bit longer and to land on Big South Cape Island and climb to the top, to get a better view of what was happening around the cape. We could see a boat moored in the harbour now so it would be helpful to speak to some locals. It proved quite tricky finding the passage through the crashing waves and rocks, but we landed and climbed up the trail to the first building and met some muttonbirders who were surprised to see us arrive. We talked about what we were doing and they weren't too hopeful about the chances of us rounding the cape safely. They'd been trying to get onto the island all week but the storm had prevented them. We went for a walk around the island and looked at the sea – it didn't seem as bad from up high so we decided to give it another nudge.

When we got to our kayaks the skipper of the vessel in the harbour was there and reckoned that it would be close to impossible to round the cape with the current seas and tides, suggesting we would be best to try in the morning. We wanted to give it a try so braved the seas once more but had to return again, it was so savage. The only way I could see a safe way around was to paddle about 5 km offshore and keep plenty of sea room between us and land, but we both knew the swells out there were monstrous and it just didn't appeal. It was an extremely exposed place. We were invited to stay overnight on the island so we did that and prepared for another try in the morning.

Back in our kayaks we were determined to get around the cape. This time we paddled with gusto towards the promontory that kept denying us passage. I sensed that Tony was fully committed, in an almost death-or-glory mindset. As we got closer, though, I didn't like it – nothing much had changed, the risks that had stopped us in previous attempts remained. I pulled the pin and we headed to a small cove to the north of South Cape. When we finally landed we had just had another epic paddling experience. We were both exhausted – it was like we were abuse victims of the ocean. A yellow-eyed penguin standing immobile on the beach as we unpacked our kayaks looked as fed up with the weather as we were. We put our tents up and slept the rest of the day while the conditions raged on. I lay there wondering how long I was going to live on the island.

The next morning we were starting back towards the cape when we came across a crayfishing boat moored in a small bay. The guys on board were waiting for the tide to round the cape and said the weather pattern was likely to last a few more weeks, maybe a month, offering to take us to Bluff but saying we'd need to leave in an hour. By now we had almost run out of food and time, so we took the ride option, both vowing to return again sometime.

After Stewart Island I headed to the North Island to run the Autumn Challenge women's adventure race in the Manawatu, but as it wasn't getting anywhere near the traction of the Spring Challenge we decided to drop the event after that. Word had got out that I was back racing at a high level so I started to get some invitations to join teams. I was happy to be back doing some races provided the team was good, there was prize money and it was a country I wanted to visit. Midway through the year, Richard Ussher gave me the call-up. China had established an adventure racing series in 2004 and since then it had grown into the most lucrative series in the world, with millions of dollars being invested in the sport annually. Given they had been producing most of the world's adventure-sporting equipment for a decade or more, it was only a matter of time before they joined in the fun.

The biggest race was a four-day stage in a city called Wulong near Chongqing in central China. Elite teams started racing there around 2005 but the race had gained a 'who doesn't get sick wins' sort of reputation. Rich warned me of the illnesses and bugs that had plagued him in previous years and how many other athletes had succumbed. I'd spent enough time in China to feel confident I could stay healthy so I signed up for the race. Sure enough, as the days went by, racers dropped like dominoes. Our team took an easy second place after two elite teams were forced out of the competition courtesy of diarrhoea and vomiting.

While racing in China I got an invite from US racer Mike Kloser, the captain of one of the most successful teams in the world, to race in his team for the World Championships in Spain. I'd never been to Spain so I was keen. Another Kiwi, Chris Forne, was in the team. We got second in the race, not far behind the winners. I hadn't had a brilliant race, developing conjunctivitis in my eyes, which at times made it difficult just to see. It was also way colder than I'd expected and I suffered like a dog for days. Mike retired after the race so I asked Chris if he'd be keen to form a New Zealand team for the next World Championships and he agreed. Once

I got home I asked Sophie if she was up for it, and she signed up too. We all agreed to invite Marcel Hagener to join us.

After Spain my energy turned to the last race of the year in Abu Dhabi. We had the same team as the previous year and were motivated to win again and bag the biggest prize purse. My focus was swim training as there would be a swim of 2 km, which caused me some concern as stage races tend to be won or lost by small margins and a poor swim could make the difference. I needn't have worried, my paddle training served me well and I attached a small tow line to my strong swimming team-mate Marcel, which kept me in his draft, and I even enjoyed it. We won the race after dominating the two-day run through the desert. At times the heat was like an inferno but the uniqueness of the environment seemed to make it worthwhile. I kept telling myself during that race, 'I only have one more desert run left in me in this lifetime.' Ironically or aptly, Jodie decided to buy a new fridge-freezer with some of the prize money I won racing in the desert.

My foremost memory, though, was not running up burning sand dunes with camels curiously watching on, it was being drug tested at the finish. I've been tested twice in my career and I don't like it as a positive test will brand someone for life even if they are innocent. I knew I was clean but testers have made mistakes in the past and will do so again. The problem with the test in Abu Dhabi was that it took place in a hotel about 30 minutes from the race finish where they'd told me I could not urinate despite the fact that's all I wished to do. I was hustled into a car and driven away. Stuck in traffic, my urge to pee became irrepressible and there were no containers in the vehicle. 'Okay,' I said to them, 'either you let me out of the car to piss right now or I swear to god, I'm going to piss right here in the back seat!' Fully exposed, I blissfully released the tension build-up in my bladder on the median strip. By the time we got to the hotel I needed to go again, pronto. A month or so later I received a letter in the mail informing me that my drug test results were negative, I was clean, good boy.

CHAPTER TWENTY-SEVEN
NATHAN'S FAULT

By 2011 our kids were four, six and eight, and we felt it was time to step up the level of adventure activities we were doing as a family. Up until this point we'd done some incredible adventures, but often it didn't engage them physically – in essence, they were more passengers along for the trip. Now that Tide was four, she was robust enough to handle some legitimate outdoor activities, but our main motive was that we felt Jessie was starting to be held back because we were limited to what we could do with her little sister.

To kick off the New Year we joined friends with children of similar ages and headed down the Clarence River, a wilderness area in the upper South Island. We got in about 50 km downstream from the source and embarked on a 180 km trip that would take us to the Pacific Ocean. We planned a 10-day trip because we didn't want to rush, and the camping in the valley is as much an attraction as the rafting itself – and as it turned out we may as well have been driving in a car, because playing on land was the highlight for the kids. On the second day we got soaked by heavy rain that swelled the river to a size that wasn't ideal for nine children aged between four and eight. Some of the rapids reached Grade 3 and there was some powerful hydraulics happening in the brown and churning water. We had highly capable adults on the rafts but after a few minor close calls we agreed to play it safe and set up camp early. By the next day the river had dropped to a perfect flow and we were treated to a week of glorious weather as we floated downstream. Sleeping in tents, flame cooking, fresh mountain water to sip, it was an exceptional trip and for most of us it marked the beginning of some fun family rafting expeditions to come.

After spending 10 days in outback isolation including New Year's Eve, our next goal was to do a week-long hiking trip. Because the kids were still too young to carry big loads, Jodie and I had to design a trip that suited the family and the fact we'd have massive packs, with enough gear and grub for a week. A downhill tramping trip was what we needed, and locally the best option I could think of was to hike the Wangapeka Valley over the relatively low saddle into the Karamea Valley, abundant with pristine swimming holes and campsites, and work our way down. The problem was that the trail ends at Karamea Bend and then it's a steady climb back to Mount Arthur and the nearest road end. The kids could do it but I wasn't sure they'd enjoy it. That's when the helicopter entered the equation. We could spend seven days hiking to Karamea Bend and then get a helicopter to pick us up and fly us home. The local helicopter company I spoke to were enthusiastic, and the pilot even said that if we weren't at Karamea Bend on the scheduled pick-up day, he'd fly around and find us.

I reckon I started the trip with the heaviest pack I've ever carried – it was 49.89 kg so I added another snack to get it over 50 kg. It was a 90-litre pack bursting at the seams with two additional bags strapped to the outside, and when we got dropped off I ended up with another bag to carry in my hand. It was a crazy load, but considering that the average Sherpa in the Himalayas carries a load heavier than themselves it barely rates a mention. The kids surprised us with their walking ability and by the end of the second day we were camping just below Wangapeka Saddle. Our packs were getting lighter already so we decided to lengthen the trip with a detour over Biggs Tops. We alpine camped by a tarn and then dropped to the Karamea Valley. After a few days of basic living and travel we arrived at Karamea Bend for our final night. The next morning the helicopter landed on the riverbank amid billowing clouds of dust, and after a soaring scenic flight over the national park we were at our favourite café in Motueka having lunch in next to no time. What I liked the most about that trip was that it was a solid mission with a fair balance of challenge, hardship and reward for the kids. By including the helicopter, Jodie and I wanted to teach them to be open to possibilities and not impose limitations on what you can do, to think big.

We squeezed in a few more day trips, mainly rock climbing and caving, before the kids started back at school. I then turned my attention to putting the final touches on Sophie's preparation for the Coast to Coast. We did a few Waimakariri River paddles to ensure she was happy with the route and knew the lines through the rapids. By now she was a very competent paddler but still lacked confidence in her ability. She was then – and still is, I guess – shy and avoids the limelight. Her biggest barrier was getting flustered by the pre-race hype and not being able to access her potential. By now Jodie knew her well and had joined her support crew, primarily as her bodyguard to make sure she kept calm and relaxed in the days leading up to the race.

Sophie won the Longest Day, setting a new record for the kayak stage and getting within 90 seconds of the race record. Flying to different parts of the course with the race media team, I saw her a few times and she was in total control. Arguably, because of course changes over the years, in 2011 she probably recorded the fastest ever race time for a woman. It wouldn't have taken much for her to break the record but she never knew just how close to it she was. They had stopped support cars from following their riders and supplying them with time splits and updates as the finish line approached.

A race is a race, you win some, you lose some, end of story. But playing a part in seeing Sophie realise her dream was more satisfying than any personal victory I had achieved and made me understand why some people coach. I must have got dust or something in my eyes, because it took a while to stop them from watering.

For a few years I had become obsessed with surf-ski paddling. I was doing about 100 to 150 km a week on the ocean in front of home and racing as much as I could. I loved it. Purely on impulse, I got in off the water one day and entered the World Championships in Molokai, Hawaii, the Mount Everest of ocean surf-ski racing. I went okay, finishing about twentieth, and was a little unlucky in the closing stages of the race when another paddler collided with me on a wave and sheared my rudder off, so that I had to paddle the final 5 km with no steering, losing a few places as a result.

I wasn't back in New Zealand for long before we headed to Australia for our winter family escape. My sister had been living backwards and forwards over the Tasman and her partner was working near Brisbane so we flew there to begin with. With a few days to fill in before we flew to the Whitsundays, we stumbled over a local orienteering event, with controls on termite mounds. We then flew north and made our way to Airlie Beach where we would start our trip. Although we had tried to rent kayaks locally, the company wasn't comfortable with the fact we had three young children, so in the end we took Incept inflatable sea kayaks from New Zealand and this gave us full freedom. Our goal was to paddle 140 km around Whitsunday and Hook islands, camping on beaches as we made our way. It was a splendid trip, up there with the best. The wildlife, including snakes and other reptiles, was fascinating for the kids, the beaches and coastline were incredible, and the snorkelling was wicked, with hundreds of fish, turtles and sharks. We even had a humpback whale swim under our kayak, so close that we could have reached down and touched it.

Midway through the year Sophie emailed me about a new race in Idaho, subject line: 'Ideal training for Tasmania?' Good idea, I thought, so I ran it past Seagate who had come back on board for the 2011 World Champs and also thought it was a good idea. I was pleased to see we went via San Francisco, relishing the change from immigration at LAX. Chris was unavailable so Nick, Sophie's partner, joined us for the race. I wasn't concerned where we placed, because the main goal was training for Tasmania, so we raced very conservatively and took second place. Sophie was highly competitive and didn't enjoy racing conservatively, certain we could have won, but I assured her that Idaho was training, whereas Tasmania was going to be different, very different.

Before I went to the World Champs I shot over to China for the Wulong Mountain Quest and two running races in the Gobi Desert. I was racing with Rich, Elina and Trevor Voyce in Wulong and we won the race comfortably. We built up a good lead in the first few days which enabled us to sit back and play it safe, just doing enough to protect our lead. We then flew to Urumqi and took part in the desert runs. The Gobi is not a pretty desert from what I could see, and the trip became somewhat of a comedy show as we'd bus for hours, days even, through the same landscape to reach parts of the desert to run in which weren't visually any different from where we had boarded the buses. Despite all the bus time in China, I wasn't worried, we'd won Wulong and made good prize money and the runs were also handy training for Tasmania.

In the midst of training for the World Champs I attended the Outward Bound International Staff Symposium in Singapore, where I was speaking as an ex-instructor, ambassador and professional adventure racer. The symposium was enjoyable and interesting but what fascinated me most was Singapore and how risk-averse the country was as a whole. I decided to travel a few days early and spend time with local friends doing some training. One day we went to a kayak training facility with the intention of me giving them tuition. There was a vast selection of kayaks including some good Olympic K1s so I tried to hire one but was asked for my kayaking certificate. My friends explained that I was from New Zealand, that I was a kayak instructor and was there to teach them some paddling technique, but I didn't have a Singapore kayak certificate. It transpired that without a certificate I could only rent a plastic kayak, a toy. There was a K1 sitting on the grass next to the water so I asked the guy in charge if I could hop in it and prove I wasn't going to drown. No, too dangerous, need certificate. There were a number of K1 paddlers out training, and they were okay but nothing flash, so I said to the guy, 'What if I can beat all those guys in a race?' No, need certificate. FFS!

When I got out to the symposium venue at Pulau Ubin Island I asked one of the staff where I could run. They told me I could run around the property but definitely not to go outside the gates. 'Why?' Too dangerous – wild pigs in the forest.

It wasn't easy, but I found a way to climb over the perimeter fence, it was 2 metres high with sharp barbs on the top, so that I could enjoy the trails in the jungle. However, the best bit was when a few of us got into the kayaks and were told under no circumstances were we to go out of sight. I was with an instructor from New Zealand, Dan Moore, and a few others from Taiwan who had found the Singapore rules stifling too. When no one was watching we bolted and spent a marvellous few hours paddling around the island. On returning we did get a mild scolding. The opposite side of the island was Malaysian waters so we weren't meant to go around there – we had crossed the border illegally. It was a fun adventure nonetheless.

It was then time to focus on the World Champs. Because it was close to New Zealand, Jodie travelled with me, to follow the race more closely as well as for the chance to have a holiday somewhere she'd always wanted to visit. Tasmania was a diverse experience, and the course went to some incredible places, starting and finishing from the small coastal town of Burnie. We traversed around Table Mountain, ran on expansive wild beaches, pushed through thick forest, and paddled ocean, rivers and lakes. However, despite the fact we dominated the competition from the starting gun, unchallenged, the race didn't go so well. The challenge in the end came from within our own team when I accidentally left our SPOT tracking device behind on stage two which earned us a four-hour penalty. We were six hours ahead at the time but then Chris ran over a stick severely damaging his mountain bike, losing all the gears as a result. We spent hours trying to fix it, looking for a spare bike, and even contemplated breaking into a mechanic's workshop at 3 a.m. one morning as we could see the tools we needed to fix the bike inside, but we had one penalty already so decided against it. The outcome of the bike problem cost us somewhere in the vicinity of eight hours. Even then we still managed to keep leading until the pressure of protecting a lead that would absorb the penalty got to us, with some minor conflicts flaring up. We ended up third. I'll admit that we didn't race to our potential but I think we also got hard done by in receiving such a big penalty. It was a very minor mistake and didn't give us any advantage.

The race had started with a short sea-kayak paddle along the coast and each team had been issued with the SPOT tracking device, which weighs about 100 grams, the same as a snack bar. They said it could go on top of a backpack but they preferred it to go on a PFD as it would send a stronger signal. I was about to toss it into my pack but then attached it to my PFD, because we were a feature team and I knew it would be helpful for the media and supporters if our tracker was transmitting. We broke away in the paddle and led off the water, arriving to the hyped-up media entourage, desperate to get photos and comments. Being a fully sponsored team, we're always obliging to the media, but transition areas are a very difficult time to be interviewed as you're trying to be as fast as you can – in this case changing from kayaking to hiking gear – but I answered what questions I could and we departed.

The stage was a short trail run with a few orienteering controls. Not far into it we arrived at a rifle range and each team nominated a shooter. Our brief was to shoot two clay pigeons from the five you were allowed before you could progress. If you called all five pigeons but didn't shoot two, you had to serve a 10-minute penalty. I was the shooter and shot the first two to pieces, then dropped the rifle and started to leave, but the staff member said I still had three to shoot. I told him that you had to shoot two birds and that was it but he insisted I shoot at the remaining three, even though there wasn't any point. Furious with the stupidity of it, I stood there and shot three rounds into the ground. 'Happy now?' When we arrived at the end of the stage the staff member there informed me that our tracking device wasn't working. Damn! It was still on my life jacket. Not to worry, he had spares, so he got me another. Back on track, this time on bikes. A ride, a caving section, more riding and a big trek that had us swimming rapids through a frigid canyon in darkness, delivering us to the end of a lake as daylight seeped through the clouds.

We knew we had a sizeable lead as we prepared the canoe for the paddle. It was bitterly cold and drizzling, we were tired, dog wet and doing our best to shiver off Jack Frost. The organisers had issued us a two-person canoe for the four of us, plus our gear. For the next few hours we grimly balanced the overloaded canoe, paddling as best we could crammed like sardines in a can, while being marinated in the cold water. Exiting the canoe to the gathered media and spectators, I announced to everyone, 'That makes it into the top ten dumbest things I've ever done in a race!' Retrospectively, it was more worthy of the top three. While we transitioned, the race director pulled me aside and informed me we had been issued a five-hour penalty for not having the tracker. I told him straight up it was ridiculous. That was a massive penalty for a minor error, especially when the SPOT trackers had been proven unreliable over and over again. The transition area after the first kayak was a melee and we were swarmed by the media due to our profile and had made an honest mistake. He did agree to discuss it with the race jury and the penalty was subsequently reduced by an hour.

We still had more paddling to go but thankfully we were given an extra canoe at that point. Back on the water the pressure started to show. Marcel and I had a heated argument when he couldn't understand why Sophie and I couldn't stay on the wash from the canoe Chris and he paddled. The problem was that Sophie and I had all the team gear so we were bogged down with weight but Marcel suggested it was my lack of ability to control the canoe. I was extremely offended and a slagging match began, broken up by Chris and Sophie. Later in the race Marcel had a few digs at Sophie which weren't helpful or respectful either. The tension was mounting as the reality of winning the race dissolved before us. We led the entire race until the penalty box which was about a 30 km bike ride from the finish line. With a lead of hours, we had to sit and wait while two teams went through. The only upside was that Chris managed to borrow a city commuter bike off a spectator for the final ride so we didn't have the hassle of towing and pushing him on his broken one. We ended up third by a few minutes and about an hour behind the winners, but the whole event was marred by the controversial penalty that had been dished out to us.

I was extremely pissed off with both the race organisers and the race jury, but I needed to accept that they made their decisions with the best intentions, and they were just out of their depth with no experienced racer of note among them. I was equally disappointed with the teams that passed us whilst we were serving the penalty. They were simply benefitting from the technical rule interpretations. I wouldn't want to win a race in those circumstances but it took me a while to acknowledge that it wasn't fair of me to project what I believed was the right thing to do onto them. It was a World Championships event and they wanted the best possible result they could get regardless of the situation. I acted poorly with bad sportsmanship. We made errors we shouldn't have made, we twice lost significant time when local people stopped us and suggested a different route to the one we were on, we argued and bickered, and if I was to reflect honestly on the race, we got third because that's what we deserved. I felt really shit, mainly for Sophie. The rest of us had all won the World Champs before but it was her first attempt and we were undoubtedly the fastest and strongest team in the event. Vowing to myself that in 11 months' time in France we would win the World Champs and she would get her title, during the awards ceremony I kept saying to myself, 'Eleven months, it's only eleven months away.'

CHAPTER TWENTY-EIGHT

NICE FRANCE

The success of the jam-packed summer we had planned for the 2012 school holidays could pretty much be measured by how many nights we slept in our tent. The tramp we planned first up was an ambitious one. We were to head up the Leatham Valley in the Marlborough high country, then climb over Severn Saddle into the Severn Valley, travel down that for a while and then pick our way through the Raglan Range into the Branch Valley, then follow the Branch down to where it joins the Leatham. The weather forecast was for a front to pass over with one or two days of heavy rain, but we decided it was safe to head into the hills as there were plenty of huts at the start and end of the trip and as we weren't required to cross any major rivers we could sit out a flood. When you're in the hills for seven to eight days, you can work around several days of rain easy enough.

The first day we walked on four-wheel-drive tracks and, while a bit boring, they were good surfaces for the kids to hike on. The kids walked faster than expected and by the end of day two we were at Top Leatham Hut. They liked the feeling of doing more than we had set out to do, the sense of achievement that they were exceeding expectations. Then the trail started to get narrow and rough, more interesting. The third day the weather started to move in but we crossed the pass into the Severn and found a great campsite in the beech forest high in an alpine basin. We were in the wilderness now – no trails, no huts, no people – but acutely aware the weather was about to change.

The next stage of the trip would be the most difficult. I had done it before when I was training years ago and recalled it being technically challenging to find a route through because it was steep, rocky, broken country with countless bluffs, but provided we took our time and stayed safe I was certain we could do it. That night the rain pelted down hard, turning the streams into small rivers. By morning the rain had eased but low cloud meant there would be no visibility to climb over the range. We stayed in the tent, safe, dry and warm, with books and a pack of cards for entertainment. By midday it had cleared enough to see the range and the route up so I decided to go and check it out. It was about a 1000-metre climb to the top, steep and rocky. After about an hour I reached the ridgeline and could see down into the Branch. Pleased to see that the Branch River was small and looked crossable, I descended about a quarter of the way and identified a route through some steep bluffs that I was happy for the kids to do. When I got back to camp I was keen to pack up and do it while the weather allowed and the route was fresh in my mind. We still had six hours of daylight which was enough to get over and down to a campsite or, more appealing, to the Upper Branch Hut.

There was no track, it was steep on loose rock, in places we were pulling ourselves up using the tussock grass, and the climb took a few hours. What worked really well was giving the kids my altimeter to set short-term goals to keep them focused. With every 100 metres of elevation gained, they could have a short rest and a snack. It was magnificent landscape with very dramatic mountains, not dissimilar to parts of the Andes or Himalayas, but much lower altitude, and everyone was in high spirits when the climb was completed. We started down fast as the top was shingle scree, fun to run and jump. When we reached the bluffs we briefed the kids on safe travel, to go slow, be mindful of rock fall and to communicate. Tide needed some help, and Jessie by nature is cautious, capable but in need of reassurance, so I teamed with Tide and Jodie with Jessie. Zefa is very nimble on his feet so he is self-sufficient in that type of country. Reaching a section where we couldn't see the way down because it was so steep, we sat the kids down while Jodie and I explored around, eventually finding a suitable route. It started to rain again and the temperature plummeted, a southerly shift with ice in the air. The exposure to the cold was a concern – we needed to get to the hut or to a campsite quickly.

Climbing down through some vertical rock terraces, we were going well, with just one more sheer tussock grass face to get past before the mountainside angled out to an easier gradient. It was very steep, wet and slippery. I went down first with Tide, and we got down okay but it wasn't ideal. If someone tripped and fell there wasn't anything to stop them for quite some way. Meanwhile, Jessie had descended to the steepest part and had stopped there, unsure about it and starting to panic a little. Jodie was quickly making her way to her when she slipped herself. She didn't fall far but crashed into Jessie and knocked her down the mountain while I stared up in horror as they tumbled down head over heels, mainly over tussock grass but also scattered boulders and rocks, in a chorus of screams and yells. It wasn't free-falling but the next closest thing, and in the space of about five seconds they crashed down around 50 metres.

Sprinting across to intersect their path, I managed to jump on Jodie as she came past. Their momentum had almost slowed anyway and Jessie was lying in the tussock all bent and twisted, both of them groaning and moaning. Certain someone must be seriously injured, I ran to Jessie first, got her to remain still and asked her to tell me where was sore. Her waterproof clothing was ripped, and some small cuts and bruises were visible. But she pushed me away, sitting up and saying, 'I'm okay, Dada, I'm just a bit frightened.' Apart from some bruises and damaged clothing, fortunately Jodie was uninjured also, but her heart didn't stop hammering until the next day. By this time Zefa had reached us but Tide was showing signs of hypothermia. The weather was getting worse and we couldn't stop where we were. There was still some distance to cover to the forest and there was no track, just big tussock that was over Tide's head in places, and she couldn't move fast in that terrain. I quickly emptied my pack, stuffed her into it and then lashed most of the gear to the outside – everything was in dry bags so that was fine. It wasn't the first time Tide had travelled in my pack and she'd warm up very quickly in there. In a matter of minutes she was merrily chatting in my ear as we hiked off the mountainside.

The hut was only a few kilometres downstream but the light was fading, and when we reached the forest it was the opposite of what we wanted to see. Often high alpine beech forest is open and easy to walk through, but this had suffered avalanche damage and was a city of tree debris – we would only move through that at about 500 metres an hour, at best. With nowhere amid the fallen trees for the tent, we had no option but to keep moving forward. Luckily, across the river, we could just make out what looked like some flat ground, so I dropped my pack and went over to inspect it. Amazingly, in the middle of a forest that had been smashed up by wind throw, there was an area big enough to erect our tent. We got the tent up swiftly, the kids into dry gear and sleeping bags, a fire roaring and cooked a hot meal. Once we were all warm, fed and cosy, the kids nodded off, exhausted. Probably in delayed reaction to the close call of the accident, Jodie and I couldn't sleep for thinking that Jessie could have sustained permanent injury. Admittedly, the trip was a bit hard, but in fine weather it would be different too. That said, we agreed to be more sensible in future and not expose the kids to unnecessary risks. You live and learn.

The next day, the kids dried their socks on the fire, and we packed up and headed off downriver, arriving at the hut (a one-bunk bivvy which we viewed as luxury) at midday. It was New Year's Eve, the sun was beaming, we had a relaxing afternoon while our gear dried out, and it was magic. We stayed the night there and completed the trip in two more days of fairly easy hiking. After a good time in the wilderness, one of the things we all love is a few treats, so we headed straight for the shops for pies and ice creams.

Once back in Nelson, we wanted to move on to our next trip – a sea kayak around D'Urville Island – as soon as possible. The forecast was for fine weather but some strong south-west winds. These don't tend to blow at night or in the early morning, and sometimes don't reach the island at all, so if we were lucky they would provide us with a tailwind and following sea. Happy to be in the wilderness again, the weather allowed us passage to attempt the circumnavigation, paddling in the mornings, exploring the coast and being land-based for the afternoons. Typically we'd find campsites on the edge of the farmed areas above the beach which is a driftwood wonderland offering a superb natural adventure playground for the kids. They'd create miles of beach art too. Beach fires, fresh fish and seafood are staples of these sea-kayaking trips.

The first committing section was up to Nile Head, one of the longer stretches where there was no landing, and added to that the outgoing tide meeting the incoming swell there creates confused waves, which we were likely to have. With strong currents and rocks awash to stay clear of, we would need to be confident in our abilities and decisions. We stopped in Greville Harbour, had a fun swim with seals and decided to try getting further up the island. We had a campsite in mind to be at for Jessie's birthday which was two days away. I was paddling a double sea kayak with all three children, Jessie and Zefa sharing the front seat and Tide sitting in the rear hatch behind my seat. The centre hatch was loaded with gear. Jodie paddled her single kayak, the compartments fully stuffed with food and camping equipment. This combination evened us out and meant we could paddle in a wider range of conditions because Jodie didn't have to paddle with one of the children in a double.

Making our way towards Nile Head, with about an hour to go before we could seek shelter in the harbour, the wind and swell started to build, whitecaps began to form and the conditions changed quickly. There had been a lingering swell already, so with wind on top of it there were breaking waves. In flattish conditions this wouldn't be an issue but the front seat wasn't sealed with a spray skirt to keep water out because with both Jessie and Zefa in the compartment a skirt wouldn't work. As we started to contend with bigger waves and more wind there began to be a real risk of a wave breaking into their seating cockpit. As it was, I was working close to maximum just to keep the boat moving – if we took on over a hundred kilos of water I wasn't sure I'd have the power to keep the kayak off the lee shore, which I was working hard to keep away from as it was. There was about 50 metres of sea room between us and the rocks on the coast, and it would be carnage if we got pushed onto them. The wind direction was preventing me from getting further from shore but I knew the outgoing tide at the head would be strong, so however far out I went it would just increase the difficulty of getting into the port. Up ahead, I could see the occasional wave crashing into the headland sending white water well over 5 metres into the air. Nor could we turn back as the wind was too strong to paddle against. We were committed.

One advantage our kids have in terms of accessing the outdoors is that their parents are both qualified and experienced outdoor instructors, but the converse of that is they can also find themselves in distressing and hazardous situations. While we try to avoid those moments, they can happen, and I respond by actively engaging my mind and body, saying to myself, 'If there was ever a time for me to utilise my skill set, this is it.' Isolated, in challenging conditions, creeping our way carefully around Nile Head while it was being battered by wind, waves and tidal currents, the kids hunkered down trying to avoid being blasted by the sea spray, it was game on. If a wave did pick us up and dump us, I could end up with a heavy capsized kayak, three children swimming, and wind blowing us onto ocean-smashed rocks. Minutes crept by as Nile Head grew closer until eventually we had to make the moves to get through. The tide was racing full speed out of Port Hardy so it was a fine balance of staying close enough to shore to avoid the main current but far enough out to avoid getting surfed onto the rocks. The massive face of a wave rearing up behind us as we were right on Nile Head, I dug the paddle deep and chased hard, surfing it a good 100 metres between the head and spiny outcrop of rocks protruding into the bay. Wahoo! We were safe.

It was still a fight to reach the beach, with another hour of battling wind gusts and tidal flow, but at least the sea was calmer and we had plenty of sea room, the pressure released. Finally we reached the tranquil waters of the port, exhausted. Tent up, fire lit, bellies full. Once the kids were in bed, Jodie and I had a cup of tea by the fire and debriefed. We'd made another poor judgement call – we shouldn't have been out there in those conditions with the kids. Neither of us slept well that night playing through worst-case scenarios of what could have happened, things going completely pear-shaped, a friggin disaster zone.

The next day we celebrated Jessie's birthday and had a relaxing morning sheltered from the wind. We were keen to get to a coastal campsite and have a hearty birthday beach fire and roast some delicious food in the embers so we ventured out again into the wind and open sea. While the conditions were less severe than the previous day, it still wasn't ideal and I was silently cursing myself as we clawed along the coast and then had to do another surf landing to get to shore. Had I been in my single kayak alone, or with experienced paddlers, the conditions were fine, but not for a family summer trip. The saving grace was that the weather was sunny and warm, and there wasn't a person in sight, so the camping was divine.

Determined to have a risk-free day – at least with the children – we decided not to kayak through Stephens Passage together. Instead, Jodie and the kids would hike over the headland to the sheltered waters on the eastern side while I would paddle the double kayak around alone and then one of us would jog back over and paddle Jodie's single kayak to the next camp. It was about a three-hour paddle and we could see from the beach that the wind was blowing strongly at Cape Stephens, the horizon line showing that there was a large swell rolling through – thankfully in the direction I wanted to go. Prior to departing, I decided to try and tow Jodie's single – a sleekly designed Nordkapp which wouldn't have much drag – to save one of us having to paddle it round later. To Jodie, this looked like trouble waiting to happen, but I was keen to try and would leave it somewhere on a beach should I strike any difficulty. It was hard work paddling a double and towing a single, both fully loaded, but the only worrying time was going around the cape itself when I turned into the following sea. Being lighter, the single kayak surfed up and very nearly hit me from behind. The tow line was 15 metres long so I got quite a fright when its bow tapped me on the shoulder. The next day we completed the trip, and while we felt we'd really achieved something of value it didn't need to be said that we all wanted an easier one next up.

The plan was to helicopter in from Nelson to the headwaters of the Pelorus River with inflatable kayaks and spend four days paddling out to the state highway bridge. We had paddled the river's lower section multiple times but the upper section was uncharted. It seemed no one had paddled it, including one stretch in particular between Roebuck and Middy Creek huts where the river went through a number of narrow gorges that I'd examined on Google Earth imagery. The weather forecast was excellent and we could expect the river flow to be low – ideal for what we wanted to do. Jodie took some convincing but in the end agreed it would be worth a shot. Thankfully the trip turned out to be an absolute gem. It was a superb journey through some incredible canyons and small gorges, the water was as clear as freshly cleaned glass, with lush deep pools and numerous small fun rapids to enjoy. After our initial uncertainty over whether to do the trip or not, we were so pleased we did. It had a perfect blend of adventure and safety in breathtaking environments.

Once the kids returned to school I flew to Argentina for the first race of the year, the Tierra Viva staged in the northern part of Patagonia. Our team for the season was to be myself, Sophie, Chris Forne and Trevor Voyce. After Tasmania, I had made the hard decision not to include Marcel, my gut feeling telling me it was time to make a change. The event was based from San Martin, a small lakeside resort town nestled amongst mountain country, servicing skiers in the winter and summer sports for the rest of the year. Driving from Bariloche to San Martin, we were blown away to see the remnants of the Puyehue Volcano eruption from 2011. The ash levels in places resembled a 2-metre snow base and the coverage was immense. With the volcano still pluming ash, any wind from the west clouded the sky and dusted everything with another coating of silver powder. We won the race comfortably, and while Trevor struggled through part of it after a mountain-bike crash left him mildly concussed, overall he coped well in his first long event.

I had hardly unpacked my gear from South America when I started to repack for GODZone in Queenstown. Jodie and the kids road-tripped down to help celebrate my fortieth birthday a few days before the race. The day started with a swim in the lake and breakfast at my favourite cafe, Vudu, followed by lunch at Arrowtown. Unbeknown to Jodie and I, while the kids were playing on a rock wall near the café, our two youngest had begun teasing another child (which is highly uncharacteristic for them) but Jessie didn't intervene. Somehow this all came out while we were driving back. I was furious and pulled over and told them to get out of the car. While Jodie drove, I walked with the kids, keeping up a brisk pace. It was about 15 km and they were tired, sore and upset, but we spoke about how the boy would have felt when they teased him. At first Jessie was annoyed because she hadn't done any teasing but I explained to her that by doing nothing she was endorsing that behaviour. They got it. The other consequence was that we were going out to a dessert restaurant for my birthday and they wouldn't get any. They'd have to sit and wait, sipping a glass of water.

Now, I know many parents would perceive that as harsh punishment but my Outward Bound experience highlighted to me that too many people grow up without any consequences for their actions, so that when they reach the independence of adulthood it's a huge adjustment. Both as an outdoor instructor and as a parent, I found that powerful teachable moments would come along now and again. These were natural chances to provide a lesson but you needed to action them at that moment. It just happened to be on my fortieth birthday that the teachable moment to get the kids thinking about teasing and its effects happened to come along, but I wasn't going to let it pass.

The GODZone race had injected excitement and energy into the New Zealand adventure-racing scene. There hadn't been an expedition race since 2005, when the

World Champs were last staged on home soil, so it was billed as the homecoming of adventure racing as Queenstown was where the sport began in 1989. The course was an incredible 11 stages from Milford Sound to Queenstown, covering 522 km, and a handful of strong and skilled teams would offer a hard battle for the win.

As darkness fell on the first night we slipped away courtesy of some challenging navigation and built a convincing lead over the days that followed. Being early April, we froze at times during the nights and early mornings but we had some glorious days. We had a highly performing team which meant we could move through the course smoothly and efficiently. My highlight was the final paddle down Lake Wakatipu at night, racing along nearing Queenstown with every stroke, and smelling the aroma of hot food as we got closer – it's funny how important food becomes (burgers and chips in this case). Finishing a race is a blessing; finishing first is jubilation. Winning the race was hugely satisfying and gave me the confidence that if our team could win GODZone, we would win the World Championships. It was a pleasing way to kick off the next decade. My fortieth would be memorable for teachable moments and the GODZone adventure race.

With our next race not until spring, it was a chance to enjoy some adventures. Sophie was keen to paddle Cook Strait and I was willing to do it if we did a double crossing. I'd never paddled it there and back. A few friends had expressed interest so we got a small team together – Richard Ussher, Dan Busch, Todd Jago, Sophie and I – and eyed up a weekend when the tides were good for the double, making sure we could get from the South Island to the North and back again in daylight hours. We could expect to be paddling for about ten hours in exposed waters.

We paddled to the end of Tory Channel the night prior to the crossing and camped where I could feel the wind movements from the strait on my cheek as I slept. I wanted to connect with the environment, get a sense of what was happening, and it was looking hopeful. In the dark of the morning we quickly had some breakfast, a sailor's-strength coffee, and readied the boats in an atmosphere of suppressed nerves and excitement. Paddling away from the South Island is always inspiring as even on the calmest of days impressive water hydraulics are at work as you transition from sheltered to open water. The trip over went well, surfing waves with a light tailwind. I was paddling my fortieth birthday present, a shining-new red Arctic Raider sea kayak handmade by Graham Sisson – it was the perfect place to launch it. After lunch on the beach in the North Island we returned. Some sea fog made the navigation important and the currents close to Arapawa Island slowed our speed but we made it back in the last of the fast-fading light, cooked up a hot meal and enjoyed the glow of satisfaction from having completed a solid mission.

Next was another kayak mission but this time with the family in Fiji. Friends Cindy and Andy owned a yacht there and had invited us to spend a week sailing around the Yasawa island group. I hadn't been to those islands since I raced the Eco Challenge in 2002, the stage of our epic victory. We had a leisurely week sailing in the tropics and then got dropped off for our kayak trip. Our aim was an 11-day paddle, circumnavigating the Yasawa Group including paddling around the main island of Yasawa, which is infrequently done due to the trade winds blowing. Afterwards I learned that the kayak base manager didn't rate our chances very highly – given our paddling team, I suspect – and summed it up dubiously as a 'very ambitious trip'. I was in a double with Tide (5) and Zefa (7), and Jodie and Jessie (9) in another double.

Approximately 130 km later, with all but empty kayaks, we completed the trip we had embarked on with a feeling of accomplishment. While it was paradise, it wasn't always a holiday. We had some hard paddling, moderate swells and surf landings. We survived a mass mosquito ambush at one camp and got drenched a few times by rapidly moving storms. Each day we would find a new campsite and then walk to the nearest village to meet with the chief. A small ceremony would take place where we would offer some kava, which we'd brought from the mainland, and request permission to camp on their beach. It was always special as the chief would welcome us as family and give us the rights of the village. They were always impressed with the kids. I guess most families head to resorts, buffets and pools for their Fiji vacation.

Once back home it was time to start training for the 2012 Adventure Racing World Championships in France. It was a race I wanted to win so I trained accordingly, putting in big efforts to clock up large volumes of training, typically 30 to 40 hours per week. En route to France we decided to do an event in China as part of our build-up. In my many years of travel and racing I have seen some intriguing things and Ordos in Inner Mongolia ranks right up there on my list of the top 10 most bizarre places I've been to. Apparently this 'ghost city' was built to cater for 10 million people, yet only two million live there. Its swathes of empty residences and desolate streets are eerily apocalyptic or reminiscent of mass alien abduction.

The race itself took us to unique areas, including a day's running in the Kubuqi Desert. Paddling on the Yellow River, horse riding and mountain biking kept us busy for four days. Success in racing in China involves the art of adaptation – the thing you least expect is bound to happen and random things are guaranteed. On the kayak down the Yellow River we were racing side by side with Richard Ussher's team when an official race boat pulled alongside, screaming at us in Mandarin and pointing for us to go back upstream. We had no idea what they meant but assumed we'd missed a channel and were paddling towards a major hazard, perhaps a dam. The flow was strong and when we turned around and pointed upstream we were going nowhere, so we paddled to the shore and climbed out. The safety boat seemed satisfied and went back upriver. Clueless as to what was going on, we surveyed downriver and couldn't see any danger, and agreed to carry on but be cautious. After wasting over 10 minutes and at risk of being caught by the chasing teams, we paddled on and came across nothing. Luckily the GPS tracking device recorded our stoppage and the race director credited us back that time, also confused by the actions of the renegade safety boat. Only in China . . . We went on to win the race, making our tally for the year three wins from three starts.

China is a strange place in which to race for a myriad of reasons. 'Contrasts' is the word I'd use to describe it. A typical day starts at the hotel, and after breakfast we load buses and travel sometimes hours to the racing location. It could be in the middle of a huge city or in remote wilderness. Normally we'll experience both locations in a day. We race through rural villages, croplands and waterways, but at other times we can race through working construction sites, polluted areas and massive bustling cities. The events in most cases are extremely well run, sometimes with military precision, and the hosting is generous and thorough. For many events the organisers subsidise the flights for foreign teams, with accommodation, meals and transport all laid on. The opening and closing ceremonies are huge affairs – with fireworks, performances, and speeches yelled by dignitaries – over the top by New Zealand standards but a small price to pay for being catered for so well. Even though there may be only 30 teams competing, they will shut a major highway or close off large areas of a city for the race. Being treated like a superstar when you're not one can be a bit comical, but we play along, smile for the cameras. Some of the safety aspects of the racing can be marginal though, especially the ropes sections, and I have seen some very unorthodox rigging of abseils and the like, which can be scary when you know they're not solid set-ups.

After winning the race in Ordos we enjoyed a night of fine dining in Beijing before flying out to Nice, France, where we quickly settled into the mountains to train for a week and prepare for the World Champs. Visiting France at any time is a most enjoyable experience, but visiting France after racing in China is sensational. I thoroughly enjoyed the training there, the highlight being riding some of the classic cycling climbs used in the grand tours – the Alpe d'Huez in the central French Alps and the Col du Galibier. The team was feeling confident having freshly won in China against the world's best teams, and in light of what had happened in Tasmania in 2011, redemption was on the cards.

The field was largely comprised of European and Scandinavian teams. Swedish athletes had scored some impressive results in recent times and they were highly represented by a large contingent of teams and supporters. At the opening ceremony, one of their team managers came up to me, looked me in the eye and said, in his thick accent, 'You must be very scared of the Swedish teams.' Holding his gaze, I calmly replied, 'No, I'm not.' But I walked away thinking, 'A fucking war has begun. Thanks for starting it!'

Soon into the race, which began with a glacier stage, it became obvious to me that we were the strongest team in the competition. Climbing and descending from the ice field, our team was in cruise mode while the teams around us were working really hard. The first day of a race can test patience as any number of teams can go 100 per cent and remain in contact for the first 12 to 20 hours, and then they invariably explode as a result of red-lining for too long. As the race progressed, the lead pack slowly diminished, and by the end of the first day only us and the defending world champions, a French/Swedish combined team, remained in the lead. They seemed content sitting behind us, saving their energy, leaving Chris to navigate, which is typical in races and very occasionally we do the same thing.

As we descended off some high mountains we joined a zig-zag track. I had the team control card which I had to clip at each checkpoint, evidence we'd been there. Most of the time I don't know where the checkpoint is and Chris will point them out to me. In this instance, we weren't using the zig-zag track but instead running directly down the fall line. Chris called out to me that there was a checkpoint to the left. I spotted it and angled off, clipped the card and started down the hill after the team to catch up. Out of the corner of my eye the other team came into view and I was fairly certain they hadn't seen me clip the checkpoint. They followed me down not paying attention to their map. Catching up to the team, I casually called to Chris to speed up, which he did. We started losing height fast and the chasing team kept pace. I whispered to the others that they hadn't got the control and to go even faster. For about 15 minutes we raced down the hill at full speed until their navigator finally checked their map and discovered they'd overshot the checkpoint. I'm not sure if they knew then that we'd already got it but climbing back up a hill can be soul-destroying.

There are times in a race where I get a strong sense that the outcome can be determined at that exact moment. I'm nearly always right and I felt it here, communicating that to the team. Despite the fact the race in France had just began, and we hadn't even completed day one of five, I sensed we needed to apply pressure while we had an advantage and force the chasing teams to make errors, which is exactly what happened. But what I didn't account for were the problems that awaited us, venturing into the unknown. Later that night I started to feel ill and accepted I was suffering in the altitude. I was getting acute mountain sickness from racing for extended periods on high ground. Feeling shit, I slowed and struggled to keep up. The team rallied, taking my gear and towing me through some sections. I was vomiting, had a splitting headache and was wiped out. Around 3 a.m. I was lying in the grass throwing up, feeling complete crap and getting my head around the nightmare I was living. Debating my needs, Sophie and Trevor were talking about putting up our tent and letting me sleep. 'No way!' I called out. 'We need to protect our lead and get me off this mountain.' Back in the valley I started to improve straight away and as we descended lower I recovered further.

We very nearly lost the lead when a checkpoint had been put in the wrong place, and after spending considerable time looking for it we eventually gave up. But when we got to the end of the stage the race staff insisted that it was in the right place and believed teams behind us had got it. We were half dressed into our rafting gear for the next stage so we started to change back into hiking gear to return and look for the checkpoint we had missed. Thankfully we were saved by the race director who had more faith in Chris's navigation abilities than the staff who set the checkpoint. Speaking to us by phone, he told us to continue racing and we maintained our lead. It turned out later that Chris was right, so it was a great on-the-spot decision by the director to insist we raced on.

It's common in races that the white water will be over-graded to make it sound better. So when they told us we would be rafting a Grade 4 gorge I figured it would likely be Grade 2 with maybe one or two Grade 3 rapids. As we approached the first rapid and could get a sense of the elevation drop ahead of us, any sleepiness we had from 24 hours of non-stop racing evaporated as we became fully submerged when the raft dropped off a small waterfall. For the next few hours we rafted the most intense and action-packed white-water stage I have ever done in a race. It was full-on, steep, technical, continuous Grade 4. Thankfully I had rafted plenty of Grade 5 in the past and guided up to Grade 4 so we didn't have any issues, but it was extremely stressful and I wasn't enjoying it. I started to wonder if we'd missed the take-out as towards the end the rapids were getting more like Grade 4+. On one rapid, which looked Grade 5 to me, I couldn't see the exit as the water cascaded down through a canyon, and desperately called commands to catch an eddy above the first drop. Stuff the race – I wasn't prepared to drop into this without a visual. However, it didn't look too bad from the riverbank, so using a throw rope we lined the raft around the first drop and then hopped back in. Once at the end of the stage I was exhausted.

Our gap back to the chase teams had lessened but we kept pushing. For the next few days we raced hard and built up a handy lead of about six hours, despite the fact Trevor had gone through a real bad patch and Sophie was biking with one pedal as the other had disintegrated. On a hiking stage we popped out onto a highway and saw a cyclist coming towards us. We waved him down and somewhat reluctantly he stopped. In a stroke of luck it turned out he was using the same pedal system as Sophie. We had stacks of cash and showed him the money and pointed to his pedal. It was clear we wanted it and were prepared to pay him extravagantly. Not at all keen, he pushed us out of his way and rode off, turning back to give us the finger and yell out, 'Fuck you, Americans!' How bizarre, for all of us I suppose. Thankfully at the end of the stage we managed to get a new pedal.

The course was outstanding as we journeyed towards the Mediterranean. We were performing splendidly, overcoming multiple curve balls, and although we certainly weren't having the perfect race we were winning and only had one more night left, one more mountain stage to complete. In high spirits and freshly stocked up after visiting a patisserie, we climbed into the mountains. As we gained elevation I started to feel strange again at around 3000 metres, and soon enough I was keeled over spewing. Oh no, the elevation profile of this stage meant we had a few passes to go over – we were going to be up high for 10 to 12 hours. This was going to be a mammoth task. Carrying nothing, I was stumbling around trying to maintain forward progress, but I was frustratingly slow and the team could sense our race unravelling. I tried to reassure them that no team would be moving fast at this end of a race, that we just needed to keep plodding, even if it was slow. We were due for a sleep, though, as we'd only managed about seven hours by this point. It was getting dark and the temperature had dropped when we arrived at a large mountain lodge and asked if we could rent a room. No. Could we just use the bathroom? No. Standing outside, I was overcome with fatigue and told the team that I needed to lie down right then and there, so we decided to sleep. Four people with minimal gear, clearly in some sort of race, curled up on the front lawn of the lodge fast asleep, would have been a curious sight for the other guests. It would have been even more of a sight when I woke vomiting copiously. Wiping my face clean I told the team I felt a bit better and we should go.

Sadly, the improvement was short-lived and I soon fell into the torment of my body being too poisoned by carbon dioxide and inadequate oxygen to function normally. For hour after hour I soldiered on, battling with my mind and body but refusing to give up. Chris was towing me so hard he kept breaking his tow line, and Trevor was feeling similar effects, which meant that Sophie and Chris were literally carrying the weight of the team. In a state of delirium, I heard Chris utter the magic words, 'That's the last pass – it's down to the ocean now.' Hallelujah!

Descending into thicker air worked a miraculous recovery. Once under 2000 metres, despite being dog-tired and debilitated, my mind was back in the game, and I resumed my captaincy and focus to win the race. Thanks primarily to Sophie and Chris, we had completed the final major hurdle. We only had a mountain bike to finish, which was predominantly downhill, then a short kayak to the end. On the ride down, Sophie crashed, splitting her knee open that would later require stitches, but the race needed to be won first. We did have some forced delays as we sped by vines laden with wild berries – yum! The final paddle stage was fantastic – sunshine in the Mediterranean, sea level, knowing we had the race sealed, we could savour the victory, and we did. I was immensely satisfied. The team dug super-deep in the Alps of France to beat the best teams in Europe and win what we believed was rightfully ours. I was immensely relieved that Sophie had bagged her first World Championships, while for Trevor, amazingly, it was his third long race and third victory, an incredible accomplishment in itself. As we approached the beach and the finish line I leapt onto the boys' boat and capsized them – it was time to celebrate! World champions – we had got what we came for. I had waited almost a year for that moment.

From France I went directly to the Spring Challenge which was being held in Methven where we had a record field. I delivered the event successfully despite being spent from the racing and travel, but it was a satisfied spent, the best feeling. Catching up with the family, Jodie informed me of her plans for us to relocate to Queenstown for 2013. We had said for years that when the kids were old enough to ski on a mountain independently we'd move there for a year, exposing them to a real winter, by New Zealand standards. While I wanted to, I wasn't convinced that 2013 was the best year, maybe it was best to wait until 2014? The main reason was that my sport had just lifted to another level, we were world champions, and I was confident we could be for a few years to follow, so I preferred to be based from home. Jodie, though, felt like she was in a rut, the routine of school and home life was becoming a burden and she wanted a change, something fresh. Seeing how important it was to her, I agreed. Quietly I didn't think it would happen, as in just a matter of months we would need to rent a house there, rent out our home, come to an arrangement with the schools, plus numerous other things, and the timeframe was limited. It was therefore a surprise when a week later she told me it was all sorted, everything was in place. I have been described as a whirlwind of efficiency in my time, but Jodie definitely impressed me with the swiftness of this move.

Before I could wrap up the racing season we had one more race to do – Wulong in China – but it turned into a disaster. We weren't fully recovered from France and Sophie had an injury to contend with, suffering to extreme levels each day. That experience is the reason why our team has never raced in China again. Sophie flat out refused. In hindsight, we shouldn't have gone.

Earlier in the year I got a phone call from Neelu Memom, a woman who'd recently done the Coast to Coast in a team and wanted to know if I would paddle the Cook Strait with her. She went on to explain that when she was 16 years old she unexpectedly fell into a coma after she had contracted what she thought was the flu. In actual fact she had a post-viral autoimmune reaction which had resulted in a brain injury and caused her body to shut down. She spent two weeks in intensive care and a further three and a half months in hospital where doctors weren't sure whether she'd live or die. But miraculously Neelu woke up and the next year of her life was spent in intensive rehab. As a result she had lost much of her sight and balance. She wasn't 100 per cent sure she could actually paddle the strait and I explained to her that she'd need to do some training and then it was just a matter of getting suitable crossing conditions.

In the lead-up we did a training trip around D'Urville Island with my racing team, which gave me and Neelu a chance to do long paddles together in a double sea kayak in exposed water. I had no doubts of her ability – she was keen, adventurous, could take a bit of hassle, and we would have a few laughs. I told her that come early summer we would be able to book a few dates when the tidal flows allowed passage and then hope for good weather. The first couple of options fell over, with storms passing through the strait, but finally in November there was a small weather window that looked promising. Three friends who were experienced ocean paddlers were going to accompany us. It is always a committing trip and given Neelu's needs I thought it could be good to notify the coastguard that we were planning to paddle the strait in a few days' time, thinking a radio schedule would be a sensible safety measure given we weren't using a support boat, much to Neelu's surprise. I explained to her that if we needed a support boat we shouldn't be out there in the first place. The conversation with the coastguard went like this:

'Good morning, I'm planning to paddle the Cook Strait by kayak in a few days' time and wondering if we could arrange a radio schedule to keep in contact regarding our progress?'

'The Cook Strait by kayak! Are you sure that's wise? How many people?'

'There will be five of us, three single kayaks and a double, and I'm paddling with a blind woman who's keen to do it.'

'A blind woman kayaking the Cook Strait? Have you seen the weather out there?'

'Yes, but it'll settle in a few days and I'm confident we can get across.'

'It's a long way. How do you expect to do it? Where are you leaving from?'

'Oh, we won't do it in one go, we'll paddle down Tory Channel on Thursday night and paddle the strait early Friday.'

'Paddling at night! That's a shipping lane – you can't paddle that at night.'

'Yes we can, we'll have lights, and besides, I've done it before many times.'

'This sounds like a crazy plan to me – what sort of support boat are you using?'

'We're not using one.'

'That's insane, every kayaking group should have a support boat, especially in the conditions we're having at the moment. You can't go out there without one.'

'I've actually paddled the strait a number of times without one, I'm okay with it.'

'I think we need to let the police know about this. When are you departing and where from?'

'Um . . . you know what, I think you're right, I don't think we'll do it now, I think we'll do something else, it'd be foolish without a support boat, thanks for your advice and time, much appreciated, goodbye.'

A few days later I called Neelu and said there was a crossing opportunity in two days, could she get a ferry the next day and meet us in Picton. We met and night-paddled the 30 km or so to the heads and camped the night, watching the southerly dying away. I think it was an eye-opener for Neelu to be on a trip with highly experienced outdoors people. It was late when we got to the heads to camp, about 10 p.m., but we got our cookers out and made a meal, then sat around drinking cups of tea until late. Here we were, the night before a major, lounging about the campsite cooking lamb chops and drinking tea, having a pleasant night under the stars. In comparison to adventure racing, a day's sea kayaking across the Cook Strait *is* a leisurely day out. Later that day, we'd be having afternoon tea at a downtown Wellington café and catching the last ferry back to the South Island.

The crossing went very well. We had a lingering southerly swell which gave us some waves to surf at times and kept it interesting, and it was a beauty day to be on the ocean, but we knew a northerly change was forecast and we'd only have a windless morning. After about four hours of kayaking we landed on the North Island, stage one complete, and it felt like a real achievement to have made it across the strait with Neelu, although before we could celebrate we needed to complete the trip. We still had three to four hours of paddling to Island Bay where we'd arranged a pick-up by some local paddling friends.

As expected, the wind started to puff from the north and in the space of an hour had built to gale strength in exposed places, blasting down the valleys offshore. The final few hours we worked hard to make progress, taking conservative lines to minimise the risk of getting blown back out into the strait again. Prodigious gusts were threatening to rip paddles from our hands and I urged Neelu, who was tired, wet and shivering with cold by this point, to dig deep. Thankfully we'd made it to Red Rocks so we landed there. Now it was time to rejoice.

I am aware that some people would deem paddling the Cook Strait without a support vessel irresponsible, especially given Neelu's condition, but that's my character. I like to be tested, and while I don't go purposely looking for trouble, I'm not afraid of having an epic. The whole reason I was paddling with Neelu was that it was an additional challenge – it elevated the stakes of what was already a serious undertaking. I think my life would be dreary if I didn't regularly test my moral fibre and fortitude.

Summertime was next on the agenda and we had some exciting family adventures planned once we moved to Queenstown.

CHAPTER TWENTY-NINE
NOT FINISHED

Queenstown was to be our home for 2013. New Year's Eve was spent on the Clutha River with our friends Mark and Wendy and their daughters, doing an overnight kayaking trip. The weather was so hot we spent most of our time paddling rivers, as being on or in the water was the best place to be. The highlight of the summer paddling was a trip on the Arawhata, a large wilderness river that drains from Mount Aspiring National Park to the Tasman Sea, on the edge of Fiordland. A local jet boater dropped us 60 km upriver and we spent the next three days tripping downstream. A heavy fast-moving storm set in on the last night flooding our campsite and making the final day exciting, paddling a flooded river into a gusting headwind with driving rain – the sort of adventure I love, braving the elements. With kids, though, it's best when these days are the last ones, heading out to the luxuries of civilisation. We paddled the Dart, sections of the Kawarau and the Lake Wakatipu islands, and spent the last day of the holidays kayaking the Upper Shotover River, quite possibly my most favourite Grade 2 section in the country. By then the kids had had enough kayaking and were ultra-keen to go back to school.

During January I was checking in regularly with Sophie as she prepared for her attempt to win the Coast to Coast Longest Day again. Come early February she called me quite concerned about a particular rapid in the river that was causing her some stress, something she didn't need in the final few weeks of preparation. I was mountain biking at the time so I told her I'd shoot up and paddle the river with her. It turns out it was a tricky little manoeuvre in a 6-metre-long racing kayak at that flow but we got the line sorted. Sophie went on to win the race by a huge margin. I took the kids to watch and Jodie was in her support crew, and I was very nervous leading into the race, as if she were to have a bad day some responsibility would fall on me as her coach. Once I saw that she was in peak condition and tearing the race apart, I could enjoy it significantly more.

During my first few years of coaching I wasn't able to separate my training from what I was getting the athletes to do, so they were doing far more than they could handle. Over time, I learned that if they did far less than I could handle, they'd get better results. I'm also a big believer in self-coaching because that has been my own pathway. Over my 25 years of sport, I have had three coaches – Greg Fraine, Nathan Dahlberg and Jon Hellemans – but only for a year, and spaced evenly throughout my career. I found I hit plateaus every so often and needed some advice in advancing. After a season of being coached I'd have the skills and set-up to self-coach for another period. I'm not a technology person when it comes to training either. Because of my heart condition a heart rate monitor has been next to useless for me. The likes of power meters and all the online training and data programmes are foreign to me too. I train by feel and time. I do easy, medium, or hard sessions, either short, medium, or long. When I want to get really fit, I race, in as many races as I can get to. I've been known to race up to six times per week in my training, typically small races of one to two hours in duration, biking, running and kayaking.

Many athletes look for a coach because it's something they think they need, rather than something they actually need. I get regular requests to coach people and I find it very difficult to say no, but I have to be careful with how much of my time I give away. I can nearly always offer people some guidance, but to coach an athlete properly is a big task because it requires training the athlete in not just the sports but the bigger picture. When I coached Sophie for the Coast to Coast, a significant part of that was sports psychology, working with her to develop a mindset and belief, and race strategy, as well as the tools to adjust it mid-race if required – the ability to troubleshoot, accept and adapt. Because we were team-mates and trained together regularly, I was able to get a good understanding of her lifestyle, energy levels and other commitments, and adjust the programme accordingly. It was good fun but came with a fair level of pressure – when an athlete puts faith in you to get them racing fast in a major event, because you've said you could, the stakes are high.

The remainder of summer was spent hiking and biking in the surrounding mountains and enjoying the festivities a resort town has to offer. It was special family time for us as life was significantly less busy than at home. The phone hardly rang and we hung out together all the time. There was something new to do each day. An added bonus was that the GODZone Adventure Race was in Queenstown again, making it really easy for me, and our team won again. It was a strange race in some respects. Coming off winning the World Championships in France we were extremely confident we would win and never really doubted that throughout the race. A Kiwi team with some great athletes wasn't far behind us but for some reason we never sensed a serious threat. In hindsight we were probably a bit complacent and could have been beaten as a result. One of the reasons we all agreed we'd won both GODZone and the World Champs was that we had some new discoveries in nutrition and possibly superior fuelling to the other teams.

Early in 2012 I'd been talking with Grant MacDonald, a keen outdoors man who developed an anti-chafe cream that our team used, who is also an award-winning food scientist. Eager to help us race further and faster for longer, he'd calculated our calorie demands for an expedition race and come to the view that the only way to efficiently carry the required calories was to use ultra-light and mega energy dense freeze-dried food. Because of a cutting-edge drying technique he'd developed, he'd produced meals that tasted great and wouldn't cause dehydration or other issues we had experienced and offered me some to try. We trialled them and immediately became convinced. They tasted amazing and had massive advantages in terms of carrying energy while racing.

At the World Champs in France it was the main thing we ate, and we showed the products to some other athletes and teams who then started using them also. By 2013, Grant and his son Andrew had started a company making the meals for commercial sale, Absolute Wilderness. Given that I had been involved with some of the product development and marketing, I jumped at the opportunity to invest in the business. The three of us now run the company which is rapidly growing, we firmly believe we have the best freeze-dried meals in the world, and we have ambitious goals for the business. It's exciting to think that we're making delicious and invigorating meals that will fuel people doing amazing things in incredible places. Our drive is to offer people around the world the ultimate food for adventure – healthy, tasty and enjoyable, and primarily made of nutritious New Zealand ingredients.

One family adventure we wanted to do while living in Otago was the Central Rail Trail. In 2010 a friend of ours, Emily, lost her husband and two of her daughters in the catastrophic Haiti earthquakes and had set up a foundation to raise money for children there through an initiative called Purple Cake Day. We wanted to show our support for that and the kids agreed to ride the Rail Trail as a fundraiser. They did exceptionally well and rode the trail in just over three days, raising over $3,000 for the charity.

Before the racing season was over I had to shoot over to China for a stage race in Wenzhou. It was only a two-person team so I went with my team-mate Trevor. We finished second after some bad luck in the first few days, and although we were never likely to win the race against another strong Kiwi male team, we had to work harder for second than normal. My next event was the Nelson 24-hour adventure race, where I teamed with Sophie, Richard Ussher and JJ Wilson, and we had a good day out, winning the race.

The ski season was soon upon us including all the reasons we wanted to live in Queenstown. It snowed heavily, shutting the roads and cancelling school, so the kids went skiing in our back yard. I had to ring a mate to ask if it was standard to put chains on the car to drive into town. Living in deep snow is normal for some people but unique for us and it was fun building snowmen and making snowballs. One reason for being there was to get the kids' skiing ability up to a level good enough for them to enjoy the sport plus introduce them to another outdoor activity they might wish to pursue. We soon discovered that it was an ideal family sport and we skied intensely for the winter. I had to go to Nelson about once a month for work commitments and it was really nice to stay with Mum and Dad while I was there. Mum often joked that they saw a lot more of me since I moved south.

On 13 July 2013, my day started in Christchurch. Over the previous few days I had been to Marlborough to do a job, speaking at a conference and scoping out a possible new event that Peter Yealands of Yealands Estate Winery wanted me to organise. There was a chance I would have to go to Nelson for a meeting on the Wednesday but that didn't eventuate, but I still flew to Nelson on Thursday, emailing Mum to let her know I needed a pick-up from the airport about midday. I had a nice flight up from Queenstown. Dad collected me and said Mum was out getting a few things for lunch. I had planned to go for a run but enjoyed lunch with Mum and Dad out on the veranda first, sitting under the Nelson sun, chatting and relaxing like you can only do at the house you grew up in. Once the food settled I went for a run, grabbed a quick shower and asked Dad to drop me off in town for my 4 p.m. pick-up. Mum told me she would take me into the city as she had bought some second-hand outdoor chairs and needed to collect them (she spent hours perusing Trade Me for bargains – the polar opposite to me, as if I need something, I'll buy the best I can get and brand new). As we drove past the SPCA, she remarked that she'd love to own a llama, having seen one grazing in the paddock. We pulled up at the iconic church steps, I gave her a quick kiss, said thanks and that'd I see her in a few weeks. I grabbed a coffee and waited for my ride. I was picked up at 4 p.m. on the dot and we drove down Trafalgar Street. Coincidentally, Mum was driving back up the street, and I was going to wave but decided not to – she wouldn't recognise the vehicle I was in. That was the last time I saw her alive.

On Friday I ran a half marathon at the Yealands vineyard and then got into a car for a ride to Christchurch airport with one of the staff. No sooner had we started driving than the airline phoned to advise my flight was cancelled and that I'd have to fly Saturday morning. I called my brother to let him know I'd be staying the night. We arranged to meet at a bar as he was having his end-of-term staff drinks. Later that night we went back to his place, he cooked a meal and we decided to Skype our good mate Andy Pohe (who's like a brother to us) living in Australia. I thought at the time I should let Mum know I was staying at Braden's, as being immensely family focused she'd like to hear that, but decided it could wait. Saturday morning I said goodbye to Braden, and his partner Enna dropped me at the airport, both of us commenting on how random such visits can be.

Because I was due to arrive in Queenstown before 11 a.m., Jodie and the kids had decided to wait for me to return and we'd go skiing for the day as a family, especially as the ski field was open until 9 p.m. on a Saturday. Our two younger children were eager to learn how to ride the T-bar so that was the goal for the day. By 12 p.m. we were all skiing. After about 30 minutes of skiing, in which I had done three leg-burning rides up the T-bar with my six-year-old daughter, who was turning seven the very next day, I could feel my phone ringing in my jacket. Moving to a chairlift, I had a moment to check my phone on the way, seeing that I'd missed a call from Braden. At first I thought I must have left something at his house, but figured he wouldn't ring for something like that. I called him. He told me Mum, Dad and our two-year-old nephew Ali had been in a car crash but didn't know any more details. I said I'd keep skiing until I heard from him. As we loaded onto the Greengates chair, a six-seater so all the family were on it, I told our kids there was some bad news, a crash, but I didn't know any more at this stage.

I'd just got off the chair when Braden called back. He suggested I sit down. I didn't. He told me it's bad. Mum is dead, Dad and Ali are in the intensive care unit. No more details. How soon could I get to Nelson? Our sister Zariana was there by herself, in the hospital with the three people she lived with all on different levels in different states. It was a waking nightmare. I sat the kids down and told them the news and that we needed to get home so we could go to Nelson. In a state of semi-shock, I skied off the mountain, gathered the family in the car and drove home, crying. Mum was gone. Surely this couldn't be true.

I called Air New Zealand immediately to book a flight, explaining the situation and that I was rushing to the airport – I love it that New Zealand is small enough that they said they'd hold the plane until we got there. At 2 p.m. I was back on a flight to Christchurch where I met Braden and Enna. I was numb. It was sur-real, like looking at the world through dirty glass. Braden had more news about the crash – their car had plunged into the river and sunk. It seemed Mum had a blackout or something where she lost consciousness. Dad was being treated for a heart attack and Ali was alive but was being treated for drowning and was to be transferred to Starship Children's Hospital in Auckland.

At 6 p.m. we landed in Nelson and were met by friends who took us to the hospital. We went to the ICU where Ali was in a coma wired to life support in a chilled room. He looked strong. If any kid was going to pull through something like this he had it in him. I embraced my sister and then went to see Dad. He looked 10 years older than his age, frail, weak and distraught. We held each other and cried. It hurt, it really, really hurt. Dad was in a panicked condition, still reliving the trauma of the accident. His wife was dead, he had nearly died, and his youngest grandchild was fighting for his life. My Aunty Tua sat beside his bed praying and summed it up perfectly: 'This is a very, very bad situation for our family – one is dead, one is in a coma, one is in critical condition.'

We sat, cried and listened to Dad painfully recount the events of the day. Zar had gone to work so Mum and Dad (known as Ma'ma and Papa to their four grandchildren) were looking after Ali, which they often did as Zar and Ali had been living with them for the previous year. During the morning, Mum had decided to drive down to the port and get some fish for the cats. Ali was keen to go too because Ma'ma often took the time to stop and look at things of interest. Dad went with them. They got some fish from one shop and then went down the wharf to see if any boats had recently arrived with a fresh catch. None had come in so they started off on the return trip, Ma'ma pointing out the moored yachts in the marina. Dad remembers the car hitting the curb as Mum made a left turn, a mistake we all make from time to time. He asked her if she was okay and she replied that she was fine. Just seconds later, Mum was unconscious, and the car accelerated and launched over a traffic island, hitting a road sign and going through an intersection, directly towards a river. Instinctively Dad grabbed the wheel and tried to steer the car away from the river, but he didn't have enough time or room. The car arched over a grass strip, passed through some bushes and plunged 3 metres down into the water and began to sink.

Mum was unresponsive and Ali was screaming with fright in the back seat. Dad tried to reach around to free him but couldn't manoeuvre inside the tight confines. It took a herculean effort to get out of the car, the weight of water on the door making it near impossible to move, but he did manage to get out and then went to open Ali's door only to find it was locked. Standing in the freezing-cold water, panic-stricken, he kept furiously trying to open Ali's door as the car filled with water. Dad was standing in soft mud and could feel himself sinking deeper as the weight of the car forced him under. Ali gazed up at Dad in terror as water covered him and the car slipped under the surface. The stress of trying to hold the car up caused Dad to have a heart attack and he collapsed into the water thinking he was going to die. That's when the rescuers arrived, dragging him to shore. Barely alive himself, with a massive effort Dad was telling them his grandson was still in the car, repeating 'kid, kid, kid' with all his remaining strength. The rescue team went to work. It was the heroic efforts of Kyle Paki Paki, Philip Walker, Adam Black and Gary Miller and others that saved Dad and Ali, otherwise they would have all died.

Identifying Mum in the morgue added another level of reality. She really was gone. Everyone cried. Next we visited Ali in ICU before he was transferred to Starship. Seeing the little fella lying on the big bed, tubes and monitoring devices all over his body, highlighted the magnitude of the experience. The doctors were unsure whether Ali's brain had been damaged in the drowning or not – the icy-cold water may have actually helped him but only time would tell. I felt weak, helpless and overwhelmed by despair. We soberly made our way back to Dad's room. Soon afterwards, Jodie arrived and that triggered another emotional breakdown for Dad – I was starting to wonder how many of these he could take. He needed rest so we went back to the family home.

That was a heavy time. It was peculiar going into the house that they had left just hours before. They had simply popped out to get fish but instead got a catastrophe. It felt strange to be walking around the house, with reminders of Mum everywhere – the washing on the line she had hung out, a crossword on the table she had not completed yet, my running gear from Thursday she had washed and folded ready waiting for me. There was a giant pot of vegetable soup on the stove she had made that morning. We heated it up and ate some, and I had tears dripping into my bowl as I sipped the hot broth, thinking, Mum had chopped these carrots, she had cut these onions. From Mum and Dad's house we could hear the air ambulance revving and taking off. Standing on the veranda and watching the plane fly through the darkness, the navigation lights flashing, I quietly whispered, 'You have to make it, Ali, for Ma'ma.' My sister was on a plane to Auckland with her son in a coma, my dad was in intensive care recovering from a heart attack, and my mum was dead. It was family triage.

Zar would have ample family support in Auckland so we had comfort knowing we could let them manage there. Dad was the one who needed our support and we knew that in many ways Ali held the key to Dad's recovery – should anything happen to him life was going to be extremely difficult for Dad to face. The next day was full on. The police needed more information from Dad, the media wanted more information, and friends and family wanted to offer their condolences and help. We spent the day rushing around, visiting Dad, checking in with Zar, and dealing with all the tasks that rolled in one after the other. The news from Starship in Auckland was that Ali was stable, still in a coma but otherwise doing well. Dad had had an extremely hard day coming to grips with the reality of the situation, but he had his brother and sisters at his side which enabled me and Braden to manage things in the background.

Adding further to the emotion of the situation, it was Tide's birthday, and birthdays are a real big deal for her, so my heart was torn again. Just two days earlier, Mum had given me Tide's birthday present from her and Papa to give to Tide on this day, which should have been in Queenstown. But we were in Nelson Hospital and I had taken the present back to Dad so he could give it to her – the last present any of the grandchildren would get from Ma'ma and another stark reminder that she was gone. Later that night when we were reporting to Zar on the day she asked a heartfelt question: 'What about Mum?' She was right, we'd been so task focused that we'd neglected to think of Mum, so we arranged to visit the morgue to sit with her, which was really peaceful and beneficial and gave us the strength to cope with the following day. We know she was telling us, 'Don't worry about me – look after Ali, Zar and your father.'

The following day news came from Zar that Ali was awake. Apparently a nurse was working in his room and heard him ask, 'Can I have some toast please?' By the end of the day he was on his feet and creating havoc in the ward. When Dad heard that news the weight of death lifted off him – you could just see the pressure dissipate. He was released the next day. Family had arrived in strength to support us through the process and we had a full house. Zar and Ali and the family entourage from Auckland returned to a profound reception. When Ali went to Dad, they embraced for an eternity. It was like Ali was saying to Dad, 'Papa, that was a really awful thing to happen, but at least we have each other.' With Dad and Ali back in the family home it meant we could turn our attention to Mum and organise a funeral. This caused a little tension for a period because, as with many things in our life, there has been a Samoan and a European way of doing things and they can conflict. So Braden, Zar and I had to negotiate that balance, working to ensure that the funeral would be something Mum would want.

One thing that I will never forget from that week was the support from family and friends. People were helping in so many ways and it really made a huge difference – never did we feel unsupported or that there wasn't someone we could turn to for help. The sacrifices people made and their willingness to be there for us was deeply touching. Countless friends immediately dropped what they were doing and said, 'We're here for you and your family.' People could identify with the accident on so many levels – losing a wife, losing a parent, losing a mother, losing a grandmother, the risk of losing a son or a grandson, the list went on. Mum came home for the final few days until the funeral and we finally started to celebrate the fact that Dad and Ali were okay and accept Mum's death but celebrate her life at the same time. We began to laugh and cry as we focused on her and what she meant to all of us. She was a very special person who'd reached a vast amount of people.

I inherited Mum's pragmatism – shit happens, move on. Mum had played her role in my life. She'd raised me and set me free. My deep sorrow was that the relationship between her and my children was essentially over. She still had so much to teach my kids, and they were just reaching ages where she would be able to support, help and influence them greatly. She would have been looking forward to those years, but now they were stolen, which was sad, for them and her. Thankfully for our children, Jodie's parents, Sally and Bill, have a close relationship with them and are always willing to help out where they can. Mum was an education pioneer and it was a fitting tribute when the Ministry of Education honoured her work with an award for services to Pasifika education.

After the funeral I flew back to Queenstown. Jodie and the kids were on a later flight. I needed space now. It had been the most intense, grievous and traumatic two weeks I'd ever had and I longed for some time in the mountains and the feeling of isolation. Getting home was a welcome respite. I felt I could process things to another level and start life again without my mother.

In August I was due to race in Brazil, another round of the Adventure Racing World Series. In two minds whether I should go, I was close to withdrawing and organising a replacement athlete when I got a phone call from Chris – he'd travelled ahead to compete in an orienteering competition in Columbia where he'd taken a bad fall and injured himself and wasn't going to be able to race in Brazil. I knew then that I'd need to go and quickly started to find a replacement. Thankfully Dougal Allan was able to race but needed a few days to sort things out before he travelled so I went ahead with Sophie and Trevor. It was therapeutic for me to get out and have an adventure, to occupy my mind with other things and enjoy myself.

The race didn't go well for us, though, which looking back does not surprise me. I wasn't ready to race hard and with Chris not being there I became the navigator. In most cases I'm keen to get the maps and do some navigation but I'd never used Brazilian maps before and it took me a long time to adjust to them, and in the meantime we lost time to the lead teams. The mapping was really poor and often didn't make sense. On one stage we had a cameraman travel with us who had a GPS and vaguely knew the way. He was a nice guy but told me a number of times that he wasn't allowed to help us in any way, which I didn't have an issue with. However, I got really mad with him at a checkpoint when a staff member was telling us something in Portuguese and he wouldn't translate what they were saying. I patiently explained to him that had we been a local team we would have got whatever information it was, so it wasn't any advantage, but he refused. As a result we spent an hour looking for a trail and ended up back at the checkpoint, the same staff member trying to give us the information again, pointing this way and that, trying to help but actually making us more confused until we eventually located the trail and off we went.

Later that night, we were travelling down a valley on the way to the checkpoint at the next town when we entered a large village that wasn't marked on the map. We were at a river confluence and nothing made sense. After a while I decided that the river must surely be mapped correctly so it must be the village that was marked wrong, most likely on the opposite bank. Despite it being about 4 a.m., a local man came out of his house to see what we were doing. I told him the name of the town I was trying to locate and he pointed off in a direction that didn't make sense either. We couldn't understand what he was saying so, once again, a local team would be getting this information. When I asked the camera guy what the old man was saying, he told me he couldn't help us. I'd had enough. Placing my hand firmly on his shoulder I quietly said to him, 'Tell me, please, what the fuck the man is saying.' He said if you follow this trail it'll lead to a bridge, cross the bridge and the trail will take you to the town. Thank you.

In the end we finished in second place, but with the poor maps, the language barrier and a sinking kayak, not many things had gone well for us. As a team we'd had fun and plenty of laughs so from that respect it had been good for me. It served as a timely reminder that if I wanted to perform well at the World Champs in Costa Rica in a few months' time I'd need to get focused. In light of what had happened in our family, I now needed to decide whether that was something I could do.

Travelling back home I was getting some strange looks passing through the airports. On the first day of the race in Brazil I'd decided to take a short cut through a small section of jungle with no trail that didn't pay off. Unbeknown to us, there were plants in there that had super-sharp edges that cut my forearms to shreds, lacerating them like I'd lost a fight with a chainsaw. The bloody gouges then had days and days of racing, more scratches and intense sunburn added to them. Not only were they sensitive and painful, but as I started to travel home the dead skin was flaking off, so they looked like something out of a horror movie.

Then, just a few weeks later, I woke one night with an almighty fever, the bed so drenched with sweat that I needed to change the sheets. Barely an hour later, I was piling extra blankets on, trying to ward off shivering spasms. I had stomach-wrenching pains and was so weak the next day that I felt like curling up and dying. After another night of torment I woke to find myself covered from head to toe in a rash of angry red spots and my stomach pains were worsening. Clearly my body was in major freak-out mode so I went to see my GP, Jo, who leapt into action after learning that I'd just been racing in Brazil. The tests he ordered for infectious tropical diseases revealed some form of threadworm in my intestine and a form of parasite resembling small fish in my blood that the lab had never seen anything quite like before. My miracle cure – ivermectin. I shouldn't have been surprised at falling so crook, as out of desperation we had drunk river water on one of our stages, adding double doses of our water purification liquid – but it was hopeless really, the waterway was so truly foul and polluted.

Once back on my feet I was full-time delivering the Spring Challenge, which was held in Gibbston, near Queenstown, with another record field. We took a risk and had the teams raft through the Dog Leg section of the Kawarau River – a big step up from any rafting we'd previously had in the race. It was eyes wide open for many. I'd decided by then that I wanted to race the World Champs, because in the history of the sport, no team had successfully defended their title, winning consecutive years. This provided a level of challenge I needed and by December I was in Costa Rica with the team ready to race. I was back in good shape having made some committed efforts – I really wanted this win.

Midway through the year I received an email out of the blue from a guy in Nelson, Matt Watson. He told me a little about himself and how he wanted to set up an organisation to help solve an issue he saw in youth in our community. He went on to explain that there were kids in the school his children went to who couldn't throw or catch, couldn't kick a ball. They didn't exercise, they didn't play much, and some of them wouldn't even go onto the grass field in bare feet. In light of the health issues the country is faced with, especially child obesity, he wanted to take action and start a non-profit organisation called No Child Left Inside. He wanted me to help him launch it, mainly to endorse what he wanted to do. I liked his enthusiasm and energy and agreed to meet for a coffee and make a plan, which we did, and credit to Matt, a few years on and it's a runaway success offering programmes to most local schools. But the one major influence Matt had on me was that he had written a book. When I quietly mentioned I was working on one myself, he was fully supportive and encouraged me to do it, giving me a copy of his book which I read, enjoyed and that gave me additional confidence to knuckle down and write mine.

As build-up to the World Champs I wanted to get some racing in my system, a few hit-outs before we travelled. There were two 24-hour races on which were perfect lead-ups to Costa Rica – one in South Canterbury and the other in Cromwell – and we won both events and felt confident heading off to the Worlds.

Unfortunately, the course designers had got carried away designing the race, clinging to a marketing hook that the course would go from border to border and coast to coast. While this sounded exotic and purposeful, it translated to a long and often boring race, focused more on covering distance than quality stages. About midway through the race a stage summited the highest mountain, Cerro Chirripó, at nearly 4000 metres. In light of our altitude experiences our plan was to race conservatively until we got over the mountain, take stock of how we were, and then make a bid to win the race. Before reaching the mountain stage we had ocean-kayaking, hiking and biking stages. We led the race a number of times early on but never managed to turn that lead into a race-winning move. We got navigationally tangled in mangroves one night and ended up sleeping in our boats until daylight. We thought we would have lost large amounts of time but no one was making good progress through the poorly mapped terrain, some teams spending three days in there.

We do crazy random stuff in some adventure races and Costa Rica had a classic. Part-way through a mountain-bike stage we had to stop and do a zip-line. The Superman de Osa is the world's longest cable ride at 2 km and has recorded speeds of 225 km/h. I don't see any place for adventure tourism thrills in an adventure race but we have to do what is set out. Because of my outdoor background I know all about rigging and rope capabilities, so whenever we do things I'm always checking out the set-up, and it's often not pleasing – the few times I've risked my life racing have been on substandard rope set-ups. This activity looked okay but I still wasn't happy about doing it. Oh well, life has to end sometime. Reluctantly I harnessed up. Being there at night the ride was somewhat placid and the speed was difficult to gauge. I was impressed, though, by how close to the trees we went – obviously an illusion, we must have been well clear of them. As I zoomed into the finish I was curious to find out how they stopped people. I was approaching the lights of the finish building at warp speed and could see two guys holding a rope which was the braking system. I seriously doubted their ability to stop me and started to prepare for impact at the end of the building. There is a similar but shorter ride in New Zealand but it has three brakes, not one. Amidst the crashing and clanging of hardware and yelling from the guys, I pulled up just short of the end of the cable and wall of the building. The guys were flapping their hands – they'd received some minor burns holding the brake. 'Wow,' they gasped in disbelief. 'We've never seen someone come in so fast! We weren't sure if we could stop you.' Ninety kilograms, thanks, boys. We heard later that the ride was stopped when an athlete hit a tree and shattered their ankle.

We raced on and made it over the high point. Once over the top we felt confident we could win the race from there. Ahead of us were days of paddling and it was clear we were the fastest team – we just needed to stop making mistakes. With 30 km left in the 90 km hiking stage that we were on we decided to run the valley out. It would be quicker than walking and less boring, and we were in second place so we wanted to get the lead and take control. Jogging down the jungle trail snacking on bananas and guavas that we snatched from trees in passing, a few hours later we caught and dropped the leading team, made up of a Kiwi, a Spaniard and two French athletes. Now leading the race, I could start to see how it could unfold. We were tantalisingly close to a race-winning opportunity. We were in very good shape, the remainder of the race course played to our strengths, and we'd just caught and passed the lead team with ease. Surely it couldn't be that easy? Foolish thought, since things then fell apart in monumental fashion.

It started with me. I had what felt like a build-up of sand and grit in my socks mainly around my toes. I told the team I'd clean them out at the next stream and catch up. I seated myself on a rock and took my shoes and socks off, rinsing them in the fresh water, but strangely, there was no grit on my feet or in my socks. How weird. I did notice some bleeding between my toes, but that wasn't uncommon as you tend to lose toenails and layers of skin off your feet during a race. I caught up to the team. Trevor commented that he too had to clean his socks at some point. Not long after this we had a compulsory medical check. The doctor told Trevor he had a foot infection but failed to tell him what to do about it. When he inspected my feet he was more occupied with talking into the television camera than inspecting me – his big chance of small-screen fame. On the next bike stage my feet started to get sore, a burning tingling sensation I hadn't experienced before. Biking was okay but standing was becoming painful. After the ride we had a rafting stage and a long kayak, so we'd be off our feet for close to 30 hours hopefully. Once off our bikes we had to walk about 30 minutes to the river. I was jogging along when Sophie said to me, 'Just walk. We're walking and keeping up with you fine.' My feet were flaming sore. The rafting was amazing but I couldn't enjoy it – whatever was happening to my feet was overriding everything else. By the end of the raft stage I could barely walk. Trevor complained of the same thing.

We were due for a sleep and in light of what we were going through we stopped for a two-hour rest on the riverbank. Despite the risk of crocodiles wandering by where we slept, we soon nodded off in the shade. After a few hours Sophie woke me up. Shaking off the sleepiness, I was trying hard to understand what she was saying. It turned out she'd woken with the same foot issues and quickly realised there was an infection at work. She went to the race staff and they confirmed we had the fungal infection more commonly known as trench foot. We needed to clean our feet thoroughly and then apply iodine to the open wounds, which were taking over our feet at rapid pace. Dousing the sores with iodine was intensely painful but needed to happen. We hoped that the treatment would work fast – we'd now spent nearly five hours on the riverbank and slipped back to second place. Miraculously, Chris escaped the trench foot, possibly because he was applying an antibacterial and fungal cream more liberally than we were.

Our foot problems were highly distracting and we struggled to stay focused on the race. In fact, it was difficult to see how we could even finish the race at that point, as we made a series of errors, both navigation and tactical, generally floundering around for the night. After paddling up a channel for hours Chris started to doubt his compass, on further inspection discovering that the compass was hovering over a can of food between his legs, the tin swinging the needle about 45 degrees off course. We had to backtrack. As the new day arrived and the sunshine, we made it to the Caribbean coast. After about 18 hours of travel by kayak, we tested our feet on land. Thankfully Sophie and I had made a pleasing recovery – our feet were tender but we could walk okay. Trevor, though, had deteriorated to the point where he couldn't bear his weight. Any attempt to stand had him collapsing in a heap. Fortunately, we were at a luxury resort with an outrageously helpful manager who gave us two rooms to use and sourced more iodine.

The following hours became a valuable learning experience for us all. I was on autopilot. I knew we needed to get the team strong before we carried on racing and we were in the ideal place for that to happen. We still had at least a day of racing to go. My plan was to overnight at the resort. Everyone would benefit from the rest and Trevor really needed it – his body wasn't going to recover without it. Before I went to sleep, Sophie, Chris and I had a talk. Chris wasn't that keen on staying the whole night – he was still driven to win the race. I felt that it was pointless trying to race until we consolidated and rested, and that we'd have a good chance of getting second or third if we rested now. In Chris's mind, if we weren't in it to win, why bother. Sophie also questioned the point of stopping overnight as she couldn't see how a night's rest would make any difference to Trevor's ability to walk. Chris and Sophie were suggesting that we either take our chances and carry on, or get Trevor out to a hospital for proper treatment because it was concerning that the infection on his feet was still worsening.

We'd been racing for five days and we were all tired. I needed to make a decision.

One of the race directors who had been in the area and seen that our GPS tracking device had stopped moving had turned up. I told him what was happening and showed him Trevor's feet. He wasn't very encouraging, admitting that things didn't look good. We discussed options, and he explained that the rescue helicopter was stranded by weather in the mountains and that if we stayed overnight but then needed Trevor evacuated, it could be another day before they could fly in. The only other way out was by boat and he said he would be leaving in an hour, and that the next boat out could be days away. He could get Trevor to hospital that night if we moved swiftly, otherwise he wasn't sure.

I made the call to abandon. 'Let's get the fuck out of here!' It seemed the right thing to do. Our friend and team-mate was in bad shape, his feet getting taken over by what appeared to be a flesh-eating fungal infection. Boats, ambulances, flashing sirens and we found ourselves in the emergency department. The reality of the situation started to set in once in hospital, when the doctors said to us there was little they could do, that we should go home, get clean, put some cream on and rest – exactly what we'd been doing at the Caribbean resort. Next thing we were back at the hotel wondering what the hell had just happened. Sophie was upset and disappointed we'd pulled out. Chris reckoned we should have just kept racing. I admitted I'd made the wrong call but I wasn't going to sweat it – shit happens. At that time, with the information I had to hand, I acted accordingly. If we could look ahead with 100 per cent accuracy, life would get rather uneventful I suspect.

Accept it and move on. Having a coffee with Sophie a few days after the race, she was still struggling to come to terms with the fact that we'd quit the race. It was eating her up and wasn't made any easier when the winning team had disintegrated and barely made it over the finish line themselves. Had we stayed in the race we still could have won, even with all the problems we had. She asked me how come I wasn't worried about it, how come I was so accepting. With tears dripping from my eyes, I said to her, 'I'm upset about my mum dying – I refuse to be upset about a race.' She got it. 'Don't worry,' I added, 'we'll win the World Champs in Ecuador.'

I arrived back in New Zealand ready for another action-packed school holidays with the kids. We had one more month in Queenstown and wanted to maximise the chance to get into Fiordland on a small expedition, flying into Preservation Inlet and doing a two-week kayaking-based adventure. Christmas was spent in Nelson and on Boxing Day the wind was blowing as Jodie and I took off to the beach to go kite boarding. Kiting is one of the safest sports I do (I did get a hae-matoma on a testicle once when the kite powered up and my harness wasn't fitted correctly – that hurt) but freakishly we both had some major wipe-outs and injured ourselves significantly. I tore some cartilage in my ribs and Jodie semi-dislocated her shoulder. We limped back to Queenstown and to some bad weather.

All our summer plans were either being stopped in their tracks or altered due to our injuries and the weather, so we just had to accept things and let go of what we had visualised. Sitting at home on New Year's Eve, the kids were in bed and Jodie and I were lounging about. My New Year's resolution entering 2014 was not to feel compelled to stay up until midnight to see 2014 in. Around ten o'clock I announced, 'This is fucked. I'm going to bed.'

CHAPTER THIRTY
NOVEMBER FESTIVITIES

Most days I have something to write in my training diary, because I rarely have days off. I just don't function well without exercise. Jodie sees it as my addiction. If working from home I'll always strive for about two hours' exercise a day, an hour minimum, but an hour hardly fulfils me. Given the choice, I enjoy training for around four hours a day. When I set up my training diary for 2014 I placed the logo for the Adventure Racing World Champs at the top so I'd be continually reminded of what I was working towards. I had a good feeling about the World Champs in Ecuador in November and Jodie and the kids were keen to travel with me, follow the race and have a holiday afterwards. We'd spend the third school term in Queenstown skiing and the fourth in Ecuador. Sorted. We spent January in Queenstown enjoying some hiking in the mountains before we moved home to Tasman. Despite the ups and downs of 2013, we'd had an awesome 13 months down there and it felt good knowing we'd be back for the ski season.

Home again at Kina Beach, I needed to get training – my injury had enforced a sedentary start to the year, the GODZone race was in early March, so I only had five weeks to get in shape. A friend mentioned they were doing the Kiwi Brevet mountain-bike event so I thought I'd do it too. Starting in Blenheim, it was an endurance event where the riders had to follow a set route of approximately 1100 km through a variety of terrain, from state highways to single track through native forest, and everything in between. While not a race, there was a start and finish line, and the fairly basic rules were that riders had to stop for six hours between 9 p.m. and 9 a.m. each day, and they couldn't finish in under four days, which worked out to be midday Wednesday. Riders take their own gear, as to do a Brevet in pure form, you cannot receive support. It is allowed, however, to stop at shops for feasting, which for most riders is the highlight.

I put in a few weeks' training for the event and lined up on the start with about 50 other riders. Endurance athletes (myself included) tend to be a slightly eccentric bunch and a glance around the start line confirmed this observation – it was a kaleidoscope of bikes, clothing and people. I was excited about the adventure and pleased there were mandatory stopping times, otherwise I would have ridden the entire course almost without stopping and suffered a great deal more. As it was, the suffering required was an honest amount. Riding about 17 hours a day, I completed the route and crossed the finish line soon after it opened. I had to endure some severe bruising on my sit bones over the last two days, and I did some nerve damage to my hands which is unlikely to repair. The biggest day I rode was 315 km, over half of it off-road, probably the single-hardest bike ride I've ever done. From a training perspective, it was money in the bank. Now I needed to lift my running and kayaking. Another Cook Strait crossing was next up, this time with three ladies.

When Mum died, many people in our community rallied around and provided amazing support. One of those people was Jane Martin, a friend in the kayak club. She organised meals and food to be dropped off to my Dad and while we were hosting family around the time of the funeral. I was really grateful for her efforts and made a mental note to acknowledge that sometime. Jane had already mentioned to me that she really wanted to kayak the Cook Strait so I offered to paddle it with her, essentially as a guide. I'd done five successful crossings by then and knew what to look for in terms of tides and weather. Jane jumped at the chance and asked if two of her friends could paddle as well. Suzie and Lynley were both strong paddlers, so I was happy with that.

There was a very small weather window in early February so I got the team to be on standby. Paddling the strait from the South Island often means you have to take a risk choosing a crossing day, as it takes a day to paddle to the Tory Channel entrance, versus starting in the North Island where you can launch directly into the strait itself. Given we were all tight on time and that the next favourable tides were another month away, we had a little less than a day if the weather forecast was correct, and there was every chance we'd have to abort if the system approached faster. But it was worth an attempt and they were keen – there was an adventure beckoning regardless.

We enjoyed an evening paddle to the heads and camped overnight. Waking early, the strait looked good – the dying southerly swell was still evident and the northerly was due to increase to gale force later. We had half a day to get over to the North Island. The plan was to paddle for an hour and see what was happening.

If it wasn't looking good, return to the South Island, if it looked okay, press on. If we chose to carry on, it required full commitment, because in another hour you're halfway, smack in the middle.

Conditions were kind to us and it was an enjoyable paddle, but the level of exposure always keeps you alert. The reality is that the strait is a very safe stretch of water when you consider how fast rescue services can reach you – in an emergency you'd have help hovering above you in 10 to 15 minutes, but no one wants that kind of scenario. We landed on the North Island in good time, but we could feel the northerly building and we still had a few hours to go to reach land where a vehicle could pick us up. We wanted to paddle into Lyall Bay, but as we rounded toward Wellington the offshore northerly was screaming and it made little sense to risk getting blown back out into the strait when we had achieved the objective. Instead we bee-lined to the westernmost vehicle access point at Red Rocks. We'd done it. Jane was thrilled to have achieved her long-time goal of paddling the strait and I was glad that I got the chance to show my appreciation for the assistance she gave our family in a time of need.

The GODZone adventure race was now less than a month away so I kept my training ticking over and squeezed in some work in between. I had a new event to deliver for Yealands Estate Winery who were interested in organising a half marathon around their huge coastal vineyard in Marlborough, which coincidentally is the exact half-marathon distance. I joined a large group of staff doing a midwinter run around the proposed course as a trial and met with the management team afterward. While it was a stunning course, it was not an original concept, as both globally and locally, there were countless similar events. Yealands struck me as a highly innovative and cutting-edge business so I challenged them to do something more creative, more unique. From touring the vineyard I'd seen that running around the perimeter meant the best parts were missed. What about doing a trail-running team relay event where runners would do a number of loops that visited each of the different grape varieties? Moreover, given that women were their main New Zealand customers, what if we created an event just for them – a women's team event based on a vineyard? Magic! The Yealands Yak was launched and 268 women turned up for the inaugural event which I'm sure will grow into a major annual fixture.

Time for the GODZone in Kaikoura – a spectacular seaside town with vast outdoor sport possibilities. After Costa Rica, Trevor Voyce had decided to step down from expedition racing for a stint, to focus on his family, his MiGym business and stage racing. We asked two-time world champion Stuart Lynch to join the team, which was perfect timing both for us and for him. Going into GODZone I felt in good shape, particularly on the back of my Brevet miles on the bike, and was eagerly anticipating the event. There wasn't a huge depth of competition so we were confident of a victory and pleased to have an easier race that we could enjoy, with less pressure. As expected, we won the race and we loved the course, the highlights being summiting Mount Tapuaenuku, biking Molesworth Station and kayaking the Hurunui River. The race included a dark zone, so we'd packed sleeping bags, tents and a cooker, and after about four hours of paddling we were forced onto land to camp for the night. It was the third night of the race and we'd not had much sleep at all, so to be able to get warm, rest, enjoy some hot food relaxing next to the river and then get a full night's sleep – well, that purely and simply was totally awesome.

One thing about the race was mildly concerning though. I had turned up with a high level of bike fitness, more than ever before, so was expecting to be super-strong biking but likely to struggle in the running and hiking. The race started with a kayak and a short run loop around the peninsula, dodging seals, and I felt okay but nothing flash – often the fast starts don't treat me kindly anyway. The first long stage was a mountain-bike ride and soon after we started I felt inexplicably fatigued. It was like I was riding with my brakes on. Nutrition, I told myself, eat and drink, suck it up, it'll be alright. But as the ride went on I was digging myself a grave while my team-mates all seemed relatively comfortable. Getting into the first long climb, I was struggling too much – it was too early in the race to be pushing that hard, I needed help. I asked Chris if he could take my gear which allowed me to recover and keep pace, but I was confused over why I wasn't coping. I made it through the ride which took about four more hours, and then we headed off into the night on a long trekking stage. I started to feel better but the whole night I felt like I was on my limit. Early the next morning, I told the team I'd need to stop at the hut for a short sleep, to allow my body some time to equalise. After the sleep and some wholesome freeze-dried meals, I improved and went on to have a strong race, but I was perplexed as to why I'd started so poorly.

Our next race was in South Africa in May so I needed to maintain a level of race fitness through to then. Autumn is my preferred season for training as the weather is cooler but the days are often fine and calm. On April Fools' Day Sophie and I circumnavigated D'Urville Island in sea kayaks in one day, just over nine hours. It was something I'd always wanted to do, especially since my first trip around the island took five days and I used to think it was a really long way – perspectives do change over time. My kids lined me up for a kayak trip as well, this time an expedition for them. In an effort to raise money for Purple Cake Day, they decided to kayak the Abel Tasman National Park under their own steam. As they fundraised and more people learned about their plan, TV ONE got wind of the story and ran a news feature which made it very real for them.

We had time set aside for the trip which could take up to five days, but a series of weather patterns kept forcing delays. Finally we got a gap and set off, starting from the northern end. The three of them paddled a double kayak that could easily accommodate them all, while Jodie and I paddled single kayaks in support. There was one time when we needed to tow them as they were crossing an open bay in a blast of gusty offshore wind that was taking them out to sea faster than they could paddle. A few times, Tide would hop into one of our kayaks for a rest, but Zefa and Jessie paddled the whole way and had to dig deep to reach the end, taking three full days to complete it. I was really proud of them, both for what they had achieved and their motive behind the challenge.

While I was training for the South African race, I was lying in bed one night and noticed that my heart was damn near leaping out of my chest. That's a bit odd, I thought, running over the day, the training I'd done, the coffee I'd drunk, nothing unusual. I paid closer attention. Fuck it, my heart was in arrhythmia! My initial response was denial. No, that can't be right, it isn't right, maybe it's just a one-off episode. Gutted, I tried to relax and get some sleep. The next day, I took my pulse, yep, still irregular, shit. This wasn't good news, my heart had now been beating irregularly for nearly 24 hours. Jodie and I agreed that I needed to see the doctor. The next morning it was still in arrhythmia so we arranged for me to be seen at Nelson Hospital and it was confirmed that I had atrial fibrillation again. The hospital staff were not very inspiring, telling me I was old, that my heart was worn out, and that I needed to accept that and change my lifestyle – in other words, give up. Thankfully I'm a fighter – quitting wasn't yet an option. That said, I was due to fly to South Africa in just a few weeks and I was really torn. The risk of racing and slowing the team down if I had heart complications was not appealing – it wouldn't be fair on them or me. I emailed the team and suggested they find someone else, but they all replied that if I could race they'd still prefer to race with me, or if I didn't go the whole team would skip the race.

It was most likely AF that I'd been having at GODZone, so it wasn't like it stopped me in my tracks, it just slowed me down. Nor am I aware of anyone with AF dropping dead from training or racing. I've never been afraid of taking risks with my heart – I guess I'm not that afraid of death. As much as I'm keen to live, I figure I'll live the life I want to, and if I get taken out, so be it. That said, I did have one episode that got me thinking. I was at home with the kids and decided to shoot out for a surf-ski paddle for an hour or so. Unless it's rough, offshore wind or cold – in other words, when I deem there to be a risk – I don't usually wear a life jacket when I'm paddle training. On this day it was quite calm when I went out so I didn't bother to wear one. I headed out towards the Abel Tasman National Park, paddling upwind for about 45 minutes, or about 3 km offshore. The wind was building so I was going to get some good runs surfing home. Then my heart went into arrhythmia and I was hit with extreme fatigue, leaving me barely enough strength to keep the boat upright. Shit, this wasn't ideal. In normal circumstances I would have been revelling in the conditions, singing out loud as I chased the waves home, but on this day I needed to stay focused and muster all the strength I could. My concern was that if I fell out and ended up in the water, I might not have the strength to remount my ski, or worse still, become separated from my boat, with little chance I'd be able to swim that far to land. I was mighty pleased to reach land safely that day.

I was severely washed out because I wasn't sleeping through the nights due to the AF. I made a few diet and lifestyle changes, drank more water, stopped all caffeine and reduced my workload, and after about a week my heart went back to normal, I started to function better, and my training productivity increased. I wanted to race in Africa so I confirmed I was going. Before flying out I popped over to Wellington with the family to do a six-hour navigation event called the City Safari. Sponsored by the public transport provider Metlink, the event blends the transport network – cable car, ferries, buses and trains – with running in urban areas, the city and parks. The goal is to score as many points as you can in the available time, and by using public transport you can reach more checkpoints. It's a super-fun event that I'd done before but this was the first time with the kids.

Six hours is a long time for them to run so we knew we'd need to utilise the transport frequently, plus for the children, that would be part of the fun. Not knowing the area well, we thought we'd start by using the ferry as there was one about to depart soon after the race started. We ran to it and hopped on just as it was leaving. Excited to be under way, we then noticed that the ferry wasn't going in the direction we expected. Damn it! We'd got on the wrong ferry. I phoned the race director who told me it wasn't as bad as it seemed, we just had to get off the ferry when it landed, catch a bus, and within 20 minutes we'd be back on the course. It was a tad embarrassing but we had to laugh, the classic part being the media headline 'World champion gets on wrong ferry' that took up half the front page of the *Dominion* newspaper the next day, which I saw as I was boarding the flight to South Africa.

Based in Port Edward on the coast, the race traversed a 500 km course involving the core sports, trekking, mountain biking and kayaking. I raced well for the first three days but then got sick, stopping hourly with diarrhoea regardless whether there was a toilet, which had the side effect of leaving me weak as I couldn't eat and drink effectively, making the final night and day miserable as hell. It was a real slog. Added to my discomfort was some extreme chafing I'd got on the first day from running in salty and sandy shorts. The skin on my upper thighs was raw and uncomfortable. Unbeknown to the team, I stopped at one point on the bike stage out of sheer desperation, downed pants and sprayed chain oil over myself. The stinging sensation made my eyes water and didn't help the chafing one bit but it gave me something else to focus on for a while. At least I didn't experience any heart issues to compound the misery.

One of the more memorable stages was a river kayak. Due to low water levels (the upper section of river had no water in it) the stage was shortened from about 80 km to 40 km. We launched into the water at night in darkness which was intensified by low cloud and fog. It was near impossible to pick the deep water and we were constantly running aground, having to get out and carry or drag the boat over shallows (idly wondering what wildlife I might step on in my bare feet), and on a few occasions Sophie and I would lose contact with Chris and Stu as fog engulfed us. We even found ourselves disorientated and paddling back upstream at one point. It was mildly humorous until we started to get cold, and then it wasn't funny any longer – we just wanted it to end so we could warm up and get some sleep. After the race we enjoyed a few relaxing days savouring our victory and touring about (the local coffee was exceptional).

It seemed like a good idea at the time but not quite so good when it came time to happen. On the way home we stopped in Australia to race their premier adventure race, a 48-hour event called the GeoQuest. I'd wanted to do it for years and it seemed a perfect opportunity, as our flight stopped in Sydney anyway. Chris didn't want to race so he continued on to New Zealand and we were joined by Jacob Roberts, a Kiwi athlete based in Australia. Sophie, Stu and myself were all unwell and trying our best to recover from the expedition race in only five days. I was slow but felt healthy so I enjoyed it, but Stu didn't recover in time and had to dig super-deep to finish. It was a small miracle really that we managed to win the race given the state we were in.

While I was away Jodie had been beavering away organising my next heart ablation procedure, which was scheduled in Christchurch during the time we'd be in Queenstown for the ski season. Once again, I needed to weigh up whether my sport was worth the risk, as I could live a reasonably normal life with the heart condition. It didn't take long to decide – my life revolved around pushing hard and challenging myself physically, I wasn't ready yet to let that go, plus I had a World Championships to win. The surgeons were really confident they'd corrected the problem this time, and told me I could expect to be up and racing again in a few months.

Driving into Arrowtown where we would live for the next three months, I remember staring up at the encircling mountains, snowcapped and grand as they towered above the basin, and feeling a shiver. These were the mountains where I would prepare for the World Champs, they would set me in good stead to handle the Andes, and I was ultra-motivated to get into them as soon as I could. It took discipline to take it easy for a little while, but I didn't ski for a week, instead going for gentle walks into the hills each day, snow underfoot, crisp air in my lungs. I felt good.

Winter sped by with all our spare time spent skiing. The kids were on the mountain four days a week – all weekend, one school skiing day each week, and Friday night they could ski from after school to 9 p.m. I enjoyed seeing the kids improve their skiing and, more importantly, develop a passion for the pleasure that could be derived from the natural beauty of the snow and ice. I used the skiing as my mountain training and spent as much time as I could at the higher elevations – given my aversion to altitude, more exposure to high country would be of benefit and Queenstown is probably the best place in New Zealand to regularly spend time at around 2000 metres. Deciding to see how many ski runs I could do in a day – my goal was a hundred – one Friday I set off on my mission. Starting when the chairs opened at 8 a.m., I skied non-stop for 13 hours through to 9 p.m. The last three hours or so my legs were jelly but I managed to ski 101 runs and record the highest number of vertical descents skied that day, perhaps even the season, or ever.

One day during the ski season some bad weather didn't make the skiing very appealing, so we popped over to Wanaka to the indoor climbing wall with the kids. While they were climbing I picked up a brochure on guided mountaineering trips around the world by local company Adventure Consultants which advertised a package to climb the Ecuador volcanoes that seemed very good value. After a quick chat with them I discovered that they could custom-design an altitude training camp for our team as build-up to the World Champs, plus they were really excited to help us out. I ran the idea past Seagate and thankfully Pat, who approves our sponsorship, is a mountaineer and saw it as an extremely valuable exercise. I flicked an email out to the team: 'Anyone keen on 10 days climbing in Ecuador?'

Wrapping up the ski season we had a very busy few weeks – we needed to shift back home, go to Hokitika and deliver the Spring Challenge, which had a record field with over 1000 women, and then get ready to travel to Ecuador for two months. Thankfully we'd been conservative with the Spring Challenge course. Jodie and I had done an event planning trip there when we were hit by torrential rain and got to see first-hand what heavy rain did to the area – it flooded and flooded fast. Leading up to the race, I kept saying to people that the event would be great provided it didn't rain heavily. Well, the night before and the morning of the race it poured not just cats and dogs, it poured cows and bulls. It became a festival of mud. Sitting all alone in the marquee early that morning with the rain pelting so hard I could hardly hear myself think, I couldn't deny I was stressed. Out on the course teams were under way, support crews were doing their job and staff were in position, so it was largely out of my control from this point on, but I wasn't sure if being an event director was worth it. As the day went on and teams started finishing the race, their smiles, jubilation and stories put things into perspective again. The event was achieving magical things for many people and was a huge success. Perhaps because the weather was so bad everyone embraced the extremity and adventure of it all. By the end of the weekend Jodie and I both knew that the 2015 event was going to be gangbusters.

I was so insanely busy around that period it was a lifesaver that Jodie and the kids were travelling to Ecuador with me. I had about two weeks to manage my workload and train before we departed. At the start of those two weeks Jodie said, 'I'll see you at the airport', and she couldn't have been more right. We travelled over ahead of the team because we wanted to spend a week there as a family beforehand, with the added advantage of more time for me to acclimatise. LAN airline was a race sponsor so we got a lovely surprise upgrade to business class, which made the travel more pleasant and a novelty for the kids (in fact, it was so relaxing, I would have been happy to keep flying around the world). We had a day in Chile before landing in Quito, our base for the next few months.

Because Quito sits in the mountains, there are some excellent hikes close to the city and we got out exploring. Being able to spend time between 3000 and 4000 metres each day, plus sleeping high, was all welcome adjustment to the thin air. Everyday living felt like training for the race. When the team arrived, Jodie and the kids headed off on their own expedition, to the Amazon forests. Our local alpine guide Eddie would take us through 10 days of altitude training, the highlight being a summit attempt on Cotopaxi, the second highest mountain in Ecuador at 5897 metres. I thoroughly enjoyed the camp, which was a blend of hiking and climbing, staying in a range of accommodation, from luxury lodges to high tent camps in the snow. Each day, I could feel my body coping better with the lack of oxygen. Summit day came around and we had fine weather for the ascent. We trudged our way up, pacing ourselves for the altitude ahead. Eddie insisted on a slow ascent so we would have time to enjoy the summit, as other athletes he'd guided up before tended to climb fast but once on the summit would start to get AMS (acute mountain sickness) and need to start descending immediately. He wanted us to enjoy the whole experience, and that suited us, especially me, as I knew that a slow climb with a controlled heart rate was the ticket for me. Standing on top of a huge volcano in the Andes with the team, soaking up the breath-taking views, was a sign for me that the race would serve us well. We returned to Quito exhausted but jubilant.

Jodie and the kids were back, too, so keen to maximise our training camp we planned to head back to the mountains for the final few days before the race started. It gave us privacy, plus my family hadn't been to the mountains yet. It was Jodie's forty-first and she was keen to climb to the Cotopaxi Glacier for her birthday. We set out to do it as a family but about halfway up, at around 4500 metres, Jessie started to feel sick and collapsed to the ground and lay there breathing hard. I knew full well what she was going through so told Jodie I'd take her back down while they continued up. Zefa had my altimeter on and he wanted to get over 5000 metres, which is partway up the glacier. On our way down I saw a number of the world's top adventure-racing teams heading up, all suited up in their race wear, looking the part. I had to chuckle because I knew they were all thinking they were doing something quite extreme, but they'd get to 5000 metres and be greeted by my eight-year-old daughter and 10-year-old son – sorry folks, it's not that hard-core!

The few days before a race can drag on a bit and the packing logistics can be tiresome, testing my patience, so I need to take deep breaths to relax. Most of the time I can live at my speed and to my levels of efficiency, but in the team environment things take longer, partly because it is a group of people, but also because of different personalities. I'm the only parent in the team and my job is largely organising so I probably place a higher value on time than my team-mates, who tend to need more time to do things. Added to that, the events themselves can often be guilty of time-wasting, especially in the lead-up. It's one aspect of the racing I don't enjoy and one of the factors in my decision to step aside from competing at the end of 2015. Once the race finally gets under way I'm far happier, especially after the first day when the teams spread out and do their own thing and we're left to our own devices and company.

Adventure racing is quite unique in that not just elite teams but also complete beginners line up at the start. For the less experienced teams, it's a real buzz to be in the exact same race as the world champions. While lacking experience, some of these teams are in fact strong and fit which means they can often keep pace for a few hours and sometimes for most of the first day. I don't like it as they typically get in the way and tend to interrupt the flow of things, but I can understand why they want a story that they can tell their friends: 'We were leading the race for a while in the first day . . .' Ecuador was slightly different because we started so high above sea level, over 4000 metres, that the starting pace quickly filtered out the teams who had adjusted to the elevation and those which hadn't. The course climbed slowly to 4200 metres and then started a gradual descent, from under the Antisana volcano to the edge of the Amazon Basin. We were comfortable in the lead pack and it was obvious that the time we'd invested in training in the mountains had paid off, not only in terms of altitude acclimatisation but in respect of team building without the pressure of being in a race environment, together with the benefit of being adjusted to the time zone as well.

The first trekking stage took about five hours, following a faint trail through alpine areas – what they call 'paramo' in Ecuador. Chris suggested we take a short cut, but we soon found ourselves wading in deep swamp, our mistake accentuated when we looked up and saw the leading teams swiftly running around the mountain on a good trail. It didn't matter, we had a very long way to go and that was the nature of things. In terms of navigation gambles it's always roulette – you win some, you lose some. However, our route choice soon became one of the highlights of the race. As we trudged across a swamp flat we spied a huge puma creeping along stealthily and scoping us out. We were too amazed to be frightened as the big cat deliberately crossed our path, never once dropping its piercing gaze as it slowly blended into the long grass and disappeared. Back on the trail we upped our speed and less than an hour later had made contact again with the leading teams.

Not long afterward, Chris started to develop symptoms of mild AMS, the effects of the body not being able to exhale enough carbon dioxide, the result a form of poisoning. The next stage was mainly a link to another hike, predominantly downhill. About five teams were still together but we got a small gap when they took a wrong trail and we started stage three in the lead. Chris was not in good shape, but at least we were down at a lower elevation. Ahead of us was mainly a long climb up a valley, it was dark, getting cold and we were tired after a day's racing. Somehow Chris still managed to find the strength to navigate while we carried his gear. Our priority was to get him strong again. The sensible thing to do was to find shelter and let him sleep for a few hours at the lower altitude, but the race had imposed eight hours of compulsory rest on the teams which could only be taken at transition areas, which was at the end of the stage, at least 12 hours away. We needed to push on to there before we could stop because any rest taken in the field wouldn't count in our required eight hours.

The only rule for the stage was 'KEEP THE OYACACHI RIVER ON YOUR LEFT' – this was the valley we were travelling up and we had marked the trail we needed to take on our map. Arriving at a bridge sooner than expected, we weren't sure whether the bridge was over the Oyacachi or if it was a tributary. We crossed but after a few minutes realised it wasn't right. Another team arrived, clearly thinking the same thing. If we used the bridge and the road, the Oyacachi River would be on our right, but it appeared the logical route. Stu wanted to radio the organisation to ask if the bridge and road could be used but none of us could see any other way to interpret the wording. Our only choice was to stay on the designated route. We hunted around and found the trail that allowed us to travel up the valley with the river on our left, as the rule book stated. The trail was very poor and difficult to follow. Meanwhile, the weather closed in and after a few miserable hours of hiking in the jungle being blasted by ice and rain without the proper clothing for such conditions we stiffly walked into the transition area. Thinking we were in second or third place, we were shocked to see about ten teams. We learned later that 50 of the 53 teams had crossed the bridge and walked up the road, saving hours of energy and exposure to the severe weather.

The race committee had a problem in that only three teams had followed the rules and two of those teams, including us, were considered the best teams in the world. They needed to rectify the situation and decided to give the other 50 teams a four-hour penalty each, the intention being to remove the advantage they had gained by taking the short cut. Amazingly, many of those teams protested against this penalty and rumours even circulated that our team had put pressure on the race committee to impose it, which was complete nonsense. I thought that four hours was not enough and explained why to the race jury but it stood firm on its decision. It didn't matter anyway as Chris had recovered and we'd moved back to the front of the field and were racing strongly. Over the five days we descended through the different ecological zones, kayaking down rivers, biking and hiking, arriving at sea level in the tropics for the final stage. This was a 60 km ocean paddle to the end, a small fishing village called Mompiche. The kids were at the finish line, super-excited to be celebrating our victory, but Jodie was recovering from a tropical illness so was barely able to offer her congratulations before returning to the sanctuary of the hotel.

For me, winning my third World Championships was more a matter of relief than jubilation. I felt like we'd been the best team in the world since we started racing again in 2011 but random things kept knocking us down – the penalty in Tasmania, footrot in Costa Rica. We just needed to race without these curve balls to win. I know other teams would say the same thing about their results and racing but I don't think it's that simple. There's a checklist that needs to be completed to win a major race: a team needs an exceptional navigator, they need speed and endurance (very few teams have both), they need supportive sponsors and reliable equipment, they need experience, and they need to know how to win, how to pace wisely and strategise – very few teams have all these attributes. The team unquestionably needs four strong, committed athletes, and while all its members need to be at the top of their sport, the female needs to be extraordinary. Expedition races are a mix of power and stamina. Females are aces at stamina, better than most males, but they often lack the power needed for carrying big heavy packs, lifting bikes over fences, and clambering through rough terrain. Sophie and the other Kiwi women I have raced with have always been powerful both in mind and body, and that's often made the difference. Not many teams can match us when you stack up the statistics.

Ecuador proved how winning a World Championships is not just about winning a race, it's more about building a campaign, an exercise in research, planning, decision-making and mapping out how it will be achieved. Ecuador was about starting at the finish line and working backwards from there, not just to the start line, but months prior, making sure all the pieces of the puzzle were there before we put it together. Using that analogy, most teams get to the finish line and realise they were missing one or more of the pieces when they started.

Mission accomplished, it was now time for our family adventure holiday. Ecuador has much to offer in a compact area but the main attraction for us was the Galapagos Islands. We had planned to spend two weeks touring around on a shoestring budget so it was a welcome gift when our team won a week-long trip on a luxury cruise ship – this was going to be the ultimate in post-race recovery. We had some good times on board the cruise, and swimming with marine iguanas, sharks, turtles and rays was a highlight. My best day of the cruise was land-based – we did a bike ride, went for a kayak and after lunch at a plantation there was a game of soccer for anyone keen. Once back on the mainland we headed to a beach called Montañita, a very hip and cool town, where there was a surfing school – it was Jessie's idea to learn to surf and the other kids wanted to attend so we booked in for five days. After a week at the beach it was time to head back to the mountains and the rivers.

While travelling in Ecuador we couldn't *not* go to Tena – one of the white-water hubs of the world – to do a rafting trip with the family. We read up on the multitude of rivers available, finally selecting the Jatunyacu (meaning 'big water' in Kichwa), and contacted a highly recommended rafting company, River People, and set up a two-day voyage with the children – happy to run a private trip, they kindly put a safety kayaker on the water to accompany us. Leaving the city, it was incredible how quickly we were in the wilderness of the jungle, which is largely protected by a number of large national parks in that area. When we got to the put-in I was surprised to see how big the river was – it was full of waves and drops. Listed as a Grade 3 trip, I suspected there would be a couple of Grade 3 rapids but mainly Grade 2. When I asked our guide Alex how many Grade 3 rapids there were, he said he didn't know for sure but guessed about twenty. I did wonder at that moment if we had chosen the most suitable trip for the kids, but how many times in your life do you get to paddle a tributary of the Amazon? The Jatunyacu had extra significance for me as the river's headwaters are found on the Cotopaxi volcano which I had climbed just a few weeks earlier.

Normally a 27 km river run, our trip was 40 km in total as the guides offered to raft us back to our lodge further downstream, which was a real bonus. The river was topped up from the previous night's rain, making it good for rafting but limiting how far we could go up a canyoning side trip on the first day. The rafting, though, was excellent and the extra flow speed was helpful given we had three children on board. After an action-packed morning of negotiating some large powerful rapids, which thankfully were mainly pressure waves and not nasty recirculating holes, we enjoyed a replenishing lunch on the riverbank. Due to the river speed and our canyoning trip being flooded out, we arrived at camp early and spent the afternoon relaxing on a glorious river beach, swimming and soaking up the sun. Amazon evenings are special and a bonfire on the beach enhanced the experience. I love going to sleep in the tropics – the warmth, scents and cacophony of insect and bird life blended with the river ambience produces a rich atmosphere – although the guide did kindly warn us that snakes and scorpions were often spotted around the camp.

Before we boarded the rafts for our second day (when we did find a stow-away scorpion), a visit to the local cacao plantation was a worthwhile excursion. Spending an hour with the kids making chocolate and then hot chocolate, served with bananas roasted on the fire, supplied the necessary sustenance to tackle the awaiting rapids. With three children on the raft, our guide took conservative lines but still ensured that the kids got splashed and tossed about. The adults all knew that flipping in a big hole wasn't going to be pretty – save that for the thrill-seeking backpackers. The morning was continuous rapids so we were kept busy with paddling commands – all forward, all back, left back, right back, all down and hold on! It was then a lazy float for the afternoon to the end. While we were only on the river for two days it felt longer and was well worth it.

With a few weeks left in Ecuador we travelled to Baños and enjoyed the adventure sport there – canyoning, hiking and soaking in the thermal pools. Our last stop was Chimborazo National Park, a distinctly unique environment. Surprisingly, after our time at sea level and the Amazon, we took a day or two to readjust to the altitude. The hiking in the region was incredible, wandering around beneath the towering mountain, which is often climbed by international climbers because due to the earth's bulge on the equator the summit of Chimborazo is in fact the furthest point from the centre of the planet. We were then New Zealand bound after a highly successful trip – the kids had experienced living in a foreign country for two months with a myriad of new experiences logged and I was an Adventure Racing World Champion again, not bad at all.

CHAPTER THIRTY-ONE

NEARLY FINISHED

As soon as 2015 kicked in it was time to get up to our usual tricks: hit the road and into the wilds. Our plan was to do a loop around the South Island linking adventure trips in amazing places, starting close to home with a two-day kayak down the Maruia River, a magic wilderness experience that's really quite accessible. Before our gear could even dry out we headed to Arthur's Pass to paddle the Wamakariri. Jodie and I had paddled this river countless times over the years as it's the paddle stage for the Coast to Coast, but it still remains one of my favourite river trips ever. Every time I paddle between the gigantic towering gorge walls I say to myself, 'There's nowhere I'd rather be right now!' I'd wanted to do a family camping trip down there for some time and the weather was intensely hot so being either on or in the river was just the ticket.

Being a month out from the Coast to Coast race we were passed by dozens of people training, many of whom I knew, which got me excited about the race. We spent more time in the region rock climbing, caving and doing some biking, and the more time I spent there the more I thought about the race. I was training for GODZone so I was fit enough and I started to wonder if it would be my last good chance to race it competitively. We headed south mixing up hiking, bike and paddling trips and back up the West Coast. Memorable moments included a fairly extreme trip over Gunsight Saddle (I don't recommend that as a family tramp, by the way), Zefa climbing onto an iceberg and it tipping over while we kayaked around the Tasman Lake beneath the glacier, and me estimating distances incorrectly – what was meant to be a 30 km cycle on the West Coast Wilderness Trail turned into 72 km (oh well, that happens, and the reward of a mince pie in Hokitika kept the kids focused).

While I was biking back to Kumara to retrieve our vehicle, I went past the start line of the Coast to Coast. The race was only a few weeks away now but I knew I had the fitness to do it so decided to contact my mate Rich, the newly appointed race director, and ask him what he thought of me racing. Coincidentally, he sent me an email that very day suggesting the same thing. At the time, I did have a running injury, so I needed to see how that would heal in the following weeks. About ten days out from the race I was happy that my running was strong enough to get me over Goat Pass. I wouldn't be quick but I wasn't worried about that anyway, what I wanted was the fastest paddle – as a paddler, there's a level of prestige that goes to the man and woman who clock the quickest river trip of the event, and that was my aim. Now 42, I entered in the veteran category, as I didn't see any sense in taking on the younger guys and felt there would be a fun competition in the old boys' division. I looked over the entry list and sized up my competition on the river. Dan Busch was the stand-out paddler entered. A former New Zealand kayak representative and incredible downriver paddler, I knew that 'Bushy' would be setting the pace. I managed a couple of training sessions with him leading up to the event and felt I had a small advantage over him in the boat – he'd worked mainly on his running and cycling and I suspected his paddling had suffered as a result. This was enough to give me the confidence to chase the fastest paddle time with gusto.

I mainly trained on the ocean in my surf ski for the race and was quite surprised at the targets I was hitting with paddle in hand. My support crew, the acclaimed Maitland brothers, Chris and Dave, were fully behind me building my race around the fastest paddle. There was no way I was going to win the Coast to Coast, so gunning for a stage time – a prestigious one at that – got us all excited. Jodie didn't share the same excitement. In her mind it was a pointless exercise going all that way with the focus on doing a fastest split but I wasn't going to be distracted by her attitude. My race plan was to go steady for the 2 km run from the beach to the bikes, conserve as much energy on the first cycling stage and mountain run without going backwards, fuel up on the short cycle to the river, and once in the kayak unleash whatever strength I had left and dump it all in the river.

Standing on the start line at the beach knowing I'd soon cross the island, the race seemed short to me – a massive contrast since I last stood there with the target of winning, 14 years earlier. Unlike most of the nervous and tense entrants around me, I was able to relax and soak up the magnificence of it all – a bunch of people poised and ready to run, bike and paddle across their country, it's a fitting statement about Kiwis I reckon. Rich counted us down and the pilgrimage began. My race plan worked well and I was particularly pleased to eat a freeze-dried meal and can of creamed rice while riding to the river. With that amount of food in the system I knew I wouldn't need to take my hands off the paddle for at least two hours. I had 4 litres of liquid meal replacement set up as hands-free drinking which would sustain me for the four hours needed. I entered the river in ninth place (in the Longest Day), where my crew said that third place had started 22 minutes ahead and encouraged me to aim to exit off the water in third. Braden Currie and Sam Clark were over 30 minutes ahead and well out of reach, especially given they're very strong paddlers.

Beginning the paddle, I felt great. I could feel power flowing through my arms and the cold windy conditions suited me. I had a fire burning and started passing people immediately, after an hour moving into sixth place, by two hours into fifth place, by three hours into fourth, and soon after that into third. But with about 15 minutes to go I took a dreadful line and ended up having to get out of my kayak and carry it over the braids back to the main channel. The wasted minutes meant I slipped back to fourth but still managed to pass my mate Trevor Voyce again to exit the boat in third, my sole focus getting over the timing mat as quickly as I could to stop the clock for the paddle time. I knew Bushy was behind me and would be storming down the river like a hurricane.

As I hobbled up to my bike, fully spent after the effort on the water, I could hear Bushy arrive on the riverbank. I glanced at my watch, pretty certain I had it in the bag, paddle time 4:19:07. My arms were so empty I had a shocking transition to my bike, unable to get my hands and fingers functioning properly after they'd been gripped to the paddle shaft for so many hours. I managed to ride well enough to take fourth overall and win the veteran category, plus I had what I wanted, the paddle stage. I crossed the line about 90 seconds behind Trevor – the gap hadn't changed for the final 70 km cycle and even though I tried to close it a few times, I knew the third placing would mean more to him than me and he was fighting hard for it. Besides, I was about to win the veteran section, place in the top five, and I was certain I'd bagged the paddle prize. I was still motivated to finish the race as quickly as I could and not be caught by riders behind, but I'd decided that if by some chance I caught Trevor, I'd suggest a draw. I didn't need to race him to the wire for third, but it never came to that anyway – he just rode better.

I was thrilled with my result. Looking back, it felt good to re-establish myself as an athlete in that stream of the sport. Given my age and association with expedition racing, I knew the younger emerging athletes considered me to be good, but old and slow, past my use-by date. Not many of them were aware of my kayaking background and were surprised when I passed them in the race, the speed I was going making it seem like we were in a different event.

Next up was the GODZone adventure race in Wanaka which has tremendous outdoor sporting options making it an exciting venue. The world number one-ranked team was competing so that was motivation for us to dish out a dominating performance. Many Kiwis found it confusing that our team was ranked number two given we were world champions and generally won the major races. But the points system is heavily weighted to World Championships, and is also somewhat of an attendance award – do enough races and sooner or later your world ranking will look good on paper. Because our team failed to finish in Costa Rica it would be years before we could regain the number one ranking, regardless of how well we raced during the season. As it turned out, we broke from the field about an hour into the course and never saw another team again, winning by a massive margin, 23 hours, nearly a full day.

My lasting memory of the race was a river crossing we did that very nearly could have been fatal. As team captain, my primary objective is to keep my team safe. I know they are all adults, all individuals, and ultimately responsible for their own safety, but the race environment can cloud judgement. Plus I'm the racer who has been in two events where people have died and another race where someone was seriously injured. I don't want a team-mate killed on my watch and I pride myself that both my team-mates and their families feel a sense of security when they're racing under my leadership. I'm very clear that sport is a recreation, a luxury of the first world, and that it's not worth risking your life for.

The terrifying incident happened at the end of the first day in the Albert Burn valley. We'd run up and around the Brewster Glacier for the morning and then canoed the Makarora River. It was cold, raining, and the rivers were noticeably rising. The race management had just set up a raft to use to cross the Wilkin River which was swelling fast. The bulk of the trekking stage was the Albert Burn, where we'd spend the whole night hiking up to the saddle and then descending down to the Matukituki. All the signs were pointing to a long and uncomfortable night out in the mountains. We were leading the race and at the mandatory crossing point on the lower Albert Burn, met the river safety staff, who instructed us where to cross and supervised our crossing. We linked up and made it across okay but it was swift and deep, up to chest height in the channel. At the opposite bank we carried on but were unclear as to what to do next. A few hundred metres upstream we could see the marked hiking trail to the Albert Burn Hut, where we needed to pass by eventually, but we were on the wrong side to use the trail. The map showed the trail crossing the river a few times before settling on the right bank. Ahead of us was a steep and rocky gorge for a few kilometres and directly in front was a huge bluff. Our options were not appealing – we either scaled the bluff or picked our way up the gorge at river level, but the river looked like technical Grade 5, meaning a fall into it would almost certainly lead to drowning, given we were in hiking gear, not river attire.

The trail on the opposite bank looked like the best way forward so we crossed the river again and started up the track. We were trying to deduce what the river safety staff had intended for us to do and that perhaps we shouldn't have even crossed the river in the first place, only to have to recross it again. Then the track rejoined the river and it all became obvious. We could see the inviting blazed track marker on the opposite bank but we stood at a rapid, with swift discoloured water rushing past, midstream rocks creating turbulence and, worst of all, just downstream the river dropped into the gorge that we had seen from the bottom, a series of drops and waterfalls.

Not wanting to backtrack, we considered options. Carrying on upstream over high rock walls on the side we were on looked epic – possible, but not inviting. The trail was just 20 metres away and lured us. Foolishly, we talked about getting in the river as high up as we could and swimming downstream aiming for the opposite bank. There were three eddies, backwaters created by rocks on the far bank, and I said to the team, 'We won't make the first eddy, we could make the second eddy, if you don't make the third eddy you'll die.' I wasn't joking and they knew it. We started upstream, Chris leading. I was behind a rock when I heard Sophie cry out – Chris had dived in and was swimming across. The river speed was alarming and he was blasted downstream but he was swimming strongly and made the second eddy, just. I wanted to go next to get a feel for it, as Chris's confidence and occasional naivety often overruled good sense in these situations. Talking Sophie through the plan and what I was going to do, I dived in and started swimming. Immediately my gaiters filled with water and dragged my legs down, I felt the power of the water and retreated before it was too late. I didn't like it. The odds of getting four people across successfully were not in our favour.

It was a serious rapid we were attempting to swim with devastating consequences if someone didn't make it. I signalled to Sophie not to try but as I was making my way back upstream she dived in. Helpless, I watched her get washed down the river and past the second eddy. It was all a bit of a blur but it looked like she was going to miss the third eddy too. I assume it was a combination of her swimming for her life and Chris's fast action scrambling over rocks and water to grab her and pull her to safety that averted disaster, a team effort. The roar of the water meant we couldn't talk and I again signalled to Stu to abort, but then he dived in too. For fuck's sake! To his credit, though, Stu had a different approach and managed to swim into the first eddy, actually making it look quite doable.

But I wasn't going to try it. After a lifetime of kayaking and river safety this was breaking just about every rule in the book – we were only missing the alcohol. I signalled to the team for them to start hiking upstream, and that I'd pick my way through the cliffs and meet them above the gorge. Despite being only separated by a deep narrow chasm, we travelled a few kilometres upstream with me on one side and the team on the other. I felt bad that I was slowing the team down and they didn't know exactly where I was for much of the time. It was dangerous country. As expected, however, once above the gorge the river was a gentle babbling brook that I crossed almost keeping my feet dry. Chris was limping severely after he'd slammed onto a rock whilst getting to Sophie. We were all relieved to be reunited and very sombre about the episode we'd just survived. It was a stark reminder of how logic and reason can be almost forgotten in the heat of competition. I still find it mildly traumatic when I think about what could have eventuated had the shit really hit the fan.

During the race I pledged to myself that this would be my last year racing. The telling time was a lakeshore hike where we had to swim sections, then once at the checkpoint, swim over an arm in the lake. We'd been racing through extremely rough terrain non-stop for over 30 hours, we'd been in cold rain for much of the time, our bodies were fatigued, and then we had to swim, exposing ourselves to more elements with only our hiking gear and packs. At that stage of a race our bodies are hypersensitive and I froze. It was nothing less than miserable and I came to the conclusion that I didn't need to subject myself to such experiences any more. I'd reached my threshold of hardship and suffering – the novelty of doing extreme things was virtually non-existent. I never fully recovered from the swim and exposure to the cold with illness setting in as the race progressed. Thankfully the course included some fantastic scenery and locations, and I was enjoying racing with my team-mates and executing a dominating display of racing nevertheless. It was great to win again, our fourth GODZone, but I was starting to dream about an easier life, an imminent exit from the sport.

I will miss many aspects of adventure racing. In general, there are good, like-minded people doing the sport, and I've met some fantastic folks and made lifelong friends, but there are some real pricks as well, people with huge egos whom I have little time for. Some of the athletes are shamefully poor losers. I won't miss race checks and gear scrutinising at all – that wears me down considerably. I'm forced to carry gear I know I won't use, wear stuff I wouldn't normally wear, typically instructed to do so by people far less qualified to make the call than me.

A classic instance where I lost it was on the shore of Lake Geneva. It was a stinking-hot day and we had to kayak the length of the lake, hours of paddling. The race rules said we must wear a wetsuit, which we had, but no one in their right mind would put a wetsuit on to paddle a flat calm lake on a scorching day. I argued with the official that it was madness, that we'd run the risk of heatstroke, but he insisted, pointing at the rule book. Sensing trouble, he radioed to all safety staff in the area to check on our team to ensure we had our wetsuits on. I was furious but was left with no option but to comply.

Another crazy incident happened at the World Champs in France, where the race rules stated that each athlete must have a knife on their life jacket, which we had. But the race official decided that my knife wasn't good enough, making up his own rule that it had to be able to be opened with one hand. That wasn't a problem, I opened my knife with one hand, but he decided that I couldn't open it fast enough. He refused to accept my knife as suitable. Boiling over, I asked him what his qualifications were – he didn't have any, he wasn't even a kayaker, yet he had made up his mind on this point. Grudgingly, I went and purchased a new knife, but at times like those I really had to ask myself what sort of event and sport I was into. Perhaps the funniest occasion occurred in a race where it was compulsory for all athletes to carry ChapStick (lip balm). I mean, really, who the hell decided dry lips were that much of a safety issue? Imagine it: 'Race HQ, we have a situation, one of our team members has dry lips, we request immediate evacuation!' I just about shook my head off in disbelief.

Being a race director myself and having been in the sport for decades, my patience can be further tested by poorly run events. Many race directors lack experience and don't seem to ask for much guidance, and I see the same mistakes being made over and over again. Thankfully, and full credit to them, the GODZone race has no such nonsense – well, 99 per cent of the time anyway – the race directors Adam and Warren are racers themselves and can apply sound logic and reason.

It was Sophie's birthday a few days after the race and we'd planned a heli-kayaking trip into the Waiatoto River with a group of friends, most of whom raced GODZone as well. It wasn't quite the relaxing recovery trip we'd hoped post an expedition race and I was still affected by the river-crossing saga, so the deafening noise of crashing white water on the Waiatoto, which had a fair chunk of Grade 4 boating, had me on edge. Still, we had some fun times and tripping into those wilderness areas is always satisfying and reinvigorating.

I needed to keep training ticking along as I had one more World Series race being held in Spain to compete in before I could take a break over winter. During GODZone I told myself not to race in 2016. I wasn't enjoying the racing enough and didn't really want to be there, my heart wasn't in it. So I told the team I wouldn't be racing it the following year and that they should think about getting a replacement if they wished to compete. I don't think they believed me, which was fair enough. It's common after such events for people to vow never to do something like that again, but the dark times fade to light and somewhere in the future they find themselves on the start line of another event.

As I trained for the Spanish race, the Raid Gallaecia, I was acutely aware of my distinct lack of motivation. I didn't have an issue with the training itself, it was more that it was pulling me away from other things I wanted to do. I live on a property that requires maintenance and I know it sounds crazy, but I was more interested in planting trees and splitting firewood than travelling to Spain for an adventure race. I lamely tried a few times to get out of going. That said, I knew I'd be into the race once we got under way and the location held a fascination for me – I've long been intrigued by the Way of St James, and the race was said to finish in Santiago de Compostela and include Cape Finisterre. I've read about the history of the pilgrimage routes and have always been keen to do it with my children one day. Leading up to the race, I managed to combine some family trips and training, the main one being a five-day hiking trip through the Richmond Range. The kids were raising money for Purple Cake Day again by climbing a mountain called Purple Top. Long days on mountain trails with a maximum-load limit in my backpack makes for ideal conditioning.

Come May we travelled to Spain for the race, opting to spend a week training on location beforehand, mainly to make the most of the long travelling hours getting there from New Zealand. Chris had opted not to participate so we invited renowned Spanish racer Albert Roca to join us. Stu and Albert had raced together a number of times and were good friends so we had a connection there. It was a big deal for me racing with a foreign athlete, as it was the first time Team Seagate had raced in a mixed nationality team. I have always been a strong advocate of teams racing as nations, but there have been so many races in South and Central America where we have had to contend with the challenges of language barriers that the prospect of having someone in the team who could speak the local language was hugely appealing. But it changed something for me – the race had less significance. I felt we were now just a team of athletes in a race, not a New Zealand team flying the flag for our supporters back home. Albert is a lovely guy and a world champion racer himself but was never going to fill Chris's role. Combined with my inability to 'give a shit', that meant that despite moments of our characteristic racing style, we performed very averagely to take second place. The Swedish team were motivated and committed, racing hard the whole way, and thoroughly deserved the victory.

Typically I don't have regrets and look for the positives. Spain was a reminder that if we want to win another World Championships, we need to extract our excellence, and I'll be flying the New Zealand flag high at that race (which, incidentally, is a flag I think we do need to change, and the national anthem while we're at it – people fought hard for our freedom and we should respect them by exercising it). When I study the teams entered in the Adventure Racing World Championships in Brazil, I'll consider both their strengths and weaknesses. I'll be able to say things like, 'We can out-navigate this team', 'We can bike faster than this team', and 'We can paddle faster than these guys'. Chris is likely the strongest male in the competition and Sophie the equivalent female. Our years of experience mean our race management and logistics are perfected. We have superior nutrition. We know how to train – you don't win three World Championships without knowing how to prepare your body. How does another team beat us? In terms of math and data, if it's a race we decide to win, we're unbeatable. The beauty of adventure racing, however, is that infinite other factors come into play – weather and climate, geographical environments, insects and animals, languages and cultures, equipment failure (which can be our gear or equipment supplied by the organisation), and so on. We're human, we make errors, and once in a while a team will have a sensational race and compete over and above expectations, driven by their mind and spirit, and luck – there is such a thing as a lucky bounce.

Back home from Spain I was full on into Spring Challenge organising. The course was designed but there was ample work to do. As expected, entries had exploded with the largest field to date – 1260 women signed up and a lengthy waiting list of teams that missed out. After nearly nine years of running the event I have discovered that women are not afraid to speak their mind, to anyone. It's funny, I'm considered by some to be unparalleled in the sport of adventure racing, I have won all the major events, all over the world, captained the best team in the world, and I'm quite possibly an expert. But the Spring Challenge ladies don't care about those kinds of minor details, and I regularly get dressed down and instructed by the women before, during, or after the event, about all the things that are wrong, explaining to me how things should be and what an adventure race should consist of. Every time we send out an event newsletter Jodie and I get a barrage of comments and complaints. It's like they're saying, 'I don't care who you are, Nathan Fa'avae, this is simply not good enough!' I applaud it, to be honest. It's humbling and demands humility which is a value I rate highly.

On the shortest day, the Matariki, I organised a corporate team-building event for Yealands Estate Winery. It was the second year I'd organised it but the first year I was involved with the delivery, in the field with the participants. The Yealands motto is 'Think boldly, tread lightly and never say it can't be done'. Jason the CEO saw the benefits of incorporating adventure racing into the company values and we devised the Y-Challenge accordingly. It was a four-day adventure-based journey for 11 staff through wilderness areas involving rafting, mountain biking and hiking, and the level of challenge was intense enough to make it feel much longer. Not only did it exceed my expectations but it is extremely pleasing to see the adventure-racing model being customised to further purpose.

CHAPTER THIRTY-TWO

NEEDED FUTURE

So what's the state of adventure racing in 2015? Adventure racing is a sport I'm passionate about and something that has provided me with wonderful opportunities. It has been an integral part of my adult life and will shape my foreseeable future. I want it to grow and prosper, to provide achievable adventures for people who want them, and to offer a monumental contest blending adventure sport with the planning and scale of an expedition for those who are seeking it. Now just over 25 years old, I think the next decade will be very defining for the sport. In New Zealand, despite Kiwi teams repeatedly being the most successful in the world, the sport is still not recognised by the government sporting body, Sport NZ. It is a testament to the athletes and teams in many regards that they have achieved so highly while being officially ignored, but it's been a wasted opportunity at the same time. For New Zealand to remain highly competitive on a global level, Sport NZ do need to pull their heads out of Wellington cafés and look seriously at how they can assist a sport that has represented New Zealand so successfully. The first steps would be to fund a youth development programme and to help build a national association.

At grass-roots level the sport is alive and well, in New Zealand and in many places around the planet, with a number of small events that encourage people to get outdoors and be active. Because mountain biking and hiking are core outdoor pursuits, adding a water activity and some orienteering captures a large audience. I believe the sport will grow steadily from the base up, the Spring Challenge event being a prime example. At the elite international level, however, I think the sport is having issues and is teetering above a crevasse. In 2015, after the first five rounds of the Adventure Racing World Series, I was left shaking my head in disbelief as to what has been delivered. Four out of five of the races had three teams or fewer finishing the full course, from fields of up to 50 teams. Two of the events had only one team finish the full course. If things carry on like this I predict a massive decline in interest from people at that level. Some will argue that teams just need to get better, but I think the chasm is too big to span, that the events need to be more achievable. If you applied some business logic to these events with an appalling rate of teams completing the race, you'd conclude that the product you're selling has an extremely small market. You could expect sales to decline or stop altogether.

Adventure racing was once marketed as the 'hardest sport on earth', and equally silly statements. But the consumers, the entrants, are more savvy and have wised up to that sort of sales pitch. Very few people want to enter an event where they know the odds are stacked heavily against them reaching the finish line, and people have been set up to fail, over and over again. The World Series races need to tone down the level of challenge, so that rather than having four- to five-day courses, they are reduced to three. For the elite teams, racing for around 75 hours is ample. I've heard race directors and some athletes say that they don't want to see the sport 'dumbed down'. But if more teams have a chance of experiencing what it feels like to complete a race and pass under the finish line, and are far more likely to return to another event, this will naturally have roll-on effects for sponsors. Over time, the level and ability of the athletes and teams will rise and more difficult competitions could be offered, but right now the sport seems intent on smashing people to their limit and preventing them from achieving. It needs to cater for the audience and quickly.

There's a lack of synergy between the World Series events. Athletes are constantly being exposed to random things, ideas that individual race directors dream up without any consultation process involving the people it affects the most, the top teams. Compulsory rest is something we're seeing more often at events, but if they actually asked the athletes what they thought, they'd find out it does not work and is counterproductive. One race this year had optional checkpoints. I tried to follow the race online but after a day I gave up. It made no sense to me who was where in the race, and if I couldn't follow it, it doesn't give people who are unfamiliar with the sport much chance. The mandatory gear list requirements can differ so much we are sometimes forced to buy additional gear that won't function any differently from what we have. Dark zone protocols (such as white water that we can't paddle at night) can be complicated and confusing, with some events trying to offer time credits for teams stuck in dark zones and so on. Some events can consume unnecessary time, requiring teams to be at the event days ahead of the race for mandatory gear checks (which are completely unnecessary) and pre-race formalities. It's expensive for a team to be in a foreign country, where each day soaks up more budget, so when we're on the other side of the world waiting for a race to start, basically wasting time, it just adds to the difficulty of being a racer for no discernible benefit. But the main problem is that many of the races are simply too long, too boring, and most teams have no chance of ever completing them.

While I acknowledge that event promoters around the globe have the best intentions, I constantly see the same mistakes repeated time after time. The reason, I believe, is because adventure racing is not unified, it lacks leadership and management, and ultimately it lacks resources. The World Championships is a good example of its 'hotchpotch' nature. At the World Champs, teams are not required to race under their nationalities, meaning the sport is a circus show of multinational teams. While this is fine at Adventure Racing World Series rounds as teams can promote their sponsors further and have flexibility, for an Adventure Racing World Championships it, by and large, defeats the whole purpose of the competition. What's special about a team of cherry-picked athletes from around the world? That would be fine if we were racing intergalactically, but since we're only racing on earth, countries are the logical way of selecting teams. The multinational nature of the teams makes it extremely difficult for the competition to be seen by the wider sporting public as legitimate. There are about 8000 sports in the world. Out of that number, around 350 have World Championships (annually, biennially, or quadrennially). Of that 350, as far as I am aware, only one sport allows multinational teams at World Championships – adventure racing. It's good to be different, but being stupid is another thing. Yes, you could argue that it gives adventure racing a point of difference, something to celebrate. I'd probably agree if there was supporting evidence, but after 25 years the sport is hardly in a strong position and without some major changes and collaboration it's hard to see how it can improve. Mark Burnett, the creator of Eco Challenge, was in my view the most visionary person the sport has seen. In the late 1990s Mark asked the question, 'How does adventure racing become an Olympic sport?' He found his answers and started to evolve the sport in that direction, the first step being to make the team national. I'd like to see 50 to 75 per cent of teams finish the full course and still protect the integrity of an expedition race. The Expedition Africa race has a winning formula. Make events more achievable, allow teams to gain experience, upskill, and then raise the bar to meet their new and improved level.

Some people have argued for a change in the team structure, to either segregate the genders, or change the ratio to two females and two males. While I like the co-ed aspect of adventure racing, there is often an underlying competition within the males in the team over who is the strongest, or the fittest. For instance, if we go paddling with our male team-mates, the boys can't let me and Sophie be in front, and if we try to stay in front the pace will continue to get faster. In cycling it's called half-wheeling, where one rider, without realising, stays half a wheel in front of their riding companion – half-wheelers tend to find themselves riding alone. I think it's the subconscious male ego, a primal instinct. Because of my heart condition, I've had to let my ego dissolve, and learn to be comfortable in my mind that I'm good enough. I think that's all the more possible when you have achieved highly, as you can rest on your laurels to a certain extent. It makes being a team captain easier, too, because you're not involved in establishing any pecking order, or the need to prove your value to the team, because you have a distinct role already. The team captain needs to be self-reliant, motivated and independent. You're often encouraging the team, offering support, putting the team ahead of self, but it rarely comes the other way, which means that only certain people are cut out for the role.

Why is New Zealand so good at adventure racing? Never having been much of a spectator, always off doing my own thing, I do believe the All Blacks set a benchmark of excellence for other sports to try to match or better – through their rugby exploits they send a strong message to other Kiwi sporting codes to toughen up and get the job done. My career in adventure racing and as a team captain has been on a similar timeline to that of All Blacks captain Richie McCaw, whom I hold in high regard as a team captain and athlete. What I most admire is his composure under pressure and ability to extract winning performances from his team when most people would have given up and accepted defeat. New Zealanders have excelled in countless exploits around the world, a testament to their technical skills, fitness and ability to endure to the end. Pioneers and high achievers like Sir Edmund Hillary and Sir Peter Blake symbolise our ability to thrive on challenges and overcome whatever limitations stand in our way, which is the essence of my chosen sport.

CHAPTER THIRTY-THREE

NEBULOUS FEELINGS

Occasionally I get asked what I think about when I'm training. Most of the time I train alone and I value that solitude. I can be running a trail for four hours, paddling on the sea for five hours, or cycling around the hills for six hours, but whatever it is I'm doing, my mind invariably drifts freely. I'll deliberately process some things, nut out something topical, but the majority of the time I'll let thoughts enter my mind randomly, not consciously thinking about anything. Wandering around in nature allows my mind to wander too. Writing this book has been a chance for me to look back and ponder what I've been doing, who I am, and a little bit of where I'm going.

I'm lucky. Some people don't believe in luck and others will say you create your own luck but I'm not so sure. I believe great things happen in life when the timing is perfect and everything comes together. You need to be at the right place at the right time with the right skills and the right window of opportunity. But you need to be looking for that window. Yep, I feel lucky about lots of things alright. Being half Samoan is one of them. It's allowed me to grow up in a multicultural environment, to regularly see different viewpoints and perspectives, to have an open mind and accept that there is more than one way of doing things. Samoans are laid-back people, typically calm and relaxed, and despite my intensity and desire to pack activity into my days, weeks and years, I do have an Islander approach to many things.

For instance, being open to both eastern and western medicine signifies my Samoan and Palangi blood, growing up in two cultures and having the best of both worlds. People will have their views on alternative medicine but I know beyond any doubt that I wouldn't have had the athletic career I've had without it, and I can say the same about modern medicine. When I was 18 years old I had a knee injury that was preventing me from running and even walking at times. After failing to see any improvement from doctors and physiotherapists it was suggested that I see Mike Addison-Saipe, at the Bushin Ryu Health and Martial Arts Centre. I limped into his clinic and walked out, and was back running the following day. Ever since, Mike has been my first stop for any injuries or illness and I have no doubt that without his treatments I wouldn't have been able to sustain the level of racing that I have, globetrotting around the world to over 50 major events.

The big part of Samoan culture that I'm not part of is religion. Church, God, and the Bible are daily life for many Samoans, and my grandfather was a minister. While not religious, I do consider myself spiritual though. I don't believe that God created the earth and I struggle to believe it's a result of a large explosion either. I believe there is a greater force or power out there but what it is remains a mystery to us. I'm comfortable with the mystery. I know what brings me happiness so I try and do that as much as I can. Provided I don't wreck the planet and upset people, I'm cool with it. I know some people dislike religion because it has been and still is responsible for multiple wars, but I'm quick to point out that people, money, oil, and land have also been the catalysts of wars, so why just single out religion? We'll be fighting over drinking water next. That doesn't make water bad.

Sadly, Samoans and other Pasifika peoples also have some alarming health statistics, in the areas of obesity, diabetes and heart disease, because while food is such a mainstay of Island cultures, the people's lifestyles have become increasingly sedentary. The food they are eating has changed dramatically too, from fresh fish and produce that required an honest effort to source, to heavily processed foods high in sugar to which their bodies have not adapted. They need to make better choices in what they eat, how much they eat, and when they eat. It's not an education or financial problem so much as a matter of discipline or habit: eat better food and exercise more. It's too easy to whizz down to the store for a loaf or two of white bread and a few bottles of Coke. I hope that I can inspire other Polynesians to pursue more active and healthy lifestyles from seeing how I have lived my life and the choices I've made.

Looking back to my childhood, having brown skin and growing up in a predominantly white town wasn't always easy but it was never a big issue for me either. I always felt it gave me something extra. It's made me stronger. Early on in my sporting career I used that as motivation. I felt like I was representing something bigger when I raced, that I was racing for my colour. It's made me more empathetic towards minorities and rebellious against majorities. Most of my closest friends are either of ethnic descent or female. Being raised a half-caste brown kid in what is typically a white male dominated society taught me strength, courage and some survival strategies. In a small way, I viewed the white guy as the enemy. I knew from a young age that I needed to put myself out there, to stand out from the crowd, and my cultural roots supported that belief. I needed to take risks so I did, and I've never stopped. I've taken so many risks in life I'm quite comfortable with risk and vulnerability now. It has had many spin-offs – in my sport, my family, and my business ventures. My ability to live with risk in my life combined with my Samoan heritage (why do today what you can do tomorrow) means I can sleep easy at night. I don't tend to bother much with stress and worry.

Jodie will use words such as 'addictive' and 'obsessive' to describe me. It's true, I don't do halves. That's why I have excelled at adventure racing. There's no moderation in adventure racing. Everything is on a grand scale. It's one epic challenge after another, for days. For someone like me, it was a dream come true. Not only were the events monstrous, the training required was of equally monstrous proportions. It meant I could actually justify exercising between 25 to 50 hours per week. I even trained 62 hours one week, which may seem absurd, but when the race you're training for is expected to take 160 hours, there is sound logic. By comparison, Tour de France riders typically take about 90 hours to complete the route, spread over three weeks. Ultramarathon runners take about 20 hours to complete a race. In Ironman events most people are finished in under 15 hours, and the winners sometimes in under eight hours. An adventure expedition race is normally about 100 hours, non-stop. When we won the Eco Challenge in Fiji it took us 167 hours. Whenever I tell people about adventure racing invariably someone asks 'Why?' My answer will depend on who's asking. If it's a youth I'll tell them it's for fun, that I get to do the sports I enjoy, travel, watch movies on planes and get free stuff from sponsors. If it's a more serious questioner, I've got an array of answers. But the answer to why I adventure race stems back, a long way back.

Since I was 10 years old I've been training, travelling to events and competing. It started off as health and exercise, teamwork, something to keep me occupied. But as I got older and drifted into individual sports I began to enjoy the suffering, the hard work, the effort of pushing myself. It was in essence the ultimate journey of self-improvement as there was instant feedback. I discovered the high of training – it made me feel good, alive, better. I started to race – running races, biking races, multisport, adventure racing. Whatever race, it was an outlet for my competitive spirit, which tends to lie dormant until a starting gun goes off. Then it's about battle, smashing it, fighting, which often means winning. Jodie, who knows me better than anyone, understands that the button people should avoid pushing is the 'disrespect' one. No one likes to be disrespected, but I tend to have an overreaction to it. If it's a competitor, they're unlikely to beat me in a sporting event ever again.

I've achieved a high percentage of what I have in sport by not giving up. I have had many come-from-behind victories in competitions where most others would have called it a day, but I've always had a 'fight to the death' attitude. Most people get to the edge of success and quit – they don't know that when they get to the hardest bit that that's the final hurdle. In one national mountain-bike series race, I was struggling like hell and the finish was nearing. A good mate was in front of me and set to win. I dug deep, as deep as I could, and used every ounce of energy I could extract to catch up, the hunter. As I drew close I knew I was spent, emptied. Composing myself and riding alongside him as we started the final approach to the finish, I casually said, 'We can draw this race or I'll sprint you in and win.' Forever the opponent. He opted to draw when he would have won easily. Some would call that over the top, I call it sporting intelligence.

'Racing – where's the fun in that?' I once heard a famous cyclist being asked. Somewhat perplexed by the question, he replied, 'Fun? I don't do it for fun – I do it for pain.' I have to admit that I seek the suffering and sometimes pain that comes with endurance challenges and hard training too. It's always satisfying afterwards. Like everyone, I enjoy a hot shower, good food and warm bed, but I enjoy them tenfold more if I'm reminded what it's like not to have those things. Doing something for pain may seem somewhat odd but it is not by any means a new concept. It has driven people to explore the earth's farthest frontiers. My sport is a chance for me to experience temporary discomfort in the midst of an all-too-comfortable modern way of life. Often I'll go outside at night, look at the distant mountains or across the ocean and say, 'It'd be a great night to be out doing an adventure!' The Lillooet Indians of British Columbia believe journeys of epic endurance cleanse the soul. They have a chant that was my mantra for many years: 'Push yourself until the pain comes and then go on, until you think you cannot survive. Here the ego will let go. Here you will be purified.'

I wasn't always drawn to the hardship and chasing the feeling of aliveness I get from sport nowadays. In my late teens I was motivated by the approval. I loved to get my name in the local paper – it felt to me that it grew my identity. As the years went by I wanted to feature in magazines and that developed into wanting to be on television, despite the fact I've never owned one. But after a while I outgrew the attention-seeking, and sport evolved into opportunity and then a business. For the last five years my sport has fed my adventurous spirit. A change is in the air though. My competitive spirit is not what it used to be, my drive to push myself is diminishing, I don't care so much about the outcome of races. After the 2014 World Championships and the last couple of GODZone events, all races I won, it didn't mean all that much to me, or at least what it used to. I'm getting older.

There is a glamour side to sport which is accentuated when you win. The jubilation, celebration, achievement, it looks and is wonderful, but it comes with a price tag. It requires copious amounts of training, inordinate time spent exercising, time that could be used doing other things. For me, 95 per cent of the time training for sport is a gift, a privilege, but there are times when I've needed to push myself, often if the weather is crap or I'm completely fatigued. But I know the sacrifices I have to make to succeed. I have learnt to perfect what others find boring and repetitive. Reviewing my adventure-racing life, I'm really proud of the contribution I have made to the sport. A few people think I'm the best adventure racer there has been, although it's important to point out that many don't too. It depends on how you measure what is the best. Is it in navigation, captaincy, results, strengths, skills? I'd never make that claim myself, but I can stand back and say with conviction, I achieved highly in that sport. I'm not the best navigator but I can navigate and have done to World Championships titles. I am highly skilled in all the disciplines from a lifetime in the outdoors but there are people with higher skills. I'm not the fittest or strongest, but in my career, I have been super-fit and strong. I'm not the fastest, but at my peak I may well have been, or certainly close to it. I've heard it said that one adventure race takes a year off your life – I hope it's not true, because I've done over 30 expedition-length races, which would mean I'll die very shortly!

One of the biggest challenges I've faced in the later years of my racing has been staying healthy. I am convinced that having school-aged children and being an athlete is one of the hardest things to manage. Almost every day they bring home new bugs to share around. Most people will know that the fitter they get the harder their immune system is working, so they are more susceptible to illnesses. I love my children immensely but they haven't helped me as I've trained for some major races in that regard. It's certainly heightened my respect for athletes who have managed major achievements whilst parenting a young family, and something I'm proud of myself. What I do believe sets me aside from most others is that not only have I excelled out on the course, but off the course as well. Being able to secure sponsorship, work with the media and run my own public relations campaigns has meant that I have made a career from the sport and provided many opportunities for my team-mates along the way. My captaincy has been successful, with almost no issues in the teams I've led. I think it's due to the respect I have gained and my composure. I can lead by example.

The services to my sport I can be credited for are captaining the top New Zealand team for a decade, and securing the biggest sponsorship deal in the sport which enabled a Kiwi team to compete at seven World Championships: New Zealand, Scotland, Australia, France, Costa Rica, Ecuador and Brazil. I served nearly eight years on the committee of the New Zealand Adventure Racing and Multisport Association. The Spring Challenge is the biggest adventure race of its type in the world, the catalyst for thousands of women to be active. I am currently exploring the feasibility of organising a Kids' Adventure Race and it was my initiative to raise funding to get a book researched and published to mark 25 years of New Zealand adventure racing, from 1989 to 2014. Throughout my sporting career, I've been able to create opportunities for others to explore their sporting prowess and chase their dreams, as my team-mates, or athletes I've either coached or mentored. My career has not gone without acknowledgement, and while I've rarely sought out such accolades, it has been satisfying to be recognised for some of my efforts. I have been the Nelson Sportsperson of the Year three times and in 2012 I became a Rotary International Paul Harris Fellow (as did Jodie), for service to the community.

While I enjoy all sport, I have always been pulled to the outdoors. For me it's not so much about going into nature, it's more about reminding myself that I am a part of nature. When I ski through powder snow, or kayak off a waterfall, sail in the salty wind, or simply camp in the wilderness, whatever it is, I can feel the connection on all levels – emotional, physical and spiritual. I like to regularly remove myself from daily routines or pressures, remind myself that I am a nano-part in a huge machine of life. People never regret making time to connect with nature – in fact, they typically say, 'I need to do that more often.' Even though I live a large percentage of my life in the outdoors, I still find it's not nearly enough time.

By nature I'm rebellious. I have a strong sense of morals and fairness, but they're based on values that I've decided are important to me, not dictated by religion, society or laws. I'm unbounded in many ways, and that's why adventure racing fitted so well with me. You don't have to go to bed at night, you can eat lollies for breakfast, and for the duration of the event, the expedition, you live in a world of different rules and boundaries. In life I'm much the same. I make up my own mind about what I'll do. Sometimes I break the speed limit, I camp where I'm not allowed to, I bike on trails where it's not permitted, I resist policy, and if I think a rule is stupid, or an expectation is unjustified, I'll simply do my own thing, and I'll suffer the consequences if I have to. The important thing for me as I go through life, deciding which rules I'll obey and which I won't, is that I always ensure that I'm not hurting anyone or anything. I'm living my life the way I want it. My intent is not to be a menace, my intent is to be happy.

I do believe that society is heading off in a wrong direction at present, and I can't help but think that we have become overprotected and risk-averse. Political correctness has gone too far – we can't live life in high-visibility vests. Somehow people are being raised so sheltered, so shut off, or so removed that they're incapable of making their own judgements. I cook meals but have hardly ever used a recipe book, and I've never read a parenting book or a book on how to do outdoor sport, but I manage to eat, raise a family and not kill myself doing sport. When you boil it down to basics, I'm really just someone motivated to get outside and play. What gets me outside is the knowledge that afterwards I'll be proud of the effort and I won't regret it. I've always believed that the 5 per cent I struggle to get motivated is what gives me an edge over my rivals, that that's the bit that counts – in a literal sense, the extra mile.

If I try and see over the horizon beyond 2015 what do I see? What I take delight from in life is seeing beautiful places and actively moving through them – the more such moments I can enjoy in my life, the better. I aim to be gentle on the planet and to teach my kids a few tricks to enjoy their lives too. I want my events company to continue to create opportunities for people to enjoy the outdoors. The Spring Challenge women's adventure race has had such a positive impact on so many women in the South Island that we're going to organise a sister event in the North Island. I want to help make our freeze-dried meals company, Absolute Wilderness, a roaring success. We are passionate about enjoying adventure and food, and believe that we provide the best, healthiest, tastiest, most nutritious freeze-dried meals in the world, meals that people can relish in amazing wilderness locations. If nothing else, at least I'll have quality meals to fuel my adventures!

I'll always be active. I've trained over 300 days a year for decades and that won't change much. What I think will change is my commitment to racing as part of a dedicated team on the Adventure Racing World Series chasing World Championships wins. I'll probably do more races but under different circumstances. I'll soon have teenage children and I want to ensure that we have some quality years as a family with travel and adventure together before they embark on their own lives of independence. I'm excited about watching them grow up and being part of that story. I don't care if they're not athletes, if they're not competitive, but I do sincerely hope they have a passion for the outdoors, always going into nature to be reminded of what is incredibly special about our world. I visualise myself as an aged adventurer, riding my electric bike down to the Patisserie Royale in Motueka each morning, reading the paper and sipping a few macchiatos. Before that happens, though, I have a long list of adventure trips I want to do with Jodie and my children that have been difficult to justify whilst I have captained Team Seagate. The time away from home or devoted to specific training has shelved them. There are trails I want to ride, waters to kayak, slopes to ski, mountains to climb, wildernesses to explore. The next challenge for me is not what I will do when I stop racing, it will be how to fit everything into this totally adventurous life . . .

ACKNOWLEDGEMENTS

It's not that I'm ungrateful or unappreciative but I'm not naturally big on thank yous. I suppose I do things in life and don't expect much in return, or know that life is a series of swings and roundabouts, that most things are cyclic. I suspect part of it is the achiever's personality – don't waste time on praise, instead, tell me how to improve. But my life wouldn't be what it has been without some key and influential people and I would like to take a moment to say, thanks.

Kicking off, Fa'afetai tele lava to Robbie Burton who believed my story was one to capture in print.

In terms of shout-outs, my family tops the list: my mum and dad, brother and sister – they're the people that have been there for me, unconditionally. To my extended family, we all know I'm quite distant, but I definitely know I represent us, and I take that responsibility seriously.

I thank all the team mates I have raced with over my career – we've always achieved highly in all the escapades and, whether it be victories or not, the adventure and learning was always absorbed. It's been a blast.

Thanks also to the people and teams I've raced against. Competition has driven me to continuously improve and that has been a most rewarding journey.

I owe my sincerest gratitude to my sponsors and supporters for their loyal faith in me. For some, it's been a relationship over decades – special mention to Mike Gane and Ross Gilchrist.

I will always be indebted to Bill, Pat and Steve. I know you're three individuals but, collectively, your support has reached far and wide, beyond what you can probably ever imagine.

To Seagate, my corporate sponsor for eons, I can't imagine how that could have been any better.

To my regular core team mates – you know who you are – I don't really need to thank you, you should be thanking me, I reckon! But I want to say a special mention to a few of you folk: to Jeff and Neil for schooling me, to Kristina for learning and discovery years of adventure racing – I think we both retired once we had nailed it, to Rich for dragging me off the couch to run 120 km through a desert and reminding me I wasn't completely washed up, and to Sophie for reigniting my fire for my 'extra' years of competing.

To my children, Jessie, Zefa and Tide – it's been awesome and epic so far, and long may it continue. I hope you all look back on your childhood with fond memories! It can't be easy having a dad whose biggest fear in life is being normal, but I'll always be there for you – I know you know that.

And to Jodie, my wife, best friend and soul mate – wow, boom! You'll be shaking your head when you read this … I feel earnestly lucky that we hooked up as teenagers, that we've been together for longer than we've been apart and created a life of shared adventure. To borrow your phrase for a sec, I love you to the moon and back, which is a lot. I promise to chill out and relax … when we're much older, you know, easy bike rides, paddles, hiking trips, relaxing trips.